OVERCOMING OBSTACLES TO PEACE

LOCAL FACTORS IN NATION-BUILDING

James Dobbins, Laurel E. Miller, Stephanie Pezard, Christopher S. Chivvis, Julie E. Taylor, Keith Crane, Calin Trenkov-Wermuth, Tewodaj Mengistu

Sponsored by the Carnegie Corporation of New York

NATIONAL SECURITY
RESEARCH DIVISION

The research described in this report was prepared for the Carnegie Corporation of New York and was conducted within the International Security and Defense Policy Center of the RAND National Security Research Division.

Library of Congress Cataloging-in-Publication Data

Dobbins, James, 1942-
  Overcoming obstacles to peace : local factors in nation-building / James Dobbins,
Laurel E. Miller, Stephanie Pezard, Christopher S. Chivvis, Julie E. Taylor, Keith
Crane, Calin Trenkov-Wermuth, Tewodaj Mengistu.
    pages cm.
    Includes bibliographical references.
    ISBN 978-0-8330-7860-5 (pbk. : alk. paper)
    1. Nation-building. 2. Nation-building--Case studies. 3. Peace-building.
  4. Democratization. I. Title.

  JZ6300.D65 2013
  327.1'72--dc23

                                                                    2013000701

The RAND Corporation is a nonprofit institution that helps improve policy and decisionmaking through research and analysis. RAND's publications do not necessarily reflect the opinions of its research clients and sponsors.

RAND® is a registered trademark.

Cover, top photo: Cambodian troops arrive to reinforce other troops engaged in fighting in Phnom Penh, 1974 (AP/Chor Yuthy). Bottom photo: Cambodian garment factory workers travel home from work in Kampong Chhnang province, north of Phnom Penh, 2009 (AP/Heng Sinith).

Published 2013 by the RAND Corporation
1776 Main Street, P.O. Box 2138, Santa Monica, CA 90407-2138
1200 South Hayes Street, Arlington, VA 22202-5050
4570 Fifth Avenue, Suite 600, Pittsburgh, PA 15213-2665
RAND URL: http://www.rand.org/
To order RAND documents or to obtain additional information, contact
Distribution Services: Telephone: (310) 451-7002;
Fax: (310) 451-6915; Email: order@rand.org

Preface

Following on a series of RAND Corporation studies of nation-building interventions in conflict-affected areas undertaken by the United Nations, United States, European Union, and others, this volume analyzes the impediments that local conditions pose to successful outcomes in these interventions. Previous RAND studies have focused on the activities of external interveners. This monograph shifts the perspective from external actors to internal circumstances, first identifying the local circumstances that gave rise to conflicts or threatened to perpetuate them, and then determining how external actors and local leaders were able to modify or work around those circumstances to promote an enduring peace. The book aims to provide policymakers with the means to judge with greater clarity how local circumstances are likely to affect their prospects for success and what sorts of outcomes might be realistically achievable.

This research was sponsored by the Carnegie Corporation of New York and conducted within the International Security and Defense Policy Center of the RAND National Security Research Division (NSRD). NSRD conducts research and analysis on defense and national security topics for the U.S. and allied defense, foreign policy, homeland security, and intelligence communities and foundations and other nongovernmental organizations that support defense and national security analysis.

For more information on the International Security and Defense Policy Center, see http://www.rand.org/nsrd/ndri/centers/isdp.html or contact the director (contact information is provided on the web page).

Contents

Preface iii

Figures xi

Tables xiii

Summary xv

Acknowledgments xxxvii

Abbreviations xxxix

CHAPTER ONE

Introduction 1

CHAPTER TWO

Which Local Factors Pose Challenges to Nation-Building? 11

Factors That Raise the Risk of Conflict Renewal 12

   Civil War Onset 12

   Civil War Recurrence 20

   How Great Is the Risk of Recurrence? 24

Structure of the Case Studies 25

Tailoring Nation-Building to Local Factors 26

CHAPTER THREE

Cambodia 29

Local Factors Before the Peace 30

   Geographical and Geopolitical 33

   Cultural and Social 35

   Economic 36

   Political 39

Institutional.. 40
Nation-Building Efforts.. 43
  Geographical and Geopolitical..................................... 45
  Cultural and Social.. 45
  Economic... 47
  Political.. 47
  Institutional.. 49
Outcomes... 51
  Local Attitudes.. 52
  Geographical and Geopolitical..................................... 54
  Cultural and Social.. 55
  Economic... 57
  Political.. 58
  Institutional.. 61
Conclusions.. 62
  What Local Factors Posed the Greatest Challenges?................. 62
  Were Local Factors Modified or Circumvented to Promote Enduring
    Peace?... 63

CHAPTER FOUR
El Salvador.. 67
Local Factors Before the Peace.. 69
  Geographical and Geopolitical..................................... 69
  Cultural and Social.. 70
  Economic... 72
  Political.. 72
  Institutional.. 73
Nation-Building Efforts.. 74
  Geographical and Geopolitical..................................... 75
  Cultural and Social.. 75
  Economic... 77
  Political.. 78
  Institutional.. 79
Outcomes... 83
  Local Attitudes.. 83
  Geographical and Geopolitical..................................... 84

Cultural and Social 85
Economic 86
Political. 87
Institutional. 87
Conclusions 89
What Local Factors Posed the Greatest Challenges? 89
Were Local Factors Modified or Circumvented to Promote Enduring
 Peace? 91

CHAPTER FIVE
Bosnia and Herzegovina. 93
Local Factors Before the Peace 95
Geographical and Geopolitical. 96
Cultural and Social 97
Economic 98
Political. 100
Institutional. 101
Nation-Building Efforts 102
Geographical and Geopolitical. 103
Cultural and Social 104
Economic 106
Political. 108
Institutional. 110
Outcomes 113
Local Attitudes 113
Geographical and Geopolitical. 114
Cultural and Social 115
Economic 117
Political. 119
Institutional. 119
Conclusions 120
What Local Factors Posed the Greatest Challenges? 120
Were Local Factors Modified or Circumvented to Promote
 Enduring Peace? 122

CHAPTER SIX
East Timor 125
Local Factors Before the Peace 127
    Geographical and Geopolitical........................... 128
    Cultural and Social..................................... 128
    Economic 129
    Political... 130
    Institutional.. 131
Nation-Building Efforts..................................... 131
    Geographical and Geopolitical........................... 132
    Cultural and Social..................................... 133
    Economic 134
    Political... 135
    Institutional.. 136
Outcomes 140
    Local Attitudes.. 140
    Geographical and Geopolitical........................... 141
    Cultural and Social..................................... 142
    Economic 142
    Political... 143
    Institutional.. 144
Conclusions... 146
    What Local Factors Posed the Greatest Challenges? 146
    Were Local Factors Modified or Circumvented to Promote
        Enduring Peace?.................................... 148

CHAPTER SEVEN
Sierra Leone... 151
Local Factors Before the Peace 152
    Geographical and Geopolitical........................... 153
    Cultural and Social..................................... 154
    Economic 156
    Political... 158
    Institutional.. 159
Nation-Building Efforts..................................... 160
    Geographical and Geopolitical........................... 160

Cultural and Social 161
Economic 163
Political 165
Institutional 166
Outcomes 170
Local Attitudes 170
Geographical and Geopolitical 171
Cultural and Social 171
Economic 172
Political 174
Institutional 174
Conclusions 176
What Local Factors Posed the Greatest Challenges? 176
Were Local Factors Modified or Circumvented to Promote
    Enduring Peace? 177

CHAPTER EIGHT
Democratic Republic of the Congo 179
Local Factors Before the Peace 180
Geographical and Geopolitical 180
Cultural and Social 181
Economic 182
Political 184
Institutional 186
Nation-Building Efforts 186
Geographical and Geopolitical 187
Cultural and Social 190
Economic 191
Political 193
Institutional 193
Outcomes 194
Local Attitudes 194
Geographical and Geopolitical 195
Cultural and Social 196
Economic 196
Political 198

Institutional.. 199
Conclusions... 199
What Local Factors Posed the Greatest Challenges? 199
Were Local Factors Modified or Circumvented to Promote
Enduring Peace?.. 200

CHAPTER NINE
Estimating the Challenges and Comparing with Outcomes 205
Sustaining Peace.. 208
Promoting Democracy 214
Improving Governance... 217
Achieving Economic Growth... 221
Advancing Human Development.. 226
Summing Up 229

CHAPTER TEN
Conclusions.. 233
The Transformational Limits of Nation-Building.......................... 234
Factors Crucial to Establishing Enduring Peace........................... 236
Geopolitics.. 237
Patronage Networks 238
The Impact of Geopolitics and Patronage Networks in 20 Cases....... 239
Dissimilar Societies, Similar Instruments................................. 241
Establishing Realistic Expectations 243

APPENDIXES
A. **Performance Indicators and Nation-Building Inputs for
20 Major Post–Cold War Nation-Building Interventions** 247
B. **Economic Growth Statistics for Nation-Building
Interventions in Comparative Perspective**.......................... 269

References... 273

Figures

3.1. Map of Cambodia 29

4.1. Map of El Salvador 67

5.1. Map of Bosnia and Herzegovina 93

5.2. Bosnia's per Capita Gross Domestic Product Based on Purchasing Power Parity (current international $) Compared with That of Some Neighbors, 2011 118

6.1. Map of East Timor 125

7.1. Map of Sierra Leone 151

8.1. Map of the Democratic Republic of the Congo 179

8.2. Annual Growth in Gross Domestic Product in the Democratic Republic of the Congo 197

8.3. Annual Inflation Rate in the Democratic Republic of the Congo as Measured by the Gross Domestic Product Deflator 197

Tables

S.1. Summary of Net Changes in Performance Indicators Following 20 Major Post–Cold War Nation-Building Interventions xxv

3.1. Postintervention Performance and Nation-Building Inputs in Cambodia 64

4.1. Postintervention Performance and Nation-Building Inputs in El Salvador 91

5.1. Postintervention Performance and Nation-Building Inputs in Bosnia 123

6.1. Postintervention Performance and Nation-Building Inputs in East Timor 149

7.1. Postintervention Performance and Nation-Building Inputs in Sierra Leone 178

8.1. Postintervention Performance and Nation-Building Inputs in the Democratic Republic of the Congo 201

9.1. Peace Endurance 209

9.2. Democratization 215

9.3. Government Effectiveness 218

9.4. Growth in per Capita Gross Domestic Product 222

9.5. Per Capita Gross National Income 224

9.6. Human Development Index Scores 227

9.7. Summary of Net Changes in Performance Indicators Following 20 Major Post–Cold War Nation-Building Interventions 230

A.1. Performance Indicators and Nation-Building Inputs for Bosnia 248

A.2. Performance Indicators and Nation-Building Inputs for Sudan 249

A.3.   Performance Indicators and Nation-Building Inputs for
       Kosovo 250
A.4.   Performance Indicators and Nation-Building Inputs for
       Sierra Leone 251
A.5.   Performance Indicators and Nation-Building Inputs for
       East Timor.. 252
A.6.   Performance Indicators and Nation-Building Inputs for
       Afghanistan... 253
A.7.   Performance Indicators and Nation-Building Inputs for
       the Democratic Republic of the Congo 254
A.8.   Performance Indicators and Nation-Building Inputs for
       Somalia... 255
A.9.   Performance Indicators and Nation-Building Inputs for
       Iraq 256
A.10. Performance Indicators and Nation-Building Inputs for
       Mozambique... 257
A.11. Performance Indicators and Nation-Building Inputs for
       Haiti.. 258
A.12. Performance Indicators and Nation-Building Inputs for
       Liberia.. 259
A.13. Performance Indicators and Nation-Building Inputs for
       El Salvador.. 260
A.14. Performance Indicators and Nation-Building Inputs for
       Namibia... 261
A.15. Performance Indicators and Nation-Building Inputs for
       Cambodia... 262
A.16. Performance Indicators and Nation-Building Inputs for
       Eastern Slavonia.. 263
A.17. Performance Indicators and Nation-Building Inputs for
       Albania... 264
A.18. Performance Indicators and Nation-Building Inputs for
       Macedonia.. 265
A.19. Performance Indicators and Nation-Building Inputs for
       Côte d'Ivoire... 266
A.20. Performance Indicators and Nation-Building Inputs for
       Solomon Islands.. 267
B.1.   Comparative Economic Growth Statistics for 20 Major
       Post–Cold War Nation-Building Interventions................ 270

Summary

In the past decade, RAND has published a series of studies on nation-building. We intend this term to describe operations conducted by external civilian and military authorities that employ armed force alongside other means of influence in the aftermath of conflict to promote enduring peace. Some prefer the term *state-building*, giving primacy to postconflict activities aimed at constructing state institutions and deemphasizing those activities intended to build a national identity. Others prefer *peace-building*, which perhaps best captures the overriding purpose of the types of externally driven operations on which we focus. Neither *state-building* nor *peace-building* necessarily implies the employment of armed force, whereas all the cases we study include this element. We have stuck with *nation-building*, the most common label in American parlance, albeit one often applied pejoratively, in order to reach a wider audience and to shed new light on an oft-misunderstood and underappreciated undertaking.

Three prior RAND studies have examined U.S., European, and United Nations (UN) performance in this field.[1] Following that work, RAND produced a practitioner's manual, titled *The Beginner's Guide*

---

[1] James Dobbins, John G. McGinn, Keith Crane, Seth G. Jones, Rollie Lal, Andrew Rathmell, Rachel M. Swanger, and Anga R. Timilsina, *America's Role in Nation-Building: From Germany to Iraq*, Santa Monica, Calif.: RAND Corporation, MR-1753-RC, 2003; James Dobbins, Seth G. Jones, Keith Crane, Christopher S. Chivvis, Andrew Radin, F. Stephen Larrabee, Nora Bensahel, Brooke Stearns Lawson, and Benjamin W. Goldsmith, *Europe's Role in Nation-Building: From the Balkans to the Congo*, Santa Monica, Calif.: RAND Corporation, MG-722-RC, 2008; James Dobbins, Seth G. Jones, Keith Crane, Andrew Rathmell, Brett Steele, Richard Teltschik, and Anga R. Timilsina, *The UN's Role in*

to Nation-Building.[2] All of these publications were intended to analyze and improve the policies adopted by the intervening parties. In this volume, we examine some of those same operations with a new focus on the indigenous societies rather than the external parties, in an effort to understand how varying local circumstances affected outcomes.

What literature there is on the impact of local factors on post-conflict stabilization and reconstruction tends to treat either individual cases or individual sources of conflict. There is, however, a more comprehensive body of work on the causes of civil war. These studies necessarily have some application to the causes of its renewal, and thus the obstacles posed to preventing the renewal of conflict, which is the central purpose of nation-building missions.

Among the factors found to contribute to the outbreak of civil war are large populations, low per capita income, lootable natural resources, recent political instability, weak democratic institutions, a small military, rough terrain, hostile or unstable neighbors, and weak government. In assessing the relative importance of these causes, political scientists tend to put an emphasis on issues of governance and societal divisions, whereas economists are prone to stress the availability of resources for rebellion, some going so far as to argue that, wherever insurgency is financially and practically feasible, it will occur. These two perspectives are sometimes referred to as the *grievance* and the *greed* schools of civil war causality.

There are also critiques that dismiss the whole concept of nation-building. Some authors argue that local circumstances are so influential and so varied from one instance to another as to render any common approach to such missions infeasible. Others feel the project too difficult and expensive to be worthwhile. Some go so far as to insist that societies are so impervious to external influence as to doom any such effort to failure. These critiques generally rest their conclusions on a very limited number of cases, which is to say those that failed.

Nation-Building: From the Congo to Iraq, Santa Monica, Calif.: RAND Corporation, MG-304-RC, 2005.

[2] James Dobbins, Seth G. Jones, Keith Crane, and Beth Cole DeGrasse, *The Beginner's Guide to Nation-Building*, Santa Monica, Calif.: RAND Corporation, MG-557-SRF, 2007.

This study looked at the effects of local circumstances on the outcomes of nation-building efforts across the full spectrum of post–Cold War operations of this type. We first examine in some detail the impact of local factors in six different cases chosen for variety of location, size, income level, demography, culture, and institutional development of the societies involved. In each case, we seek to determine how local factors affected efforts of international actors to promote security, democratization, better governance, and economic development and vice versa—that is, how the behavior of the interveners affected these factors. We then expand our analysis, using statistical data, to a larger set of 20 post–Cold War interventions led by the United Nations, the United States, and Europe.

Six Case Studies

Cambodia

Invasions by U.S., South Vietnamese, and North Vietnamese armed forces triggered this country's two-decade civil war, including genocide at the hands of the Khmer Rouge. The society was poor to start with; the government weak; and the population homogenous, historically rather passive, and generally respectful of authority. In 1991, UN peacekeepers arrived with an expansive mandate but only limited time and means to fulfill it. Although a signatory of the peace agreement, the Khmer Rouge refused to disarm. Denied external support, however, it soon faded away. UN forces departed two years after their entry, leaving behind a poorly governed and undemocratic state, but one at peace and with a slowly improving economy.

El Salvador

The 1992 peace accord between the government of El Salvador and the Farabundo Martí National Liberation Front (Frente Farabundo Martí para la Liberación Nacional, or FMLN) ended 12 years of civil war. That conflict had opened with a military coup d'état and was fueled by social and economic disparities between large landowners and a mostly landless rural population. The opposing sides in the civil war received external support from the Soviet Union and its allies on the one hand and the United States on the other. With the end of the Cold War, these external parties collaborated in promoting a peace accord and dispatching UN peacekeepers. The United Nations oversaw the demobilization of former combatants, encouraged land reform, and helped reorganize the police and army. El Salvador has since remained at peace, although suffering high levels of criminal violence. Its democracy has been strengthened, its government performance improved marginally, and its economy expanded.

Bosnia and Herzegovina

With the breakup of Yugoslavia, Bosnia fractured along ethnic and religious lines. The main impetus for Bosnia's breakup came from the efforts of neighboring states, Croatia and Serbia, to carve up the newly independent Bosnia and incorporate its Croat and Serb populations. Eventually, the three contending parties fought to a stalemate, at which point the international community led by the United States was able to broker a settlement that the leaderships in Belgrade and Zagreb persuaded their respective clients in Bosnia to accept. The international community has since proved unable to reverse the ethnic divisions that the war had solidified, but peace has been preserved, democratization significantly advanced, and the economy greatly expanded. Governance was also somewhat strengthened, but not to the point at which the Bosnian state can function without continued international oversight.

East Timor

Under international political and economic pressure, Indonesia agreed in 1999 to let go of the former Portuguese colony of East Timor,[3] which it had annexed in the mid-1970s. The Indonesian Army, unreconciled to this outcome, then instigated a brief punitive campaign of revenge on the inhabitants. Australian-led troops restored order, and a UN peacekeeping mission governed the territory for three years while preparing it for full independence. Civil conflict broke out soon after

---

[3]   East Timor is also known as Timor-Leste.

the UN troops departed, however, and international forces had to be reintroduced. Despite its tiny size, the country remains divided along linguistic and geographic lines, but peace has since been maintained, indigenous governance (for the first time ever) established, democratization advanced, and the economy strengthened.

Sierra Leone

The war in Sierra Leone began with an invasion by dissident elements operating out of neighboring Liberia, supported by one of that country's also warring factions. The society was very poor, divided along tribal lines, and badly misgoverned. The war was fueled by revenue from the extraction of alluvial diamonds. Several peace accords failed in implementation, but eventually UN troops, with aid from the United Kingdom, succeeded in suppressing violent spoilers and establishing security. Consolidation of peace in Sierra Leone was aided by a similarly successful international effort to end the civil war in Liberia. Sierra Leone has since remained at peace. It has seen only slight improvement in governance but a more significant advance in democratization and a healthy increase in per capita income, though its level of socioeconomic development remains very low.

Democratic Republic of the Congo

In the early 1960s, UN peacekeepers had suppressed three separate insurgencies, leaving this very large and very poor country at peace but terribly misgoverned. In 1997, its longtime dictator, Mobutu Sese Seko, was overthrown, his government disintegrated, and the country descended into civil war. The Democratic Republic of the Congo's (DRC's) population is concentrated around the capital in the far west and several population centers in the east, with very limited transportation links in between. Neighboring Uganda and Rwanda both sent armed forces across that border and otherwise involved themselves in the civil war, the cost of their interventions more than covered by their resultant access to Congolese diamonds, cobalt, gold, and other mineral resources. International pressures were eventually able to secure the termination of this interference. The DRC subsequently enjoyed a very fragile peace, but this was broken in late 2012 as rebel forces, reportedly backed by Rwanda, surged in the eastern DRC. During the period of relative peace, the country saw no significant improvement in the quality of governance, little advance in democratization, and very little economic growth or socioeconomic improvement.

The Most-Influential Factors

In the six cases, many local factors that contributed to one degree or another to conflict defied modification or elimination. In El Salvador, landlessness remained a problem; in Cambodia, nationalism and xenophobia endured; the inequitable distribution of resources persisted in Sierra Leone; ethnic divisions hardened in Bosnia; regional and political identity differences continued to produce civil unrest in East Timor; and institutions continued to be extremely weak in the DRC. Though improvements were achieved to varying degrees in these countries, governments largely remained ineffective deliverers of public services, poor societies remained poor, lootable resources continued to be looted, security institution capabilities were still weak, and in none of the cases was corruption seriously diminished. Nevertheless, the nation-building operations in these six countries succeeded in improving security, increasing democratization, expanding economic activity, and increasing human development, as did most of the 20 post–Cold War operations we analyze statistically.

Although the causes of conflict and the results of nation-building efforts varied somewhat among the six cases, two common factors go far toward explaining what first caused, or at least enabled, the wars and then helped establish and sustained the peace. The first factor was the powerful role played by outside actors in promoting both war and peace; the second was the tenacity of entrenched patronage networks.

Geopolitics

Civil war in Cambodia was sparked by U.S., North Vietnamese, and South Vietnamese invasions and then sustained by Vietnamese, Chinese, Soviet, and U.S. support for contending factions. Peace came largely as a result of détente, not so much between the United States and the Soviet Union as between China and the Soviet Union.

The civil war in El Salvador grew out of extreme economic disparities but soon became enmeshed in the wider regional competition between the United States and the Soviet Union. Once this superpower competition ended, the war in El Salvador was quickly brought to an end.

The war in Bosnia was fought along ethnic lines, but these divisions were manipulated by nationalist leaders in the two neighboring states, both of which wished to carve up the new state. Bombing by the North Atlantic Treaty Organization (NATO) and international political pressures finally brought the fighting to a stop, with the leaderships in Zagreb and Belgrade persuading their local proxies to make peace.

Tiny East Timor was always at the mercy of larger powers. It was abandoned by Portugal, misgoverned and brutalized for decades by Indonesia, liberated by Australia, and then governed for several years by the United Nations. International political and economic pressures on the government of Indonesia caused it to abandon its claims to East Timor and subsequently to halt its army's campaign of retribution.

The civil war in Sierra Leone was sparked by an invasion of dissident elements operating out of neighboring Liberia. The UN peacekeeping operation gained traction only once the former colonial power, the United Kingdom, stepped in to sharply suppress continued insurgent elements. The deployment of UN peacekeepers to neighboring Liberia helped stabilize both societies.

Conflict in the DRC stemmed from the disintegration of the Mobutu regime but was perpetuated by repeated military incursions from neighboring states. Although international troops and economic assistance were certainly important in restoring some degree of security, the decisive factor was the decision of neighboring governments, usually under international pressure, to withdraw their troops and cease their support for contending factions within the DRC. Such fighting as continues in the DRC at this writing seems to be backed by neighboring Rwanda.

Patronage Networks

Regional and country experts tend to view local patronage networks as more or less unique cultural or historical phenomena, emphasizing their ethnic, religious, tribal, clan, or linguistic origins and sources of support. Yet, across very different societies, some quite heterogeneous and some not, these networks, however organized, seem to behave quite similarly.

Whereas the international community has had considerable success in altering the geopolitical sources of conflict in each of the six cases, it had much less success in weakening the hold of patronage networks that blocked institutional development. These patronage networks could be and often were co-opted into power-sharing arrangements that produced peace, economic growth, and even a modicum of democracy, but they could almost never be persuaded to support institutional reforms that would limit their access to power and ability to extract wealth from the society.

In Bosnia, these networks, some formed in the former Yugoslavia, were strengthened, criminalized, and recast along ethnic lines during the civil war. They continued to dominate the political and economic life of the country once peace was reestablished. In Cambodia, patronage networks reemerged after the war initially as a survival strategy in a context of very limited resources and ineffective government institutions.

In Sierra Leone and the DRC, patronage was organized around tribes, in El Salvador around social class, and in East Timor along linguistic and geographic lines. Although these competing factions sometimes collaborated to divide the political and economic pies, they all resisted strengthening of any national institutions they could not capture and exploit.

The ability of a more or less united international community to alter geopolitical realities and co-opt local patronage networks largely explains the progress registered in these six cases toward peace, some democratization, and varying levels of economic growth. The resistance of these networks to strengthening the state, which would curb their own ability to tap its resources, largely explains the lack of similarly significant advances in government effectiveness.

Measuring Degrees of Difficulty and Levels of Success

Looking to a larger universe of 20 post–Cold War nation-building operations, we find the outcomes of our six case studies largely mirrored in the additional 14 cases. That is to say, there were, in most cases, improvements in security, some democratization, economic growth, and socioeconomic advances (often from quite low starting points) but much less progress in government effectiveness.

For each of these 20 cases, we first calculate the risk of renewed conflict at the onset of the intervention, and then the progress achieved over the next decade in security, democratization, government effectiveness, economic growth, and human development.

We calculate the risk of renewed conflict at the start of each mission by employing a model developed by Fearon and Laitin (2003) that incorporates the many factors thought by them to contribute to the outbreak of civil war. This model yields a percentage indicating the likelihood of civil war onset within five years, for instance, 39.8 percent in the case of Bosnia. Although the resultant figures probably understate the chance of renewed conflict in countries that just concluded civil wars, which, in many cases, was probably closer to 100 percent in the absence of any peacekeeping deployment, the figures do provide a useful way to rank the 20 cases as regards degrees of anticipatable difficulty, based on local circumstances, in promoting enduring peace at the start of each nation-building mission.

Alongside these levels of difficulty, we list the eventual outcomes in five areas: security (i.e., whether the country is at peace), democratization, government effectiveness, economic growth, and human development. We define *peace* as the absence of international or civil conflict, the threshold usually being more than 1,000 battle deaths per year. We rate as peaceful those societies falling below this threshold. We employ the Freedom Index updated annually by Freedom House to measure progress in democratization. We employ the Word Bank government effectiveness indicator to do the same in that field. We employ mostly International Monetary Fund statistics to measure per capita growth in gross domestic product (GDP). We use the UN Development Programme's Human Development Index (HDI) as a measure of progress in socioeconomic development. In order to facilitate cross-comparisons, we convert each of the above indices to a 1-to-10 scale, with 1 being the worst score and 10 the best.

By juxtaposing chances of renewed conflict based on an evaluation of local factors thought to make that likely and the outcomes of these 20 nation-building operations, we can begin to draw some conclusions regarding the impact of these factors on the five identified outcomes: peace, democratization, government effectiveness, economic growth, and socioeconomic development.

Sustaining Peace

Table S.1 reveals no strong correlation between the calculated risk of renewed civil war and success in preventing such a renewal. All four of the failures were among the top half of the list in terms of anticipatable difficulty but not among the most-difficult cases. A clear correlation can be seen, however, between consent of the warring parties to an international intervention and successful establishment of peace. All but one of the peacekeeping missions produced peace, and none of the peace-enforcement missions has yet done so. That is to say, all but one (the DRC) of the interventions that were initiated on the basis of a peace agreement and with the consent of the parties to the conflict subsequently succeeded in establishing peace, whereas the three that lacked such prior consent—Somalia, Afghanistan, and Iraq—did not.

The table thus indicates that peacekeeping is less difficult than peace enforcement, hardly a revelation. It also suggests, however, that, aside from consent of the parties, there are no other local conditions that preclude at least some degree of success in achieving peace, the prime objective of any nation-building operation, except perhaps size. Peace was achieved in most of the 20 cases regardless of variation in level of difficulty calculated on the basis of varied local conditions.

This observation needs some qualification, however, because the two largest societies, the DRC and Sudan, enjoyed the most-precarious security, in each case experiencing renewed fighting at several points during the peacekeeping operations. As of late 2012, the DRC seems plunged into civil war once again, while a divided Sudan could easily descend into what would now be a cross-border international conflict.

Table S.1
Summary of Net Changes in Performance Indicators Following 20 Major Post-Cold War Nation-Building Interventions

Difficulty Rankings: Countries Ordered from Highest to Lowest Probability of Renewed Civil War Within 5 Years	Probability of Civil War Onset Within 5 Years from Start of Intervention (%)	At Peace in 2012	In First 10 Years After Intervention			
			Net Change in Freedom Index (10-point scale)	Net Change in Government Effectiveness (10-point scale)	Net Change in HDI Score (10-point scale)	Cumulative Growth in per Capita GDP (%)
1. Bosnia	39.80	Yes	+3.75	+1.95	NA	213.7
2. Sudan	17.50	Yes	0	+0.07	+0.3	NA
3. Kosovo	15.10	Yes	+3.75[a]	NA	NA	83.2
4. Sierra Leone	12.70	Yes	+2.25	+0.49	+0.8	72.7
5. East Timor	11.40	Yes	+6.25[a]	NA	+0.9	42.7
6. Afghanistan	10.30	No	+1.5	+1.53	+1.7	130.9
7. DRC	8.80	No	+0.75	-0.25	+0.6	8.2
8. Somalia	0.30	No	+0.75	+0.89	NA	NA
9. Iraq	6.70	No	+2.25	+0.85	+0.2	84.4[b]
10. Mozambique	6.20	Yes	+2.25	-0.53	+0.5	68.8
11. Haiti	5.40	Yes	+2.25	+0.06	+0.2	-5.3[b]

Table S.1—Continued

Difficulty Rankings: Countries Ordered from Highest to Lowest Probability of Renewed Civil War Within 5 Years	Probability of Civil War Onset Within 5 Years from Start of Intervention (%)	At Peace in 2012	In First 10 Years After Intervention			
			Net Change in Freedom Index (10-point scale)	Net Change in Government Effectiveness (10-point scale)	Net Change in HDI Score (10-point scale)	Cumulative Growth in per Capita GDP (%)
12. Liberia	5.30	Yes	+3.75	+0.55	+0.3	16.4[c]
13. El Salvador	5.30	Yes	+0.75	+0.36	+0.7	20.6
14. Namibia	5.00	Yes	+1.5	NA	+0.5	14.2
15. Cambodia	4.30	Yes	+0.75	+0.07	NA	53.6
16. Eastern Slavonia	3.60	Yes	+3	+0.83	+0.8	54.5
17. Albania	2.70	Yes	+1.5	+0.77	+0.4	75.3
18. Macedonia	2.60	Yes	+1.5	+1.09	NA	35.9
19. Côte d'Ivoire	2.30	Yes	0	-0.7	+0.2	-7.4[d]
20. Solomon Islands	0.60	Yes	+4.5	+2.38	+0.1	20.8[b]
Mean			+2.15	+0.61	+0.6	54.6
Median			+1.875	+0.55	+0.5	48.1

Table S.1—Continued

Difficulty Rankings: Countries Ordered from Highest to Lowest Probability of Renewed Civil War Within 5 Years	Probability of Civil War Onset Within 5 Years from Start of Intervention (%)	At Peace in 2012	In First 10 Years After Intervention			
			Net Change in Freedom Index (10-point scale)	Net Change in Government Effectiveness (10-point scale)	Net Change in HDI Score (10-point scale)	Cumulative Growth in per Capita GDP (%)

SOURCES: Freedom House, *Freedom in the World* reports, various years; World Bank, "Worldwide Governance Indicators," undated (d); UN Development Programme, "International Human Development Indicators: Do-It-Yourself Data Tables," undated; International Monetary Fund, "International Financial Statistics: Query Builder," undated.

[a] For Kosovo and East Timor, we assume a Freedom Index rating of 1 (the lowest) for the condition at the time of intervention because both societies had suffered massive repression in the period immediately prior to the arrival of international forces.

[b] Based on the most-recent data available (2009).

[c] Based on the most-recent data available (2010).

[d] Based on the most-recent data available (2008).

NOTE: See text for explanation of difficulty rankings. NA = not available.

These developments highlight both the limited abilities of weak governments to control extensive territory and widespread populations and the difficulty of deploying adequately sized peacekeeping missions in very populous societies. Size, then, is a serious risk factor for renewed conflict, and one that is especially difficult (or at least especially expensive) to counteract.

Nevertheless, even with these caveats, the record of 16 of the peacekeeping-type interventions in sustaining peace is notable, as is the failure of the three peace-enforcement actions to do the same.

Promoting Democracy

With the exceptions of Sudan and Côte d'Ivoire, these 20 societies, even those that remained in conflict, registered advances in democratization over ten years and, in some cases, quite significant progress. On a ten-point scale, these societies experienced an average (mean) improvement of 2.15 points in their Freedom Index scores. Again, these figures indicate no correlation between the degree of anticipatable difficulty and the degree of progress toward democratization. Indeed, Bosnia, the hardest case, registered the second-greatest gain. The highest gain, in contrast, was in the easiest case, Solomon Islands. There was even some improvement in the four societies in which peace has still not been established—the DRC, Somalia, Afghanistan, and Iraq—although, even with some progress, none of these four yet qualifies as a democracy.

The table does indicate a slight inverse correlation between absolute Freedom Index scores and relative degree of anticipatable difficulty in preventing renewed conflict. This reflects the fact that many of the easier cases were more democratic to start with.

Improving Governance

Most of these societies showed only modest improvement in government effectiveness; indeed, three societies showed regression in their scores. Again, there is no observable correlation between levels of anticipatable difficulty in forestalling renewed conflict and advances in governance effectiveness.

Achieving Economic Growth

All of these societies except Haiti and Côte d'Ivoire experienced economic growth—in many cases, considerably so. Indeed, the majority of these societies' economies grew more quickly than those of their income group globally or their region or, in eight cases, both. Our data show a definite but inverse correlation between level of anticipatable difficulty and degree of improvement in terms of per capita national income, with several of the most-difficult cases achieving the highest growth rates. In Bosnia and Kosovo and perhaps other instances, this higher growth can be at least partly explained by the abundant international assistance these societies received. In other words, the level of difficulty was appreciated and a corresponding increase in international aid provided. Nevertheless, aid levels do not fully explain the disparities in economic performance. Negative growth in Haiti can be explained by major hurricanes and a massive earthquake. Côte d'Ivoire was in civil war until 2011.

Advancing Human Development

This index tracks health and education alongside economic indicators. In this sphere, all societies for which data were available achieved progress, even Haiti and Côte d'Ivoire. Interestingly, some of the most-difficult cases achieved the greatest improvement. This includes Afghanistan, which recorded nearly a two-point improvement in its score (on a ten-point scale), although, because it started from such a low base, it did not rise out of the low human development category.

Reasons for Failure

The ability of a more or less united international community to alter geopolitical realities and co-opt local patronage networks largely explains the progress registered in five of our six case studies toward peace, democratization, and economic growth. The resistance of these networks to strengthening the state and curbing their own ability to tap its resources largely explains the more-modest improvement in government effectiveness. These same factors would seem to explain the similar pattern of results in the larger set of 20 societies. Other circumstances usually cited as sources of conflict—poverty, geography, size, lack of fully democratic institutions, and ethnic or religious fractionalization—certainly affected absolute levels of achievement in these societies, yet none of these factors except perhaps size would seem to explain most of the disparities in results, and none prevented some degree of success in all categories.

Geopolitics and the strength of patronage networks also help explain the clear failures to achieve enduring peace among these 20 cases. Afghanistan and Iraq were both invaded by the United States; thus, there was neither a peace agreement in place when international forces arrived nor did the presence of foreign forces enjoy the consent of the parties to the preceding conflicts. In both cases, the United States chose to exclude rather than co-opt the dominant patronage networks. Denied their accustomed access to wealth and power, these networks chose to fight back. Equally, and perhaps even more importantly, these disgruntled elements were able to receive substantial external support in order to do so.

The United States enjoyed some degree of regional support for its invasion of Afghanistan. Pakistan was very reluctantly acquiescent, but all the other regional states backed the intervention. No sooner was the Taliban routed than Washington rebuffed Iranian offers of continued cooperation, nor was the United States able to discourage renewed Pakistani support for its old clients.

The United States had almost no regional support for its invasion of Iraq. Among that country's six neighbors, only Kuwait favored the U.S. intervention. Washington's oft-expressed hope that a democratic Iraq would serve as a model for regime change throughout the Middle East was not a project likely to appeal to neighboring governments. Iran and Syria began supporting Sunni and Shi'a extremists respectively; Turkey staged several small military incursions into the Kurdish north and threatened larger such actions; and Saudi Arabia and the other Sunni states withheld relations with the new Shi'a-dominated government in Baghdad, while individuals within those societies financed Sunni insurgents and the influx of foreign fighters.

Interference from neighbors has been a continuous factor in the DRC's civil conflict. Such interference was also a factor in Somalia's conflict, but the main failure, back in 1993, was the decision to scale back the U.S. military commitment while simultaneously initiating a bottom-up democratization campaign that was bound to antagonize every warlord in the country.

Thus, in three of these cases, the intervening parties sought to exclude the hitherto most-powerful patronage networks in the country from any access to power, influence, or wealth, while, in all four, they failed to secure the support of neighboring states.

Despite the failure to forestall renewed conflict in Afghanistan, there has been remarkable progress there across several of the other indices. That society achieved slightly less than the median improvement in democratization but was the second among all 20 in improved government effectiveness and economic growth and showed the greatest improvement of all in human development. These results, which contrast sharply with the popular image of present-day Afghanistan, cannot be entirely explained by external aid flows because Afghanistan was not among the largest foreign aid recipients on a per capita basis. Neither is it simply that Afghanistan started from a lower base because Liberia, Sierra Leone, and the DRC were all poorer to begin with and grew less rapidly. Dramatic advances in Afghanistan's school enrollment and life expectancy, declines in infant mortality, and rapid economic growth even in some of the most-conflicted areas of the country do reflect the emphasis of the Afghan government's counterinsurgency and development strategies in pushing resources and public services out into the hinterland.

Dissimilar Societies, Similar Instruments

None of the foregoing analysis is meant to suggest that such factors as geography, culture, and level of development made no difference to the outcomes in these 20 cases. These factors clearly imposed limits to absolute levels of achievement. Yet, to the extent that these circumstances presented impediments to peace, democratization, and economic growth, they were, to some considerable degree, circumvented or overcome. Nation-builders became reasonably adept at altering the behavior of neighboring states, tracing local power structures, and co-opting feuding patronage networks into more-peaceful, to somewhat more-democratic, and almost always more–economically productive forms of competition. On the other hand, nation-builders had less success in improving government effectiveness.

They achieved these results using a limited set of tools. Although every society is, to some degree, unique, the instruments with which the intervening powers seek to promote peace are few in number and largely similar from one mission to the next, consisting of compulsion (military force), persuasion (diplomacy), and various forms of technical advice and economic assistance. The quantity and quality of such tools do make a difference to the outcomes, as we have emphasized in prior publications, but so does the skill with which they are employed and their responsiveness to the local context, as we try to illustrate in our six case studies here.

Among these tools, diplomacy seems to be the most decisive, when backed by economic and sometimes military assets. Thus, just as geopolitics proved to be the most important factor in either sparking or sustaining conflict in each of our six case studies, so diplomacy proved decisive not just in mediating peace agreements but also, perhaps more importantly, in altering for the better the behavior of external actors that gave rise to or perpetuated the conflicts.

It should not be surprising that it is easier to alter the behavior of governments than to reengineer societies. Neither should it be surprising that an altered geopolitical environment can greatly improve the prospects for peace. It is also important to recognize, however, that even the most-skillful diplomacy and the most-favorable regional environments would not have sufficed to bring enduring peace to these societies had the international community not also been willing to commit military manpower and economic assistance in order to disengage adversaries, demobilize combatants, reintegrate former fighters into civilian life, and create new political and economic avenues through which formerly warring factions could continue to compete for power and wealth via peaceful rather than violent means. Prior RAND studies, in particular *The Beginner's Guide to Nation-Building*, explored the instruments and policies through which the international community effectuated these changes.[4]

Where such efforts have been inadequately resourced or unwisely executed, the result has been subpar outcomes, even in favorable geopolitical circumstances. Inadequate attention to reintegration of former combatants, for instance, left a legacy of heightened criminal violence in El Salvador. UN forces in Sierra Leone were outmatched by local insurgents until rescued by UK troops. Foreign forces left East Timor prematurely and had to be returned once conflict resumed. International resources for the DRC were never enough to fully overcome the challenges of size, distance, and difficult terrain.

In sum, operations that have enjoyed local consent and regional support almost always have achieved peace, even when a degree of coercion was employed to secure both. Nearly all these operations have also helped produce freer, more-democratic, and more-prosperous societies. Clearly, local conditions limited absolute outcomes, and, clearly, some of these indigenous obstacles have not been subject to rapid alteration, but neither have most of the oft-cited barriers to nation-building operations blocked significant progress.

Establishing More-Realistic Expectations

This monograph suggests benchmarks by which to measure progress in current and future nation-building–type operations. Any mission that results in, for instance, better than a 21.5-percentage-point rise in a country's Freedom Index over ten years (that is, an improvement greater than 2.15 points on a ten-point scale), more than 55-percent growth in its per capita income, or better than a 6-percentage-point improvement in either its HDI or government effectiveness scores will be doing better than the post–Cold War averages to date.

Other measures of progress may also become available. Transparency International's Corruption Perceptions Index does not extend far enough back to cover the older cases we examined but should be

---

[4] Dobbins, Jones, Crane, and DeGrasse, 2007.

available to benchmark future operations. Better statistics are gradually being developed to measure violent conflict, and these too should ultimately enable more-precise measurement of progress in promoting security than the binary judgment we have employed in this study.

Establishing more-realistic expectations may, over time, lead to more-balanced appraisals of individual missions and the nation-building enterprise more generally. The prominence in memory of a few spectacular nation-building failures has created the impression among the general Western public, and even among many more-informed audiences, that these missions seldom succeed. In the United States, both Democratic and Republican presidents have routinely insisted that they will not do nation-building because of this negative reputation, even as they repeatedly engage in just such activity. Both firsthand accounts of field operatives and academic appraisals of even relatively successful operations tend to be more critical than otherwise, reflecting exaggerated expectations and resultant frustration on the part of both disappointed practitioners and interested observers at the slow pace and limited nature of the resulting societal changes. Five or ten years on with almost all of these operations, poor populations remain poor and bad governments remain bad. A war-torn West African state is at best transformed into a peaceful West African state, not an applicant for membership in the European Union. (On the other hand, all of the European states covered herein are indeed in the queue for EU membership.)

Yet, as this report illustrates, the great majority of postconflict nation-building operations over the past two decades have resulted in improved security, progress in democratization, significant economic growth, and advances in human development, and most have done so with a modest commitment of international military manpower and economic assistance. In the six cases we examine in detail, many of the factors that contributed to conflict in the past were not significantly modified, but, overall, enough changed that the conflicts did not resume. Among the set of 20 cases, operations that enjoyed local consent and regional support invariably achieved some significant measure of success, even when a degree of coercion was employed to secure both. The result has been more-peaceful, freer, more-prosperous societies with healthier and better-educated populations, although not, in most cases, significantly more-competent governments. Operations that did not secure local consent and regional support did not achieve peace, although even these efforts so far have produced improvements in most of these other fields, particularly in the case of Afghanistan.

Acknowledgments

We wish to thank Stephen J. Del Rosso Jr. and the Carnegie Corporation of New York for their support of the RAND team's efforts culminating in this volume. Our RAND colleague, Stephen Watts, helped us in important ways in developing our analytical approach. We are also indebted to our peer reviewers, Chester A. Crocker, the James R. Schlesinger professor of strategic studies at Georgetown University's Walsh School of Foreign Service, and Larry Hanauer of RAND. Both reviewers provided valuable comments that helped us to improve this volume, and we are grateful for their detailed and thoughtful reviews.

Abbreviations

ACC	Anti-Corruption Commission
AIDS	acquired immunodeficiency syndrome
ANS	Armée Nationaliste Sihanoukienne
APC	All People's Congress
APODETI	Associação Popular Democrática Timorense
ARENA	Alianza Republicana Nacionalista (National Republican Alliance)
ASEAN	Association of Southeast Asian Nations
CGDK	Coalition Government of Democratic Kampuchea
CIA	Central Intelligence Agency
CIVPOL	civilian police
CNDP	Congrès national pour la défense du peuple (National Congress for the Defence of the People)
CNRM	Conselho Nacional da Resistência Maubere (National Council of Maubere Resistance)
CNRT	Conselho Nacional de Resistência Timorense (National Council of Timorese Resistance)

CPP	Cambodian People's Party
DACDF	Diamond Area Community Development Fund
DDR	disarmament, demobilization, and reintegration
DFID	UK Department for International Development
DRC	Democratic Republic of the Congo
EBRD	European Bank for Reconstruction and Development
ECCC	Extraordinary Chambers in the Courts of Cambodia
EU	European Union
EUFOR	European Union Force
FAES	Fuerza Armada de El Salvador (Armed Forces of El Salvador)
FDLR	Forces démocratiques de libération du Rwanda (Democratic Forces for the Liberation of Rwanda)
F-FDTL	FALINTIL-Forças de Defesa de Timor Leste
FMLN	Frente Farabundo Martí para la Liberación Nacional (Farabundo Martí National Liberation Front)
FRETILIN	Frente Revolucionária de Timor-Leste Independente
FUNCINPEC	Front Uni National pour un Cambodge Indépendant, Neutre, Pacifique, et Coopératif (United Front for an Independent, Neutral, Peaceful, and Co-operative Cambodia)
GDP	gross domestic product
GNI	gross national income

GPS	Global Positioning System
HDI	Human Development Index
HDZ	Hrvatska demokratska zajednica (Croatian Democratic Union)
HIV	human immunodeficiency virus
ICITAP	International Criminal Investigative Training Assistance Program
ICTY	International Criminal Tribunal for the Former Yugoslavia
IDB	Inter-American Development Bank
IDMP	Integrated Diamond Management Program
IFOR	Implementation Force
IMF	International Monetary Fund
INTERFET	International Force for East Timor
IRI	International Republican Institute
KPNLF	Khmer People's National Liberation Front
MILGROUP	military group
MINUSAL	Misión de las Naciones Unidas en El Salvador (United Nations Mission in El Salvador)
MONUC	United Nations Organization Mission in the Democratic Republic of the Congo
MONUSCO	United Nations Organization Stabilization Mission in the Democratic Republic of the Congo
NATO	North Atlantic Treaty Organization
NCC	National Consultative Council

NGO	nongovernmental organization
NPFL	National Patriotic Front of Liberia
NSRD	RAND National Security Research Division
OECD	Organisation for Economic Co-operation and Development
OHR	Office of the High Representative
ONUSAL	United Nations Observer Mission in El Salvador
OSCE	Organization for Security and Co-operation in Europe
PCRP	Paramount Chiefs Restoration Program
PDA	Kono Peace Diamond Alliance
PIC	Peace Implementation Council
PNC	Policia Nacional Civil, or National Civilian Police
PNTL	Policia Nacional de Timor-Leste (National Police of East Timor)
PPP	purchasing power parity
PRK	People's Republic of Kampuchea
PTT	Programa de Transferencia de Tierras
RCAF	Royal Cambodian Armed Forces
RUF	Revolutionary United Front
SFOR	Stabilization Force
SLP	Sierra Leone Police
SLPP	Sierra Leone People's Party
SNC	Supreme National Council
SOC	State of Cambodia

SRSG	Special Representative of the Secretary-General
TSE	Tribunal Supremo Electoral (Supreme Electoral Court)
UDT	União Democrática Timorense
UIS	United Nations Educational, Scientific and Cultural Organization Institute for Statistics
UN	United Nations
UNAMET	United Nations Mission in East Timor
UNAMSIL	United Nations Mission in Sierra Leone
UNDP	United Nations Development Programme
UNESCO	United Nations Educational, Scientific and Cultural Organization
UNHCR	United Nations High Commissioner for Refugees
UNMIL	United Nations Mission in Liberia
UNODC	United Nations Office on Drugs and Crime
UNTAC	United Nations Transitional Authority in Cambodia
UNTAET	United Nations Transitional Administration in East Timor
USAID	U.S. Agency for International Development
WGI	Worldwide Governance Indicators

CHAPTER ONE

Introduction

During the Cold War, civil and regional conflicts often resulted in the two superpowers taking opposing sides, perpetuating rather than resolving the violence. Since the end of the Cold War, the international community has found it politically possible on several occasions to intervene collectively using military, as well as political and economic, means to help end conflicts and prevent their reoccurrence. In these instances, keeping the peace has required more than putting a stop to the fighting. Combatants needed to demobilize and reintegrate into society. Competition for wealth and power needed to be redirected from violent into peaceful channels. Institutions for governance needed to be reformed and strengthened. In some cases, indeed, such institutions had to be created anew.

For more than two decades, the international community has joined together repeatedly for these purposes. The United States has led United Nations (UN)–sanctioned coalitions of the willing into Somalia, Haiti, Bosnia, Kosovo, and Afghanistan. The European Union (EU) and the African Union have each organized multiple such missions, usually on a somewhat smaller scale. Most numerous have been the peacekeeping operations conducted by the United Nations itself.

During the Cold War, peacekeepers tended to confine their efforts to separating combatants, usually seeking to freeze, rather than resolve, the underlying conflicts. Since 1989, most peacekeeping missions have gone well beyond simply observing or enforcing cease-fires, with mandates to promote reconciliation among contending populations, create functioning national institutions, and rebuild shattered societies. In the United States, this broader panoply of postconflict activities has often been labeled *nation-building*. In Europe, the preferred term is *state-building*, and, at the United Nations, *peace-building*. The international missions that engage in such activities are often referred to as *peace operations*; most often these operations are regarded as *peacekeeping* among more or less willing parties, but, occasionally, they are characterized as *peace enforcement*, involving one or more parties that must first be compelled to stop fighting. When such operations fail to maintain peace, they sometimes degenerate into prolonged counterinsurgency campaigns, an activity that this volume does not address.

RAND has devoted three volumes of case studies to the activities of the United States, Europe, and the United Nations in the realm of nation-building.[1] We employ the term *nation-building* to describe operations conducted by external civilian and military authorities that employ armed force alongside other means of influence in the aftermath of conflict to promote enduring peace. The alternative term *state-building* gives primacy to postconflict activities aimed at constructing state institutions and deemphasizes those activities intended to build a national identity. *Peace-building* perhaps best captures the overriding purpose of the types of externally directed operations on which we focus. We have stuck with *nation-building*, the most common label in American parlance, albeit one often applied pejoratively, and we include in our definition of nation-building operations only those that include at least some element of armed force—the deployment of foreign troops or armed foreign police or both—as part of a full array of

---

[1] See James Dobbins, John G. McGinn, Keith Crane, Seth G. Jones, Rollie Lal, Andrew Rathmell, Rachel M. Swanger, and Anga R. Timilsina, *America's Role in Nation-Building: From Germany to* Iraq, Santa Monica, Calif.: RAND Corporation, MR-1753-RC, 2003; James Dobbins, Seth G. Jones, Keith Crane, Andrew Rathmell, Brett Steele, Richard Teltschik, and Anga R. Timilsina, *The UN's Role in Nation-Building: From the Congo to Iraq*, Santa Monica, Calif.: RAND Corporation, MG-304-RC, 2005; and James Dobbins, Seth G. Jones, Keith Crane, Christopher S. Chivvis, Andrew Radin, F. Stephen Larrabee, Nora Bensahel, Brooke Stearns Lawson, and Benjamin W. Goldsmith, *Europe's Role in Nation-Building: From the Balkans to the Congo*, Santa Monica, Calif.: RAND Corporation, MG-722-RC, 2008.

levers of influence.[2] We do not mean to suggest that external military intervention is always necessary or desirable in a postconflict environment but simply that these are the universe of cases we intend to study.

In each of the prior RAND volumes, the authors examined half a dozen instances in which international coalitions employed armed force and various forms of diplomatic, humanitarian, and economic instruments to end conflicts and prevent their reoccurrence. Each case study described the initial conditions that the interveners faced, the strategies they adopted, the resources they committed (such as troops, foreign aid, and technical assistance), and the results they achieved. Based on these case studies, conclusions were reached regarding the resource and policy requirements for successful intervention. These conclusions led to a fourth RAND volume, *The Beginner's Guide to Nation-Building*, which sought to provide general guidelines for the conduct of such missions that would be applicable across a broad range of future cases.[3]

The prime objective of peace operations, is, as the term suggests, peace. International interventions are not launched to make poor countries rich, or even to make authoritarian societies democratic. The spur to such interventions is international or civil conflict, and their main purpose is to bring such conflict to an enduring end or, where a conflict has ended, to minimize the risk of it resuming.[4] Prosperity and social justice are valid goals in their own right, but they are not the criteria by which the decision to launch and to terminate nation-building interventions utilizing armed force are made. There are many contexts in which foreign aid is offered in support of economic devel-

---

[2] We do not include within our definition military interventions whose primary purpose is the achievement of military objectives for the direct benefit of the intervener.

[3] James Dobbins, Seth G. Jones, Keith Crane, and Beth Cole DeGrasse, *The Beginner's Guide to Nation-Building*, Santa Monica, Calif.: RAND Corporation, MG-557-SRF, 2007.

[4] In Iraq and Afghanistan, the U.S.-led military interventions were not intended to end a conflict, but the nation-building activities that followed—while conflict was ongoing—were intended to shape conditions in ways that would foster peace. In Albania and Macedonia (among the 20 post–Cold War interventions discussed in Chapter Nine), interventions were precipitated by low-level conflicts that did not meet the threshold of civil war but had the potential for escalation.

opment and political reform as goals in themselves, but, in the context of nation-building, progress in these areas is promoted as a means by which violent competition can be redirected into peaceful channels. It is the degree to which violent societies have been transformed into peaceful ones that should be the primary measure of success for operations that had that as their prime purpose. Achieving subsidiary objectives, such as improving governance, advancing democracy, fostering economic growth, and promoting human development, is important but of enduring value only so long as war does not resume and reverse such progress.

Scholarly studies have undertaken statistical analyses of the factors that may make countries prone to civil war.[5] These factors include various geopolitical and geographic, social and cultural, political, and economic characteristics and conditions. For example, one study found that the factors that raise the risk of civil war include large populations, low per capita incomes, recent political instability, poor democratic institutions, small militaries, rough terrain, war-prone neighbors, and low economic growth.[6] These and related findings are discussed in Chapter Two.

Measures taken to alter, mitigate, or even eliminate these factors offer means of reducing the risk of renewed conflict. In general terms, such measures may include improving the provision of public services, establishing democratic government, fostering economic growth, and changing the behavior of neighboring states. Studies from the international development, foreign aid, and democracy-promotion fields pro-

---

[5]   Two of the most prominent such studies are Paul Collier, Anke Hoeffler, and Dominic Rohner, "Beyond Greed and Grievance: Feasibility and Civil War," *Oxford Economic Papers*, Vol. 61, No. 1, 2009, pp. 1–27, and James D. Fearon and David D. Laitin, "Ethnicity, Insurgency, and Civil War," *American Political Science Review*, Vol. 97, No. 1, February 2003, pp. 75–90.

[6]   Håvard Hegre and Nicholas Sambanis, "Sensitivity Analysis of Empirical Results on Civil War Onset," *Journal of Conflict Resolution*, Vol. 50, No. 4, August 2006, pp. 508–535; see also Michael W. Doyle and Nicholas Sambanis, *Making War and Building Peace: United Nations Peace Operations*, Princeton, N.J.: Princeton University Press, 2006.

vide insights into reasons that achieving these goals is especially difficult in fragile and conflict-affected states.[7]

RAND's previous studies on nation-building have aimed to provide guidance for the planning and implementation of such interventions. These studies discern from historical cases widely applicable lessons that can be used to help identify realistic ends for nation-building missions and design the means to achieve those ends. Some analysts have argued that these and other studies of nation-building have focused too heavily on the actions taken by the nation-building interveners, without fully considering the *local factors* that are central to determining whether the nation-building means applied will produce the ends desired. In particular, prior RAND and other studies have sometimes been criticized for proposing "one-size-fits-all" solutions that ignore widely differing local environments.[8]

Some scholars and institutions have warned that generic strategies for nation-building are more likely to end in failure than those that are tailored to the specific and perhaps unique conditions in the society emerging from civil war.[9] The OECD's 2010 *Do No Harm* report highlights the potentially damaging effects of routinely pursuing such objectives as electoral competition or decentralization, which do not necessarily result in less confrontational political outcomes.[10]

---

[7] See, for instance, Paul Collier, *The Bottom Billion: Why the Poorest Countries Are Failing and What Can Be Done About It*, Oxford, UK: Oxford University Press, 2007.

[8] Herein, we use the term *local factors* to refer to the conditions in and around and the characteristics of the country that is the subject of an intervention. We do not address in this study domestic factors related to states that are the interveners, many of which also may affect nation-building plans, actions, and outcomes.

[9] See, for instance, Organisation for Economic Co-operation and Development (OECD), *Concepts and Dilemmas of State Building in Fragile Situations: From Fragility to Resilience*, Paris, 2009, p. 8.

[10] OECD, *Do No Harm: International Support for Statebuilding*, Paris, November 1, 2010, p. 11. See also Edward D. Mansfield and Jack Snyder, "Democratization and the Danger of War," *International Security*, Vol. 20, No. 1, Summer 1995, pp. 5–38; Paul Collier and Dominic Rohner, "Democracy, Development, and Conflict," *Journal of the European Economic Association*, Vol. 6, No. 2–3, April–May 2008, pp. 531–540; and Rory Stewart and Gerald Knaus, *Can Intervention Work?* New York: W. W. Norton and Company, 2011, p. 136.

A 2008 report from the UK Department for International Development (DFID) states that "the work on nation-building has underlined the centrality of states within development, and has also highlighted the potential for donors to both help and hinder their improvement."[11] These studies and others note that nation-builders' "footprint" may disrupt local skilled-labor markets,[12] create new grievances now directed against the interveners,[13] or prove a destabilizing, rather than empowering, force.[14]

Occasionally, criticism of generic nation-building guidelines goes so far as to maintain that each case is so different from the others that each must be treated as sui generis. Critics have claimed that local conditions confound any so-called "cookie-cutter" approaches to planning for these missions, making general "guides" to nation-building highly problematic.[15] This criticism is most frequently made by those engaged in program implementation in the field (or academics who dedicate most of their research to interviewing field personnel), and, unsurprisingly, their narrative tends to adopt the tone of committed field work-

---

[11] Alan Whaites, *States in Development: Understanding State-Building*, UK Department for International Development, working paper, 2008, p. 3.

[12] OECD, 2010, p. 16.

[13] Doyle and Sambanis, 2006; David M. Edelstein, "Occupational Hazards: Why Military Occupations Succeed or Fail," *International Security*, Vol. 29, No. 1, Summer 2004, pp. 49–91; David Kilcullen, *The Accidental Guerrilla: Fighting Small Wars in the Midst of a Big One*, Oxford, UK: Oxford University Press, 2009.

[14] See, for instance, Roland Paris, *At War's End: Building Peace After Civil Conflict*, Cambridge, UK: Cambridge University Press, 2004.

[15] Gerald Knaus, for instance, writes that

> interveners are never in a good position to understand what objectives are actually achievable or how to achieve them before a mission starts. It is by trial and error—by learning from failure as well as success—that a mission understands gradually what it might be able to achieve. (Stewart and Knaus, 2011, p. 188)

Lise Morjé Howard argues that,

> rather than seeking to impose preconceived notions about how the missions should unfold, peacekeeping is at its best when the peacekeepers—both civilian and military— take their cues from the local population, and not UN headquarters, about how best to implement mandates. (Lise Morjé Howard, *UN Peacekeeping in Civil Wars*, Cambridge, UK: Cambridge University Press, 2008, p. 2)

ers battling rigid headquarters bureaucracies far removed from the realities on the ground.

International interventions, however, require considerable effort from headquarters bureaucracies to raise and sustain the necessary troops and civilian personnel, defend expenditures to skeptical domestic audiences, and develop international consensus on mandates and rules of engagement, among other responsibilities. The efforts of forward-deployed personnel are important but are not the whole story of how nation-building missions succeed or fail. Guidance aimed at headquarters-level policymakers is needed—and, indeed, actively sought.

A broader strain of critique implicitly rejects generalized guidance for nation-builders by questioning the very enterprise of nation-building. These criticisms take many forms but, at their core, cast doubt on the ability of external actors to transform foreign societies. In this view, nation-building is seen as capable at best of restoring the status quo ante—that is, the conditions in the host nation that prevailed before the onset of the conflict that precipitated international intervention. If this view is accurate, then any effort to overcome the "root causes" of conflict by transforming host-nation political, economic, and social structures is misguided, and the societies in question will be as prone to civil war at the conclusion of such efforts as they were when the previous conflict started.

Local circumstances are not immutable, however. Social, political, economic, and institutional change may come slowly, but come it does and often measurably over even a few years. Even the effects of geography can be altered. Roads, bridges, airports, power lines, dams, and ports not only alter the landscape; they can profoundly change the way people interact with each other and their environment. Even more mutable can be a country's geopolitical environment—that is to say the behavior of its neighbors and of other foreign powers with influence over the country's policies and its population.

Previous RAND studies have focused on the activities of external interveners. In this volume, we seek to turn around the telescope, shifting the perspective from external actors to internal circumstances, first identifying the local circumstances that gave rise to conflicts or threatened to perpetuate them, and then determining whether and how external actors were able to modify or work around those circumstances to promote an enduring peace.

We begin by reviewing the literature on the causes of conflict (specifically, civil wars) and identifying the characteristics of societies most at risk of falling into it. We then look in more detail at the role local factors have played in causing six different conflicts and in threatening their repetition. In the order of their occurrences, we examine a geographically, culturally, and socioeconomically diverse set of post-conflict interventions in Cambodia, El Salvador, Bosnia, East Timor, Sierra Leone, and the Democratic Republic of the Congo (DRC). In each case, a first section describes the local factors that nation-builders encountered at the time of intervention, including those that existed prior to the conflict and those that developed in the course of the conflict. We then describe whether and how the interveners sought to alter or circumvent these factors through nation-building activities and the degree of success they achieved. Where data were available, we have tried to describe how the local populations viewed this process.

In our penultimate chapter, we widen the aperture, looking at the fuller range of substantial nation-building interventions in the years after the Cold War—20 in all, including all those examined in RAND's prior three-volume analysis of U.S., European, and UN operations in this field. We measure the degree of success in maintaining peace, establishing democracy, improving the quality of governance, expanding the economy, and advancing human development using widely available and generally accepted yardsticks in each of these categories.

We also compare the degree of success with the degree of difficulty in each case. Using parameters estimated by Fearon and Laitin (2003), we estimate the probabilities of civil war occurring for each of these 20 countries. Our estimate is for the probability of civil war onset (which, in these cases, would be a recurrence of civil war) at the point in time when the intervention was launched. Because the primary goal of nation-building interventions is to prevent the recurrence of civil conflict, this probability—that is, the risk that conditions in the country will cause renewed civil war—should provide a rough approximation of the degree of challenge that the interveners and local leaders face. We use these estimations of each country's propensity for conflict to rank the 20 countries in terms of the approximate difficulty of each case.

The concluding chapter provides policymakers with the means to judge with greater clarity both the chances that a particular nation-building operation will succeed and the means by which nation-building can be more effectively pursued in the light of local circumstances.

CHAPTER TWO

Which Local Factors Pose Challenges to Nation-Building?

States and international organizations that intervene in conflict-affected countries to establish security, help build representative government institutions, and promote economic growth and social well-being do so principally for the purpose of trying to foster durable peace. The basic premise underlying nation-building interventions is that conditions in and around the country subject to an intervention can be changed in ways that reduce the risk of conflict resuming or new conflict emerging. Thus, nation-building interveners need to understand the factors that elevate those risks and affect the outcomes they can reasonably expect to achieve, and they should tailor their plans and actions to resolving or mitigating those factors.

It is necessary, therefore, to identify the general types of conditions in and around and characteristics of a country with which nation-builders need to concern themselves. The specific conditions and characteristics that actually influence a particular country's propensity for conflict will vary case by case and will demand variation in approaches to nation-building, as the case studies in this volume illustrate.

Scholars have sought to discern types of factors that, on average, raise the risk of conflict. We begin, therefore, by exploring the literature that seeks to identify these factors and that informs the analytical framework for the case studies in this volume.

Factors That Raise the Risk of Conflict Renewal

Civil War Onset

Because the purpose of nation-building is to promote durable peace in countries emerging from violent conflict, the most-relevant local factors nation-builders ought to understand and in some way address are those most likely to stand in the way of achieving that purpose—in other words, the factors associated with the risk of renewed conflict. These local factors that threaten intervention success are the ones that nation-builders will want to modify, overcome, or circumvent. To find out which are, on average, the most-important risk factors, we look to several statistical analyses of the causes of civil war that use large sets of data and statistical methods.

The body of academic literature that seeks to isolate the factors that affect proneness to civil war is large but fraught with both theoretical and empirical uncertainty.[1] Beyond the statistical analyses, there are many qualitative examinations of this issue and individual case studies that reach varying conclusions about which factors are most important. A study by Hegre and Sambanis examined 88 variables used to explain civil war onset in the empirical literature and found only two points of consensus among scholars: The risk of civil war decreases as average income increases and as the size of a country's population decreases. Beyond these two points—that wealthier and smaller countries are at lower risk of civil war—discrepancies in empirical findings abound, and the effects of different variables are heavily debated. Hegre and Sambanis argue that some of the discrepancies are due to failures to adequately test the fragility of empirical results, some due to differences in the statistical models used, and some due to differences in the definition of *civil war* used in different studies.[2]

---

[1]   We focus on the extensive, if unsettled, body of literature that studies the causes of civil war, not lower-level conflict, though we use the term *conflict* here as well as *civil war*.

[2]   Hegre and Sambanis, 2006, pp. 508–509, 515. They define *civil war* as

> an armed conflict between an internationally recognized state and (mainly) domestic challengers able to mount an organized military opposition to the state. The war must have caused more than 1,000 deaths in total and in at least a three-year period. (p. 523)

Hegre and Sambanis themselves also used statistical methods to test the most–frequently cited and influential findings in the scholarly literature and concluded that only nine variables have robust positive relationships with the onset of civil war: a large population, low per capita income, recent political instability, inconsistent democratic institutions (i.e., institutions with a mix of democratic and autocratic features), a small military, rough terrain, war-prone neighbors, undemocratic regions, and low rates of economic growth. In other words, civil wars are more likely to occur in countries with these conditions.[3] Among the heavily debated explanations for civil war for which they did *not* find robust empirical results was ethnic heterogeneity.[4]

Among the sets of findings that Hegre and Sambanis test are two especially influential ones. These include Fearon and Laitin's findings that proneness to civil war is principally attributable to the structural conditions that favor insurgency.[5] According to Fearon and Laitin, the main risk factors are poverty (the lower the per capita income, the greater the risk of civil war), large populations, political instability, and rough terrain. Weak governments render insurgency more feasible and more attractive. In addition, new states are especially at risk,[6] and dependence on oil exports heightens the risk as well. Ethnic and religious diversity, and grievances (such as income inequality, lack of democracy or civil liberties, or state discrimination against minorities), they find, are *not* good predictors of which countries are at risk for civil war.

Using a different statistical model from that used by Fearon and Laitin, influential work by Paul Collier and various colleagues has pro-

---

[3] Hegre and Sambanis, 2006, p. 531.

[4] Specifically, they found that ethnic fractionalization is associated with low-intensity armed conflict but not civil war and that ethnic dominance seems to raise the risk of the most-serious conflicts but not the lower-level ones (Hegre and Sambanis, 2006, p. 529).

[5] Fearon and Laitin, 2003.

[6] The odds of civil war onset are estimated as 5.25 times greater in the first two years of a state's independent existence than in other years (Fearon and Laitin, 2003, p. 85). This factor is evident in the estimated probabilities for Bosnia and Kosovo shown in Table 9.1 in Chapter Nine.

duced findings that both coincide and conflict with Fearon and Laitin's.[7] Collier and his colleagues also find that, where rebellion is financially and militarily feasible, it will occur and that the likelihood of civil war is most affected by nine factors: low gross domestic product (GDP) per capita; low GDP growth; primary commodity–export dependence (not just oil); peace duration (risks decline as duration lengthens, but the effect is very slow);[8] large population size; ethno-linguistic and religious fractionalization; being a former French colony in Africa; having a large number of young males (aged 15 to 29); and, though based on a weaker statistical result, mountainous terrain. Collier and colleagues conclude that reducing the incidence of civil war requires making it more difficult (or expensive) to engage in such conflict.

We have highlighted here the above sets of findings from statistical analyses that are very widely cited and regarded as especially rigorous and thus merit focused attention. Reviewing the full body of literature on the causes of civil war can tend to produce a laundry list of possible risk factors. Nevertheless, looking more broadly at the statistical and other literature, we find a variety of explanations for civil war onset—with mixed theoretical and empirical support—that are useful to consider in assessing the challenges that local factors pose for nation-building.

Geopolitical context has been seen as an important factor because states surrounded by other states at war have been shown to be more susceptible to collapse.[9] State failure, in other words, can spill across

---

[7]   Collier, Hoeffler, and Rohner, 2009. This paper revisits, overturns, and extends results from an earlier, widely cited one: Paul Collier and Anke Hoeffler, "Greed and Grievance in Civil War," *Oxford Economic Papers*, Vol. 56, No. 4, October 2004b, pp. 563–595. Though widely influential, Collier's work has been subject to some sharp criticism. See, e.g., David Keen, "Greed and Grievance in Civil War," *International Affairs*, Vol. 88, No. 4, July 2012, pp. 757–777.

[8]   They find in this study that, ten years postconflict, a country has a 14.2-percent risk of civil war onset and, 20 years postconflict, an 8.6-percent risk (Collier, Hoeffler, and Rohner, 2009, p. 13).

[9]   Nicholas Sambanis, "Do Ethnic and Nonethnic Civil Wars Have the Same Causes? A Theoretical and Empirical Inquiry (Part 1)," *Journal of Conflict Resolution*, Vol. 45, No. 3, June 2001, pp. 259–282; Kristian Skrede Gleditsch, *All International Politics Is Local: The*

borders.[10] At the same time, however, geopolitical context may also encourage stability if there is an external threat that encourages local elites to cooperate with international authorities, as was the case most notably after World War II in West Germany.[11]

One widely recognized conflict risk factor relates to a country's geography. A country's physical terrain or geographical location may offer safe haven for insurgents. Safe haven might come in the form of neighboring countries sympathetic to a rebel cause or in the form of rugged terrain that provides ready cover for rebel forces.[12] This problem is especially acute when the armed forces of the state in question are weak.[13]

There is considerable debate about the extent to which history, culture, and society shape postconflict challenges, but many scholars see these types of factors as having some impact. The work of some scholars suggests that certain cultures may be more violent than others. In these instances, violence is easier to legitimate, generally expected, and thus more apt to take place. Some cultures appear to enable intra-state violence in ways that are unexpected and significant.[14]

Ethnic composition of the population is perhaps the single most prominent social factor in contemporary conflict, although its precise impact is much debated. Here, the question of whether ethnically heterogeneous societies are more susceptible to conflict must be disaggregated from questions concerning the particular nature of conflicts that

---

Diffusion of Conflict, Integration, and Democratization, Ann Arbor, Mich.: University of Michigan Press, 2002; Hegre and Sambanis, 2006, p. 508.

[10] René Lemarchand, *The Dynamics of Violence in Central Africa*, Philadelphia, Pa.: University of Pennsylvania Press, 2009, p. 221.

[11] Edelstein, 2004.

[12] Fearon and Laitin, 2003; Halvard Buhaug, Scott Gates, and Päivi Lujala, "Geography, Rebel Capability, and the Duration of Civil Conflict," *Journal of Conflict Resolution*, Vol. 53, No. 4, August 2009, pp. 544–569.

[13] Nicholas Sambanis, "Partition as a Solution to Ethnic War: An Empirical Critique of the Theoretical Literature," *World Politics*, Vol. 52, No. 4, 2000, pp. 437–483; Hegre and Sambanis, 2006.

[14] Mats R. Berdal, *Building Peace After War*, Abingdon, UK: Routledge, 2009, pp. 72–75.

take on an ethnic character. There is nothing about ethnic diversity in and of itself that causes conflict, and few scholars would argue that ethnicity matters significantly in the sense that "ethnic hatreds" alone can give rise to violence.[15] The evidence that ethnically heterogeneous societies are prone to war is mixed.[16] Evidence seems to suggest that, although heterogeneous societies are no more prone to war than others, societies in which the population is polarized into a few large groups may be.[17]

When combined with other catalyzing factors, however, conflict along ethnic lines can and often does occur. Ethnic divisions may be rooted in long-standing conflicts or more-recent struggles, but many of these conflicts are latent until the state weakens and local elites seize on them as opportunities to galvanize support.[18] Moreover, although the parties to the conflict may be defined along ethnic lines, the issues at stake may be economic or political in nature. In other words, context matters.

After a war has been fought along ethnic lines, distrust among such groups naturally becomes a powerful impediment to peace-building, especially if it contributes to physical insecurity or undermines economic recovery. Intermingled populations can make self-defense problematic, thus increasing fears and insecurity. Moreover, ethnic conflicts, by contrast with ideological conflicts, often draw the

---

[15] For a summary of scholarship on ethnic conflict, see Chaim Kaufmann, "Rational Choice and Progress in the Study of Ethnic Conflict: A Review Essay," *Security Studies*, Vol. 14, No. 1, January–March 2005, pp. 178–207.

[16] Fearon and Laitin, 2003; José G. Montalvo and Marta Reynal-Querol, "Ethnic Polarization, Potential Conflict, and Civil Wars," *American Economic Review*, Vol. 95, No. 3, June 2005, pp. 797–816; Lars-Erik Cederman and Luc Girardin, "Beyond Fractionalization: Mapping Ethnicity onto Nationalist Insurgencies," *American Political Science Review*, Vol. 101, No. 1, February 2007, pp. 173–185.

[17] Montalvo and Reynal-Querol, 2005; Christopher Blattman and Edward Miguel, *Civil War: A Review of Fifty Years of Research*, Washington, D.C.: Center for Global Development, Working Paper 166, March 21, 2009, p. 43.

[18] Robert H. Bates, *When Things Fell Apart: State Failure in Late-Century Africa*, New York: Cambridge University Press, 2008.

very existence of the country as a political community into question, thereby complicating postconflict nation-building.[19]

As with culture, ethnicity can also matter if the content of an ethnic group's mythology and ethos tends to legitimize violence. When one party to a conflict is reputed to have a warrior ethos that rewards violence, the fears of its former adversaries will intensify.[20]

When a particular ethnic group straddles a border, the feasibility of sustaining a conflict increases because the ethnic group will have a safe haven and possible external sources of financing.[21] Ethnic diasporas living farther away sometimes provide financial support for rebel causes as well.[22] Although the impact of diasporas is difficult to measure systematically across cases, particular cases suggest that diasporas can play an important role in perpetuating a conflict, as, for example, diaspora support for the Kosovo Liberation Army did in the Kosovo conflict of the later 1990s.

The extent to which war is caused by economic forces is a perennial subject in political science. Economic factors are widely agreed to be important when it comes to state collapse and civil war. Many, although not all, of the conflicts in which the international community has intervened since the end of the Cold War have occurred in low-income countries. However, the impact of economic forces varies.

In general, economic factors can be either direct causes of conflict or contributing factors that facilitate conflict. On the most basic level, in agricultural societies, population pressure on the land, or differences between pastoral and farming modes of production, can lead to con-

---

[19] Daniel Byman and Taylor Seybolt, "Humanitarian Intervention and Communal Civil Wars," *Security Studies*, Vol. 13, No. 1, 2003, pp. 33–78; compare Stathis N. Kalyvas, "Civil Wars," in Carles Boix and Susan Carol Stokes, eds., *The Oxford Handbook of Comparative Politics*, Oxford, UK: Oxford University Press, 2007, pp. 416–434.

[20] Stuart J. Kaufman, *Modern Hatreds: The Symbolic Politics of Ethnic War*, New York: Cornell University Press, 2001.

[21] Kristian Skrede Gleditsch, "Transnational Dimensions of Civil War," *Journal of Peace Research*, Vol. 44, No. 3, May 2007, pp. 293–309.

[22] Collier and Hoeffler, 2004b; Blattman and Miguel, 2009, p. 42.

flicts between tribes and ethnic groups.[23] In other cases, rebel factions fight to control natural resources, such as diamonds.[24] Economic factors can also play a facilitating role, as when poverty makes it easier to recruit rebel soldiers for insurgencies.[25] Sometimes the distinction is unclear, however: Lootable resources can serve as direct causes of conflict, as well as facilitating factors when they pay for rebel armies.

Economic fragility can also weaken the fiscal foundation of a state and thereby increase dissatisfaction with the quality of government services and governance in general while undermining the state's capacity to defend itself and provide security and other public goods.[26] Fiscal weakness constrains public-sector salaries, and hence the quality of public services, and often is associated with corruption.

Exogenous shocks—for example, a drought, an increase in the price of an important consumable, or decrease in the price of an important export—can also trigger violence.[27] More broadly, economic growth or decline can have disproportionate effects on different groups in societies, thereby creating or intensifying existing frictions.[28] Economic modernization can also, in some instances, pose a threat

---

[23] Bates, 2008, pp. 75–93.

[24] Michael L. Ross, "What Do We Know About Natural Resources and Civil War?" *Journal of Peace Research*, Vol. 41, No. 3, May 2004, pp. 337–356; James Ron, "Paradigm in Distress? Primary Commodities and Civil War," *Journal of Conflict Resolution*, Vol. 49, No. 4, August 2005, pp. 443–450; Macartan Humphreys, "Natural Resources, Conflict, and Conflict Resolution: Uncovering the Mechanisms," *Journal of Conflict Resolution*, Vol. 49, No. 4, August 2005, pp. 508–537.

[25] Collier, Hoeffler, and Rohner, 2009; Collier and Hoeffler, 2004b; Fearon and Laitin, 2003.

[26] James D. Fearon, "Economic Development, Insurgency, and Civil War," in Elhanan Helpman, ed., *Institutions and Economic Performance*, Cambridge, Mass.: Harvard University Press, 2008, pp. 292–328.

[27] Edward Miguel, Shanker Satyanath, and Ernest Sergenti, "Economic Shocks and Civil Conflict: An Instrumental Variables Approach," *Journal of Political Economy*, Vol. 122, No. 4, August 2004, pp. 725–753; Oeindrila Dube and Juan Vargas, *Commodity Price Shocks and Civil Conflict: Evidence from Colombia*, Cambridge, Mass.: Harvard University Press, 2008.

[28] The evidence regarding the relationship between inequality and violence is weak, however (Blattman and Miguel, 2009, p. 37; Barbara F. Walter, "Does Conflict Beget Con-

to group identities, although the evidence for this is less strong. Most scholars agree that economic development is generally helpful in preventing the outbreak of war. Both rates of growth and levels of national income seem to matter.[29]

There is no ironclad relationship between economic development and reduced violence, however, and a lack of development obviously does not necessarily result in war. The causal relationship between poverty and violence is often indirect and depends on context.[30] Poor countries with large populations, for example, appear to be more fragile than poor, small countries.[31] Countries that are poor but small have a better chance of maintaining political order than large countries with sparse population and low incomes, where the fiscal requirements of sustaining a monopoly on violence—the classic Weberian definition of state control—are higher.[32]

State weakness is a cause as much as a consequence of violent conflict, and some conflicts are best understood as the result of a breakdown in the state's ability to provide security for its citizens. State failure may force citizens to take care of their own security by arming themselves. This then gives rise to the so-called security dilemma.[33] The fears of one group lead it to arm itself to enhance its security, but, in so doing, the group increases the sense of insecurity among other groups, encouraging them to arm in turn. The security dilemma tends to be more severe when groups have little information about each other's intentions and therefore assume the worst. Widespread access to small arms, certain ethnic geographies, and other factors can exac-

---

flict? Explaining Recurring Civil War," *Journal of Peace Research*, Vol. 41, No. 3, May 2004, pp. 371–388).

[29] Collier and Hoeffler, 2004b.

[30] Blattman and Miguel, 2009, p. 2; Berdal, 2009, p. 80.

[31] Hegre and Sambanis, 2006, p. 508.

[32] Jeffrey Ira Herbst, *States and Power in Africa: Comparative Lessons in Authority and Control*, Princeton, N.J.: Princeton University Press, 2000.

[33] Kenneth Neal Waltz, *Theory of International Politics*, New York: McGraw-Hill, 1979.

erbate insecurity.[34] Inherently weak states that are unable to provide security for their populations are thus a necessary precondition for the security dilemma to exist.

Finally, political contests among different social or ideological groups are far more likely to lead to violence if a country's political institutions are weak and the country is only partially democratic. There is evidence that these so-called anocracies are more susceptible to violence, perhaps because they offer freedom to associate and opportunities for dissent, but at the same time are mostly unresponsive to grievances that are voiced through political channels.[35]

Civil War Recurrence

The studies discussed above search for the factors associated with *onset* of civil war, but nation-builders are more specifically concerned with preventing the *recurrence* of civil war in countries where civil wars were recently fought and ended. Logically, recent experience with violent conflict could alter social, political, and economic conditions in ways that change the risk factors. Collier et al. found that the risk of conflict recurrence is greater than the risk of conflict onset,[36] which suggests that the factors contributing to the risk of civil war recidivism are either different from those for conflict onset or the same but more powerful.

The empirical literature focused on civil war *recurrence* is limited and lacks an agreed theory of the causes.[37] One statistical study by

---

[34] Barry R. Posen, "The Security Dilemma and Ethnic Conflict," *Survival*, Vol. 35, No. 1, Spring 1993, pp. 27–47; William Rose, "The Security Dilemma and Ethnic Conflict: Some New Hypotheses," *Security Studies*, Vol. 9, No. 4, Summer 2000, pp. 1–51; Daniel Byman, *Keeping the Peace: Lasting Solutions to Ethnic Conflicts*, Baltimore, Md.: Johns Hopkins University Press, 2002.

[35] Håvard Hegre, Tanja Ellingsen, Scott Gates, and Nils Petter Gleditsch, "Toward a Democratic Civil Peace? Democracy, Political Change, and Civil War, 1816–1992," *American Political Science Review*, Vol. 95, No. 1, March 2001, pp. 33–48; Fearon and Laitin, 2003; Blattman and Miguel, 2009, pp. 38–39; Gleditsch, 2007.

[36] Collier, Hoeffler, and Rohner, 2009, pp. 13–14.

[37] See Paul Collier, Anke Hoeffler, and Måns Söderbom, "Post-Conflict Risks," *Journal of Peace Research*, Vol. 45, No. 4, July 2008, pp. 461–478, p. 462 (noting that there is a large case-study literature on postconflict situations but few quantitative comparative studies of postconflict risks); Barbara F. Walter, *Conflict Relapse and the Sustainability of Post-Conflict*

Collier and others found that postconflict peace appears to depend on a gradual economic recovery and an external military presence, with political design playing a lesser role. Specifically, they found that the risk of conflict renewal is considerably higher in low-income countries; faster economic growth significantly reduces risk in the year in which it occurs, as well as cumulating into a higher level of income; highly autocratic states have a significantly lower risk; postconflict elections modestly increase risk; a large diaspora lowers risk; and peacekeeping expenditures significantly reduce risk. The ethnic composition of society, they found, was not a significant factor.[38]

Two of these variables associated with civil war recurrence— income level and growth—coincide with Collier and his colleagues' findings regarding civil war onset, discussed above, but the rest of the findings are different.[39] The two sets of findings are based on different statistical methodologies, which makes the divergence between Collier et al.'s onset and recurrence findings difficult to explain. The authors suggest that reasons for recurrence may include circumstances related to the legacies of conflict, including the residual organizational capacity of rebel armies, the plenitude of armaments, and erosion of income levels.[40]

Although many postconflict countries will have many of the conditions associated with risk of civil war recurrence, it is apparent that not all of them will actually experience recurrence. This raises the question of what distinguishes those countries that do actually experience renewed conflict from those that do not. In contrast to Collier (an economist) and his colleagues, who emphasize economic factors, Walter (a political scientist) points to state weakness militarily and institutionally as a principal factor explaining variation in the outbreak

Peace, World Bank, World Development Report 2011, background paper, September 13, 2010, p. 5.

[38] Collier, Hoeffler, and Söderbom, 2008, pp. 467–473.

[39] See Collier, Hoeffler, and Söderbom, 2008, p. 466.

[40] Collier, Hoeffler, and Rohner, 2009, pp. 13–14, 23.

of violence across countries that have a similar risk of returning to civil war.[41]

Walter's findings regarding civil war renewal differ from those of Collier and his colleagues in several other respects as well: She finds that ethnic, religious, and ethno-linguistic fractionalization significantly increase the risk; that peacekeeping does not appear to reduce the risk; and that autocratic states are not more resistant to renewed conflict. Governance plays a more important role in her analysis. She finds that governments that follow good governance practices are much less likely to face renewed conflict.[42] Walter's and Collier et al.'s studies of recurrence use different data sets and different statistical models and analytical approaches. Moreover, their theoretical orientations differ.

Some scholars have focused attention on the impact that the length of a conflict has on the chances of recurrence. A long and violent conflict can have contradictory effects not only on the risk of renewed conflict but also on the difficulty of implementing nation-building programs. On the one hand, a high level of conflict can lead different sides to entrench their positions, thereby reducing the chances of reconciliation. This effect could be expected to be greater where the conflict has an ethnic character and where there was no negotiated settlement. A long conflict also destroys infrastructure and resources and can make the challenge of rebuilding all the greater for that reason alone.[43] At the same time, however, long and intense conflicts also lead to war weariness and, for this reason, are thought to increase participants' willingness to cooperate with a peace process and stabilization effort.[44]

---

[41] Walter, 2010, p. 8.

[42] Similar to Collier, Hoeffler, and Rohner's findings regarding civil war onset, Walter also finds that poor economic conditions, large population size, and mountainous terrain are associated with civil war renewal (Walter, 2010, pp. 15–17).

[43] Doyle and Sambanis find this to be the case, although they note the weakness of the data and must make some adjustments for the finding to be robust. See Doyle and Sambanis, 2006, p. 98.

[44] Doyle and Sambanis, 2006, also note this potentially positive effect of war duration, p. 100.

Another body of literature that explores the causes of war has focused on the factors that make a conflict intractable, asking the question of why some "conflicts have persisted over time and refused to yield to efforts—through either negotiations by the parties or mediation with third-party assistance—to arrive at a political settlement."[45] Sources of intractability are various and include the increased polarization that results from war, leaders benefiting from conflict, or the normalization of violence[46]—all factors that result from what could be called an acclimatization to war, its benefits (for a fraction of the population), and the social identities it created or solidified. Intractability can also be caused by the involvement of a third party that ensures that the conflict does not get resolved; this is the case for so-called "frozen conflicts."[47] It is important to note, however, that sources of intractability are different from initial sources of conflict,[48] as well as from sources of conflict recurrence. The fact that a conflict has ended once suggests that factors producing intractability have been overcome. Conflict recurrence, when it takes place, is therefore likely to emerge from a different set of issues that is linked either to the initial causes of conflict or to new ones created by an unsatisfactory postconflict set of circumstances.

---

[45] Chester A. Crocker, Fen Osler Hampson, and Pamela R. Aall, *Grasping the Nettle: Analyzing Cases of Intractable Conflict*, Washington, D.C.: U.S. Institute of Peace Press, 2005, p. 5. International and civil wars are not the only types of conflicts that can be "intractable." The literature on "intractable conflicts" also examines environmental, social, and interpersonal conflicts. See, for instance, Louis Kriesberg, Terrell A. Northrup, and Stuart J. Thorson, *Intractable Conflicts and Their Transformation*, Syracuse, N.Y.: Syracuse University Press, 1989; and Peter T. Coleman, "Characteristics of Protracted, Intractable Conflict: Toward the Development of a Metaframework—I," *Peace and Conflict: Journal of Peace Psychology*, Vol. 9, No. 1, 2003, pp. 1–37.

[46] Crocker, Hampson, and Aall, 2005, pp. 6–7.

[47] See, for instance, Kevin G. Kennelly, *The Role of NATO and the EU in Resolving Frozen Conflicts*, Monterey, Calif.: Naval Postgraduate School, 2006, pp. 1–2.

[48] Crocker, Hampson, and Aall, 2005, p. 5.

How Great Is the Risk of Recurrence?

In addition to searching for the factors associated with civil war onset and renewal, scholars have sought to calculate *how great* the risk is that conflict will recur in a country that already has experienced conflict. Surprisingly, scholars have not offered a stable answer, and, in some instances, the answers they have provided have been treated as firmer than warranted.

In a widely referenced 2003 World Bank report titled *Breaking the Conflict Trap*, Paul Collier and his co-authors stated that the "typical country reaching the end of a civil war faces around a 44 percent risk of returning to conflict within five years."[49] This figure (and a similar finding of 50-percent risk within five years from a 2002 article by Collier and Hoeffler) has gained considerable currency in both policy debates and academic literature. Indeed, it has been widely and loosely stated that about half of postconflict countries fall back into civil war within five years.[50] But Collier and co-authors later offered a different estimate: 40-percent likelihood of reversion to war in the first *decade* postconflict.[51] An earlier version of the revised estimate indicated a recurrence rate of 23 percent within the first four years.[52]

What would seem to be a matter of straightforward accounting turns out not to be so; instead, estimates of civil war recurrence appear to be easily affected by changes in definitions, data, time periods, and analytical methods.[53] Nevertheless, even if the probability

---

[49] Paul Collier, V. L. Elliott, Håvard Hegre, Anke Hoeffler, Marta Reynal-Querol, and Nicholas Sambanis, *Breaking the Conflict Trap: Civil War and Development Policy*, Washington, D.C.: World Bank, 2003, p. 83.

[50] Astri Suhrke and Ingrid Samset, "What's in a Figure? Estimating Recurrence of Civil War," *International Peacekeeping*, Vol. 14, No. 2, April 2007, pp. 195–203.

[51] Collier, Hoeffler, and Söderbom, 2008, p. 465. This estimate was based on a sample of 68 postconflict episodes during the period 1960–2002.

[52] Suhrke and Samset, 2007, p. 198.

[53] Suhrke and Samset, 2007, p. 201. Walter (2010) finds that, of the 103 countries that experienced some form of civil war between 1945 and 2009 (from minor to major, all above 25 battle deaths per year threshold), 57 percent experienced at least one subsequent conflict— but not within any specified time limit. Without the temporal dimension, this figure cannot readily be compared with Collier, Hoeffler, and Söderbom's. In an earlier analysis, based on

of recurrence cannot be pinpointed with precision—and these figures are only average probabilities in any event—it is apparent that conflicts frequently recur. Nation-builders may not be able to assess with certainty the *degree* of risk that civil war will break out anew in particular countries subject to intervention, but, because many post-conflict countries do experience renewed conflict, nation-builders can be confident that the risk is genuine and that their actions should be geared to improving the odds that conflict will not recur. Simply as a matter of logic, the risk of internal dynamics producing renewed conflict should be considered particularly great in countries where external actors imposed an end to the conflict, such as in Bosnia, Kosovo, and East Timor.

Structure of the Case Studies

Because of the empirical discrepancies and theoretical uncertainty in the scholarly literature regarding which factors raise the risk of civil war occurrence and recurrence, we regard the results of the studies discussed above as suggestive of the types of factors that should matter to nation-builders but not as hard and fast predictors of the potential for renewed conflict. Nevertheless, it can fairly be concluded that, collectively, these are the types of factors that are, on average, most likely to affect the risk of civil war and thus pose challenges to nation-builders, whose primary goal is to make endurance of peace more likely.[54] With respect to the statistical analyses discussed above, even to the extent that their findings are robust, the relationships they describe are proba-

---

the period 1945 to 1996, Walter found that only 36 percent of civil wars were followed by an additional war (Walter, 2004, p. 371).

[54] Though they are the most-influential statistical examinations of the causes of civil war, the Fearon and Laitin and Collier and Hoeffler models are not without critics. Ward et al. find that both models do a "surprisingly poor job" of actually predicting civil war onsets, with Fearon and Laitin doing the worse job, and that certain variables contribute disproportionately to the models' predictive power (GDP per capita for Fearon and Laitin, and population size for Collier and Hoeffler) (Michael D. Ward, Brian D. Greenhill, and Kristin M. Bakke, "The Perils of Policy by P-Value: Predicting Civil Conflicts," *Journal of Peace Research*, Vol. 47, No. 4, July 2010, pp. 363–375).

bilistic, not determinative, and caution must be exercised in drawing inferences from these findings and applying those inferences to particular cases. But, together with the broader literature, they are useful as a starting place for canvassing the factors most likely to pose challenges to nation-building.

In the case studies in this volume, we organize our analyses of local factors into several broad categories—geographical and geopolitical, social and cultural, economic, political, and institutional. This approach enables us to explore the impact of the types of factors discussed above while focusing in each case on the specific local factors that posed challenges to nation-building and affected outcomes.

Tailoring Nation-Building to Local Factors

As noted in Chapter One, some critiques of nation-building operations charge that the most they can achieve is restoration of the status quo ante—that is, the local conditions that prevailed before the onset of the conflict—and that they cannot resolve the causes of conflict. An extended return to the status quo ante may be a significant achievement, however. Because many countries emerging from civil war return to civil war, a prolonged period of nonviolence may be an improvement over what would have happened in the absence of intervention, even if no further transformation of local conditions were achieved.[55] Moreover, if it is true that war is "development in reverse,"[56] then an intervention that reestablishes the status quo ante again represents an improvement over nonintervention. As we show in Chapter Nine, it is apparent that nation-building interventions, on the whole, set countries on positive trajectories in which local conditions improve. In the

---

[55] This argument has already been made and fairly compelling empirical support provided by several academics. See, for instance, Virginia Page Fortna, *Does Peacekeeping Work? Shaping Belligerents' Choices After Civil War*, Princeton, N.J.: Princeton University Press, 2008; and Doyle and Sambanis, 2006.

[56] Collier et al., 2003.

vast majority of cases, peace is sustained after intervention, and some improvement is made in other conditions as well.

Skeptics of nation-building are no doubt correct that political, economic, and social transformation of conflict-affected states and thorough uprooting of the seeds of conflict are generations-long endeavors. It does not follow, however, that successful nation-building requires effecting complete transformation while interveners' troops are on the ground. Would-be nation-builders must instead succeed only in staving off renewal of conflict and putting in place the framework in which nonviolent transformation can gradually occur.

The essential elements of such a framework are open to debate, but at least four are crucial. First, a return to violence should be made so costly that local actors are unlikely to return to mass violence to pursue their political agendas. This generally requires a period of deployment of foreign forces and reform and development of the nation's security institutions—both of which make it less likely that any effort to advance a group's interests by force would be defeated. Second, the nation-builders should seek to create a political system, and the institutional infrastructure supporting it, in which nonviolent alternation of executive power on the basis of popular political participation is possible without posing a critical threat to any of the major communities in the country. Parties to a conflict must see that political institutions offer an opportunity to advance their interests rather than a mechanism for other groups to dominate them.[57] Third, the international community should help to lay the groundwork for economic growth well in excess of population growth. Finally, if geopolitical factors played an important role in provoking or sustaining the conflict, then these factors will need to be mitigated or resolved, primarily through diplomatic means.

The details of these elements can and should vary in accordance with local context, including the specific political institutions established, the balance between services provided by the state and those

---

[57] On the importance of alternation of executive office, see Nicolas Van de Walle, *Overcoming Stagnation in Aid-Dependent Countries*, Washington, D.C.: Center for Global Development, 2005; and Samuel P. Huntington, *The Third Wave: Democratization in the Late Twentieth Century*, Norman, Okla.: University of Oklahoma Press, 1991.

provided by nonstate actors, privatization policies, and so on. Thus, guidance is needed to help nation-builders decide how to tailor the basic framework for nation-building to the local context. The security dimension of nation-building does not require significant variation because security dynamics tend to be consistent across a wide range of social contexts.[58] But the political, social, and economic dimensions of nation-building interventions should be adapted to local circumstances. The chapters that follow explore how well nation-builders have tailored their efforts to the local factors in each case and the lessons that can be drawn from these experiences for future interventions.

---

[58] Stathis N. Kalyvas, *The Logic of Violence in Civil War*, Cambridge, UK: Cambridge University Press, 2006.

CHAPTER THREE

Cambodia

In 1991, warring Cambodian parties signed the Paris Peace Agreements, agreeing to end the conflict and hold democratic elections. For more than two decades, Cambodia had been ripped apart by three successive conflicts that devastated all aspects of Khmer society: (1) civil

Figure 3.1
Map of Cambodia

SOURCE: Central Intelligence Agency (CIA), "Cambodia," *The World Factbook*, 2012b.
RAND RR167-3.1

war and U.S. aerial bombardment in the early 1970s, (2) genocide at the hands of the Khmer Rouge in the late 1970s, and (3) a Vietnamese invasion and subsequent civil conflict throughout the 1980s. In all, more than 2 million Cambodians died either as a direct result of war or from war-related famine or disease.[1] By the time the civil war officially ended in 1991—though low-level hostilities continued until 1997—the Cambodian population was severely traumatized, the country had lost nearly one-fifth of its population, and the economy was in ruins. To ensure implementation of the peace agreement, the United Nations launched its most expansive postconflict mission up to that point in time: the United Nations Transitional Authority in Cambodia (UNTAC). The mission was charged with addressing a host of security, administrative, and humanitarian concerns, from disarming combatants to promoting human rights to conducting elections. The UN Security Council granted the mission very broad authorities, far more than it proved capable of fully discharging.

UNTAC failed to demobilize warring factions, and some level of conflict continued for a time. However, the operation succeeded in resettling refuges and overseeing a national election. Today, Cambodia is a peaceful and relatively stable country with a growing and increasingly mixed economy, even though corruption is rampant, rural development is stagnant, and the governing Cambodian People's Party (CPP) has won elections that were neither free nor fair.

Local Factors Before the Peace

Cambodians commonly refer to the period after independence from France (in 1953) and prior to the Vietnam War as "the Golden Years." For the majority of this period, the country was stable, and most Cambodians were relatively self-sufficient, though poor. Most Cambodians held their leader, Prince Norodom Sihanouk, in high esteem, although leftist opponents, the Khmer Rouge, fought a small-scale insurgency

---

[1]   Milton Leitenberg, *Death in Wars and Conflicts in the 20th Century*, Ithaca, N.Y.: Cornell University, Peace Studies Program, 2006, p. 76.

against the regime for much of the 1950s and 1960s.[2] Cambodia attempted to remain neutral as the war in neighboring Vietnam escalated in the 1960s but ultimately did not succeed. U.S. aerial bombardment of North Vietnamese and Vietcong forces on Cambodia's eastern border in the late 1960s destabilized Sihanouk's regime and swelled the Khmer Rouge's ranks. The Cambodian military, led by Lon Nol, launched a coup that brought down Prince Sihanouk and ended Cambodia's policy of nonalignment.[3]

Upon coming to power, Lon Nol brought Cambodia into the Vietnam War, focusing on eliminating North Vietnamese and Vietcong bases in the east and on rooting out the Khmer Rouge and its leader, Pol Pot. Lon Nol's actions transformed a low-level domestic conflict into an all-out civil war. The U.S. bombing of Cambodian targets increased substantially under Lon Nol, causing widespread devastation.[4] The bombing, coupled with U.S. and South Vietnamese incursions, stripped the Lon Nol government of supporters.[5] Khmer Rouge forces steadily whittled away territory from the government's control until April 1975, when they marched into the capital, Phnom Penh, and seized power.

---

[2] Sihanouk was king from 1941 until 1955, when he abdicated his throne in favor of his father and assumed the title of prince in order to be elected the country's political leader. Following his father's death in 1960, he was elected head of state but retained the title of prince. He regained the title of king when the country promulgated a new constitution and officially became the Kingdom of Cambodia in 1993. Under the constitution, the king is officially the head of state, a largely ceremonial position. In 2004, Sihanouk abdicated the throne in favor of his son, King Norodom Sihamoni. Since his abdication, Sihanouk has been referred to by the honorific title "King-Father of Cambodia."

[3] Members of the Cambodian Army supported the coup in part because Sihanouk had rejected U.S. aid and officers feared that any deterioration of Cambodian forces would invite an invasion by Thailand or Vietnam.

[4] In terms of tonnage, it is estimated that more bombs were dropped on Cambodia than the Allies dropped during all of World War II (Taylor Owen and Ben Kiernan, "Bombs over Cambodia," *Walrus*, October 2006, pp. 62–69, p. 67).

[5] By the end of 1971, 2 million Cambodians were displaced and Phnom Penh's population doubled to 1.2 million, containing nearly one-seventh of Cambodia's population of 7.9 million (William Shawcross, *Sideshow: Kissinger, Nixon and the Destruction of Cambodia*, New York: Simon and Schuster, 1979, p. 222).

The Khmer Rouge enacted a plan to radically deconstruct Khmer society and return it to "Year Zero": a peasant society without money, education, property, religion, or anything else it considered a hindrance to Khmer unity. Cambodians were ordered out of the cities and into the countryside, where they lived in collectives and were forced to work in the rice paddies. Individuals associated with the previous regime or identified as elites were branded enemies of the state and, in most cases, executed. Harsh living conditions and meager food rations resulted in mass starvation and disease. Nearly 2 million people perished under the Khmer Rouge.

Despite having received aid from Hanoi during the civil war, the Khmer Rouge, with assistance from China, launched cross-border raids into Vietnam over a period of two years.[6] In 1979, Vietnamese troops invaded and overthrew the Khmer Rouge government, establishing the People's Republic of Kampuchea (PRK) with a Marxist-Leninist government headed by Cambodians opposed to the Khmer Rouge (though most were former members) and backed by 200,000 Vietnamese troops. PRK leaders replaced the Khmer Rouge's radical Maoist ideology with a Soviet-style administration and party organization.

The Khmer Rouge retreated to the northwestern jungles and reconstituted its remaining forces in refugee camps on the Thai border.[7] Forces loyal to Prince Sihanouk, under the banner of the United Front for an Independent, Neutral, Peaceful, and Co-operative Cambodia (Front Uni National pour un Cambodge Indépendant, Neutre, Pacifique, et Coopératif, or FUNCINPEC), and forces loyal to republican leader Son Sann, the Khmer People's National Liberation Front (KPNLF) were also entrenched along the border. Consequently, many of the camps, especially those under Khmer Rouge control, effectively became paramilitary training centers. With support from China, Association of Southeast Asian Nations (ASEAN) countries, and the West, the groups opposed to the Vietnamese-backed PRK organized into a

---

[6]   China supported the Khmer Rouge because its chief foreign policy aim was the defeat of Soviet proxies in Asia, such as Vietnam.

[7]   Evan Gottesman, *Cambodia After the Khmer Rouge: Inside the Politics of Nation Building*, New Haven, Conn.: Yale University Press, 2003, p. 4.

government in exile named the Coalition Government of Democratic Kampuchea (CGDK). The United States and China ignored the atrocities committed by the Khmer Rouge and managed to seat the CGDK at the United Nations as the representative of the Cambodian people. The conflict between the resistance groups and the PRK dragged on for 13 years, resulting in further loss of life and dislocations. During the 1980s, more than 370,000 Cambodians sought refuge on the Thai border.[8]

The war wound down after Vietnamese forces withdrew from Cambodia in 1989. In the same year, the PRK, seeking to remove the stigma of being a Vietnamese puppet, changed its name to State of Cambodia (SOC) and adopted free-market economic policies. In July 1990, the United States announced that it would no longer support the seating of the CGDK at the United Nations, thus signaling U.S. endorsement of a comprehensive peace settlement. The United Nations began brokering peace negotiations among warring factions in 1987, but progress was slow. It was not until October 23, 1991, that Cambodia's four main political factions—the FUNCINPEC, KPNLF, the Khmer Rouge, and the CPP (the party of the SOC)—came together in Paris to sign a series of accords that formally ended the civil war and transferred considerable authority to UNTAC.

Geographical and Geopolitical

Cambodia's conflicts can be attributed largely to the geopolitical struggle among the superpowers—the United States, the Soviet Union, and China. Cambodia's neighbors were a persistent source of insecurity as well (see Figure 3.1).[9] A largely agrarian society with a small population, Cambodia is located between Thailand and Vietnam, two more populous and industrialized countries with, historically, penchants for

---

[8] Michael W. Doyle, *UN Peacekeeping in Cambodia: UNTAC's Civil Mandate*, Boulder, Colo.: Lynne Reinner Publishers, 1995, p. 18.

[9] Dylan Hendrickson, *Safeguarding Peace: Cambodia's Constitutional Challenge*, London, UK: Conciliation Resources, 1998, p. 14.

expansionism (see Figure 3.1).[10] Early Khmer empires ruled over what are today large portions of Thailand, Vietnam, and Laos. But, over the centuries, Siam (Thailand) and Vietnam whittled away Khmer-controlled territory. Cambodians view border disputes, which have been frequent in the country's history, as not merely struggles for territory but as battles for the survival of the Khmer people. They viewed the Vietnamese invasion of 1979 in this light, and fear of Vietnamese domination contributed significantly to sustaining the conflict throughout the 1980s.

Though immediate neighbors were a historical threat, the superpower rivalries of the Cold War catalyzed the conflicts that Cambodia endured between 1970 and 1991. U.S. bombing of Soviet- and Chinese-backed Vietnamese fighters boosted support for the Khmer Rouge. China then funded the Khmer Rouge to counter Soviet influence in Vietnam, which enabled the Khmer Rouge to overthrow the U.S.-supported Lon Nol government. Chinese support kept the Khmer Rouge afloat and bankrolled its raids on Soviet-sponsored Vietnam. China and the United States interpreted the Vietnamese invasion as an expansion of Soviet influence, causing them to overlook the Khmer Rouge's crimes. The United States and China justified funding the resistance groups in the refugee camps by claiming that Vietnam and, by extension, the Soviet Union were attempting to annex Cambodia.[11] Moreover, the United States, China, and ASEAN countries bear partial responsibility for the many years that more than 350,000 refugees languished in camps; resistance groups in the border camps supported by these countries did not allow refugees to leave the camps because the refugee crisis served to delegitimize the PRK government.[12]

---

[10] In 1965, Cambodia's population was 6.1 million, Thailand's 31.2 million, and Vietnam's 38.3 million. Cambodia's population as of 2011 was 14.7 million, Thailand's 66.7 million, and Vietnam's 87.4 million (NationMaster, undated home page).

[11] Gottesman, 2003, p. 43.

[12] Courtland Robinson, "Refugee Warriors at the Thai-Cambodian Border," *Refugee Survey Quarterly*, Vol. 19, No. 1, 2000, pp. 23–37.

Cultural and Social

Most observers of modern Cambodia comment on the population's political apathy and deference to authority. In Khmer culture, elders are venerated, as is the monarch, who is treated as the leader of a large family.[13] Some experts claim that Cambodians' "ingrained habit of deference" comes from the respect for authority taught in Theravada Buddhism, the religion of 90 percent of the population.[14] Regardless of its origins, submitting to political authority has been a survival strategy born of necessity for Cambodians, who, for most of their history, have had few opportunities to control their destiny.

Although a tradition of deference may in part explain why political activity in Cambodia rarely went beyond selecting a protector to line up behind, it seems to confound explanations for how the same society produced one of the most-brutal political movements of the 20th century. And yet, Cambodian deference and the Khmer Rouge's extreme violence may have similar origins.

Angkor Wat, the seat of the ancient Khmer society, features prominently in the Cambodian psyche as an example of Khmer nationalism and greatness. It symbolizes the monumental achievements that are possible if people sacrifice personal needs for collective works. Yet, there is a flip side to this narrative that inspires chauvinism, xenophobia, and the devaluation of human life.[15] According to the ultranationalist interpretation, the existence of Angkor Wat proves Cambodians' superiority; the fact that it was built through communal sacrifice (in reality, slave labor) demonstrates the value of anti-individualism; and the fact that Angkor Wat succumbed to foreign invasion demonstrates modern Cambodians' need to be ever vigilant or risk suffering the same

---

[13] Kate Frieson, "Revolution and Rural Response in Cambodia, 1970–1975," in Ben Kiernan, ed., *Genocide and Democracy in Cambodia: The Khmer Rouge, the United Nations, and the International Community*, New Haven, Conn.: Yale University Southeast Asia Studies, 1993, pp. 33–50, p. 39.

[14] Elizabeth Becker, *When the War Was Over: Cambodia and the Khmer Rouge Revolution*, New York: PublicAffairs, 1998, p. 5.

[15] Karl D. Jackson, "The Ideology of Total Revolution," in Karl D. Jackson, ed., *Cambodia 1975–1978: Rendezvous with Death*, Princeton, N.J.: Princeton University Press, 1989, pp. 37–78, p. 72.

fate. This interpretation predated the Khmer Rouge and contributed to numerous pogroms against ethnic Vietnamese living in Cambodia.[16]

The Khmer Rouge's ideology took these nationalist ideas and fears to new extremes in order to justify heinous acts. The Khmer Rouge instituted a policy of extreme collectivism, in which any notion of the individual was officially obliterated. People who deviated from the Khmer Rouge's perverse notion of the norm (e.g., minorities, elites, people who wore glasses) were considered contaminants that had to be purged. Pol Pot espoused the view that Vietnam sought the total destruction of Cambodia and that its only hope for survival was the centralization of power and national submission to the common cause.[17] Hence, even though most Cambodians came to despise the Khmer Rouge, the widespread acceptance of many of the assumptions underpinning the Khmer Rouge's philosophy helped the group maintain at least marginal support well after its removal from power. This acceptance also helps explain why, even though most Cambodians welcomed the removal of Pol Pot, they never accepted the Vietnamese occupation or its puppet government. The Cold War created the opportunity for Cambodia's troubles to rise to the surface; however, the population's xenophobia increased the violence of these conflicts and made them harder to resolve.

Economic

Two decades of war eviscerated the Cambodian economy, which was not well developed to begin with. Before the conflicts, Sihanouk discouraged foreign ventures and avoided grand industrial projects in an effort to ensure Cambodian neutrality and hinder urbanization. These policies discouraged civic organization.[18] Cambodia had been largely

---

[16] David P. Chandler, "Seeing Red," in David P. Chandler and Ben Kiernan, eds., *Revolution and Its Aftermath in Kampuchea: Eight Essays*, New Haven, Conn.: Yale University Southeast Asia Studies, 1983, pp. 34–56, p. 46; Timothy Carney, "The Organization of Power," in Karl D. Jackson, ed., *Cambodia, 1975–1978: Rendezvous with Death*, Princeton, N.J.: Princeton University Press, 1989, pp. 13–35, p. 96.

[17] Carney, 1989, p. 96; Nate Thayer, "'I'm Tired of Talking About It': Excerpts from Interview with Pol Pot October 16, 1997," *Nate Thayer*, November 9, 2011.

[18] Becker, 1998, p. 6.

self-sufficient in food until Lon Nol brought the country into the Viet-nam War. After that, Cambodia became highly dependent on imports of food and U.S. foreign aid. In the agricultural sector, rice cultivation dropped from 6 million to 1 million acres, creating food shortages.[19] By 1973, total imports, much of them agricultural products, reached $42 million, while exports dropped to $4.9 million.[20]

The vestiges of the Cambodian economy that remained after the Vietnam War were wiped out under the Khmer Rouge. Infrastructure was left to crumble. The Khmer Rouge largely cut ties to the outside world. What limited production occurred was dedicated to local con-sumption. Even with the entire population working in the rice paddies, food production fell. Instead of importing foodstuffs to feed the popu-lation, the Khmer Rouge let mass starvation take its toll.

The loss of life and, consequently, human capital under the Khmer Rouge was staggering. It is estimated that at least 21 percent of Cam-bodia's pre–Khmer Rouge population of roughly 8 million perished.[21] An additional 218,000 were lost to migration.[22] After the Khmer Rouge, there was no educational system left to rebuild depleted human resources. The Khmer Rouge had considered those who were educated to be enemies of the state; 75–80 percent of Cambodian teachers and higher-education students are believed to have perished or fled,[23] as are many of the doctors, lawyers, and other professionals with skills needed to rebuild the country. According to UNTAC estimates, by 1979, "there were no more than 300 qualified persons from all disci-

---

[19] Michael Haas, *Genocide by Proxy: Cambodian Pawn on a Superpower Chessboard*, New York: Praeger, 1991, p. 16.

[20] Kamputsea-tutkimuskomission, *Kampuchea in the Seventies: Report of a Finnish Inquiry Commission*, Helsinki: Kampuchean Inquiry Commission, 1982, p. 13.

[21] Bruce Sharp, "Counting Hell," *Mekong.net*, last updated June 9, 2008.

[22] Sharp, 2008.

[23] Stephen J. Duggan, "Education, Teacher Training and Prospects for Economic Recov-ery in Cambodia," *Comparative Education*, Vol. 32, No. 3, November 1996, pp. 361–375, p. 365.

plines left in the entire country [and] all educational books, equipment and facilities had been destroyed."[24]

When Vietnam invaded, it inherited a society of dependents living in a country without means. Buildings, factories, schools, hospitals, roads, and bridges all needed to be rehabilitated. Rural areas were so riddled with land mines and unexploded ordnance that cultivation became too dangerous in many regions, and the country could barely feed itself.[25]

The Vietnamese-backed PRK tried to initiate reconstruction and development programs but lacked adequate funding. Because the CGDK was internationally recognized as the legitimate representative of the Cambodian people, the PRK was denied access to most external grants and loans. New communities were established in order for devastated families and the many war widows to work together to provide for their basic needs. Reconstructing the educational system became a national priority under the PRK/SOC; however, as with all government programs, the effort lacked funding. So few teacher trainees had completed their basic education that they ultimately emerged from the programs unqualified.[26] Schools were built and enrollment expanded, yet students gained little beyond basic literacy because of the poor quality of the teaching.[27]

After Vietnamese forces withdrew and the Soviet Union reduced its assistance in the late 1980s, the recently renamed SOC government tried to generate income by abandoning Marxism and adopting a market-based economic system. Little progress occurred, however, because Cambodia lacked the capital needed to create private enterprises and continued fighting sapped government resources. To pay for the war effort and the civil service, SOC leader Hun Sen trans-

---

[24] UN Department of Public Information, *United Nations Transitional Authority in Cambodia*, New York, 1992, p. 19, as quoted in Duggan, 1996, p. 365.

[25] Deepa Narayan and Patti Petesch, eds., *Moving Out of Poverty*, Vol. 4: *Rising from the Ashes of Conflict*, Washington, D.C.: World Bank, 2009, p. 341; Gottesman, 2003, pp. 231, 272, 280.

[26] Duggan, 1996, p. 369.

[27] Duggan, 1996, p. 368.

ferred all public assets to the ruling party and began to sell them off.[28] At the same time, the Khmer Rouge was financing its battle against SOC forces by plundering natural resources, such as gemstones and timber. After China stopped funding the Khmer Rouge in 1990, the plunder accelerated: The Khmer Rouge is estimated to have generated revenue of between $100 million and $150 million from selling timber and gems—more than the SOC's entire 1990–1991 budget.[29] By the time UNTAC arrived, economic activity in Cambodia was insufficient for developing the society, or even supporting the government, and its human and natural resources were severely depleted.

Political

Politics in Cambodia have historically been based on patron-client relationships in which loyalty is exchanged for money, positions, or protection. During the decades of conflict, patrons changed, but political practices remained largely the same and were reinforced by a heritage of deference to authority. Until recently, Cambodians maintained low expectations of their government because it rarely featured in their lives.[30] Consequently, they did not develop the organizations or tools with which to influence their government. Cambodia's lack of "intermediary structures" between the population and ruling elites has "left the way open for the unfettered exercise of dictatorial power."[31]

When the Vietnamese-backed PRK came to power in January 1979, party leaders seemed to genuinely believe that, by imposing a Marxist-Leninist model of centralized state control, they could mobilize the masses in a national effort to rebuild the country. Instead, they planted the roots of what became a kleptocracy and inculcated

---

[28] Discussion with American journalist, Phnom Penh, February 2, 2010; discussion with Cambodian political analyst, Phnom Penh, February 2, 2010.

[29] Tom Fawthrop and Helen Jarvis, *Getting Away with Genocide? Elusive Justice and the Khmer Rouge Tribunal*, Sydney, New South Wales: University of New South Wales Press, 2005, p. 105.

[30] Becker, 1998, p. 4.

[31] Serge Thion, *Watching Cambodia: Ten Paths to Enter the Cambodian Tangle*, Bangkok, Thailand: Cheney, 1993, p. 176.

widespread disrespect for the rule of law. At the time that the PRK government was established, the entire society was fighting for survival, including Cambodian officials who were elites in name only. At first, only top officials received more than food rations as remuneration because currency was not reintroduced until March 1980.[32] Because the new government was ill-equipped to recreate an entire society and exercised weak control, individuals ignored state edicts and established practices and institutions outside of government control. The PRK had to adapt to what emerged organically—essentially, the traditional Cambodian patronage system.

Over time, the country stabilized and the PRK/SOC created a judiciary, media, and educational system, all of which became vehicles for spreading and imposing party ideology. The remnants of institutions that survived the Khmer Rouge, such as the Buddhist wats, were bureaucratized and brought under state control. Over time, citizens increasingly cooperated with state authorities, but instead of their behavior being based on party loyalty, as originally intended, it was based on the distribution of direct material benefits and official positions from which supporters reaped illicit gains.[33]

Institutional

When Vietnamese troops invaded, Cambodia had no organized security forces. The task of building new security organs from scratch was difficult for several reasons. First, Cambodians were tired of war and needed able-bodied men to stay home and rebuild. Second, they did not see the point of fighting other Khmer, especially because rebel forces were supported by the still-revered Prince Sihanouk and because they would be fighting under the reviled Vietnamese. Third, whereas, in the past, members of the military were handsomely rewarded, the PRK lacked the resources to make military service sufficiently attractive.[34]

---

[32] Russell R. Ross, *Cambodia: A Country Study*, Washington, D.C.: Federal Research Division, 1990.

[33] Caroline Hughes, *UNTAC in Cambodia: The Impact on Human Rights*, Singapore: Indochina Programme, Institute of Southeast Asian Studies, 1996, p. 18.

[34] Gottesman, 2003, p. 227.

To resolve these issues, the PRK instituted conscription, which, by official estimates, enlisted 80,000 Cambodians, a number sufficient to fight the purported 40,000 Khmer Rouge troops, the 14,000 KPNLF troops, and the 10,000-strong Armée Nationaliste Sihanoukienne (ANS), the forces of FUNCINPEC.[35] The policy was extremely unpopular. Cambodians did all that they could to avoid conscription. Officials decided to "inspire" greater enthusiasm by making service more lucrative; however, because the government lacked funds for sufficient remuneration, it allowed units to instead exploit natural resources and "tax" the population in their assigned sectors. Forces engaged in fishing, mining, and logging and set up checkpoints to demand road tolls. Although the policy only added to the PRK's disfavor in the provinces, allowing local military units to become autonomous, profit-seeking enterprises finally provided the necessary incentive for forces to actively deter rebel incursions into their territory. Although these incentives gave the SOC a relatively effective fighting force, once the armed forces became autonomous, the government no longer fully controlled them, and rule of law was further undermined.[36]

The PRK/SOC also had to create a legal system from scratch. Under the Khmer Rouge, there had been "no pretense of legality": The judicial system was disbanded and the law of the land consisted of arbitrary dictates issued by Angkar ("the organization").[37] By the time that the PRK came to power, most Cambodians with legal training had either been killed or fled. According to a UN report, even as late as 2004, there were no more than 200 judges and 275 lawyers in the country, and most were poorly trained.[38] The PRK set up training pro-

---

[35] Gottesman, 2003, p. 227.

[36] Gottesman, 2003, pp. 230–231.

[37] Kheang Un, "The Judicial System and Democratization in Post-Conflict Cambodia," in Joakim Öjendal and Mona Lilja, eds., *Beyond Democracy in Cambodia: Political Reconstruction in a Post-Conflict Society*, Copenhagen: NIAS Press, 2009, pp. 70–100, p. 74.

[38] Laura McGrew, "Re-Establishing Legitimacy Through the Extraordinary Chambers in the Courts of Cambodia," in Joakim Öjendal and Mona Lilja, eds., *Beyond Democracy in Cambodia: Political Reconstruction in a Post-Conflict Society*, Copenhagen: NIAS Press, 2009, pp. 250–296, p. 252.

grams, but they emphasized Marxist-Leninist ideology over legal procedures, and the only qualifications for would-be judges and prosecutors were literacy and proper ideological credentials (in particular, no connection to the Pol Pot regime). As with all institutions in the PRK, the courts were completely subordinate to the CPP (the party of the PRK), and party officials frequently interfered in the judicial process, often at the invitation of judges.[39]

Another obstacle to PRK/SOC institution-building efforts was the dearth of experienced civil servants: "The Khmer Rouge's extermination of civil servants had nearly erased a national memory of how government works."[40] Government infrastructure was equally devastated. When new ministers were appointed, their first task was to search the capital for a functioning building to house their ministry. Staff were sent out to search for furniture and books. Because of the widespread suffering in Cambodian society, the priority of government officials was to hire family and friends, and ministry staffs soon ballooned. Government employment was literally a "meal ticket"—staff received an allotment of rice—and, as soon as currency was reintroduced, the civil service offered the only salaried employment in Cambodia.[41]

To stymie the trend and provide proper administrative training and greater control, Vietnamese advisers were brought in to oversee day-to-day operations. Administration slowly improved over time, but nepotism did not abate, and, as soon as officials had access to resources, corruption also became a problem. Officials ignored party and government demands to curtail nepotistic hiring, in large part because most Cambodians who survived the Khmer Rouge had done so by relying on family and friends to share what little they had and by protecting each other, often at great risk. This survivor's mentality lingered long after the PRK took power and hampered the government's ability to build an effective bureaucracy that could meet Cambodians' needs.

---

[39] McGrew, 2009, p.74.

[40] Gottesman, 2003, p. 50.

[41] Gottesman, 2003, p. 51.

Nation-Building Efforts

The Agreements on a Comprehensive Political Settlement of the Cambodia Conflict, more commonly known as the Paris Peace Accords, were signed by all four of Cambodia's combatant factions on October 23, 1991. The accords established two bodies: the Supreme National Council (SNC) and UNTAC. The SNC had 13 members representing the four signatories of the accords: six from the CPP, two from each of the other three factions (Khmer Rouge, KPNLF, and FUNCINPEC), and Prince Sihanouk, who headed the council.[42] Nominally, the SNC was to act as the "unique legitimate body and source of authority in which throughout the transitional period, the sovereignty, independence and unity of Cambodia are enshrined."[43] However, the executive and oversight powers of the council were weak. The SNC was nonetheless a symbolically important mechanism during the period in which UNTAC temporarily exercised real authority.[44]

UNTAC's mandate went well beyond those of typical prior peacekeeping operations. Its mandate encompassed (1) supervision of the cease-fire, the withdrawal of foreign forces, and the cessation of foreign military assistance; (2) cantoning, disarming, and demobilizing the armed forces of Cambodia's warring parties; (3) controlling and supervising the activities of state administrative structures, including the police; (4) ensuring respect for human rights; (5) settling Cambodian refugees; and (6) organizing and conducting free and fair elections.[45] In effect, this accord established, on paper at least, a UN-administered occupation authority, with plenary powers to direct the activities of subordinate Cambodian government organs.

---

[42] Frederick Z. Brown and David G. Timberman, eds., *Cambodia and the International Community: The Quest for Peace, Development, and Democracy,* Singapore: Institute of Southeast Asian Studies, 1998, p. 90.

[43] As quoted in Doyle, 1995, p. 25.

[44] F. Brown and Timberman, 1998, p. 90.

[45] The texts of the Paris Peace Accords are available at U.S. Institute of Peace, "Peace Agreements: Cambodia," undated.

Although the logistical scale of the operation was substantial, UNTAC was given less than two years to achieve its ambitious objectives. When fully deployed, UNTAC included a military contingent of 15,900 troops, 3,900 civilian police (CIVPOL), 2,500 international staff members, 8,000 Cambodian support-staff members, and an additional 50,000 Cambodians hired to staff polling stations during elections.[46] Although the mandate was for two years, UNTAC personnel did not begin to arrive in Cambodia until April 1992, and the operation was not fully deployed until five to six months later, leaving UNTAC a little more than a year to fulfill its mandate.

Of its many tasks, UNTAC's primary goal was rebuilding the Cambodian state's legitimacy through elections. Fulfilling this goal was contingent upon demobilizing troops and establishing security and order.[47] Unfortunately, before UNTAC was even fully deployed, the Khmer Rouge refused to canton its forces and denied the United Nations access to areas under its control, thus exposing UNTAC as a "paper tiger" without enforcement capabilities.[48] Without the cantoning of Khmer Rouge forces, the CPP also stopped cooperating after demobilizing and disarming only 25 percent of its forces. Soon after, both the Khmer Rouge and the CPP were violating the cease-fire agreement.[49] The breach set the tone for the rest of the operation, creating an uphill battle for UNTAC as it tried to gain cooperation from the other factions and convince Cambodians that the elections would be free and fair. Nonetheless, parliamentary elections were held in May 1993, and the new assembly prepared and then promulgated a new constitution by the end of September 1993.

---

[46] Steven R. Ratner, *The New UN Peacekeeping: Building Peace in Lands of Conflict After the Cold War*, New York: St. Martin's Press, 1995, p. 166.

[47] Ratner, 1995, p. 159.

[48] Benny Widyono, *Dancing in Shadows: Sihanouk, the Khmer Rouge, and the United Nations in Cambodia*, Lanham, Md.: Rowman and Littlefield Publishers, 2008, p. 77.

[49] United Nations, "Cambodia–UNTAC: Background," undated.

Geographical and Geopolitical

A solution to the Cambodian conflict became possible when geopolitical changes shifted the priorities of the outside powers that had initiated and were perpetuating the conflict. As communism collapsed in Europe, the Soviet Union reduced its international commitments. The drastic reduction of Soviet support to Vietnam and the PRK, and the subsequent withdrawal of Vietnamese troops, meant that China had achieved most of its strategic objectives and was now willing to consider supporting a settlement. With the Soviets downgrading their regional entanglements, the United States lost its motivation to continue supporting anti-SOC forces. Meanwhile, Vietnam, facing economic problems and growing discontent at home, wanted to end the conflict and build better relations with China and the United States.[50]

Although international cooperation may have made UNTAC possible, the operation's full success depended on the mutual consent of the combatant groups—something that was tenuous even as the accords were signed.[51] The SOC and resistance factions begrudgingly signed the accords because of pressure from their respective patrons and the fear that they would be cut out of a final settlement if they did not cooperate. Geopolitical changes may have reduced the resources of the SOC and Khmer Rouge, but, because both groups viewed the conflict in zero-sum terms, they found sharing authority in the SNC unsatisfactory: "With such tenuous consent, the smallest action by the UN against the interests of a party would be met with entrenched resistance, accusations of bias or violations of the accord, or impasse."[52]

Cultural and Social

UNTAC's efforts to foster respect for human rights were hamstrung from the beginning.[53] The political compromises made to placate the Khmer Rouge—such as euphemistically referring to their crimes as

---

[50] F. Brown and Timberman, 1998, p. 89.

[51] Ratner, 1995, p. 158.

[52] Ratner, 1995, p. 158.

[53] Dobbins, Jones, Crane, Rathmell, et al., 2005, pp. 81–82.

"the policies and practices of the past" and declining to bring those responsible to justice—constrained any honest discussion of human rights abuses. UNTAC, international nongovernmental organizations (NGOs), and a burgeoning number of domestic NGOs had some success educating Cambodians about their rights but failed to create institutions to which citizens could appeal for protection and legal recourse. UNTAC sent human rights monitors to the provinces, but there were numerous violations, most notably repeated massacres of ethnic Vietnamese by the Khmer Rouge and CPP assassinations of political rivals.[54]

One of UNTAC's most impressive efforts was the repatriation of nearly 370,000 refugees before elections were held. UN High Commissioner for Refugees (UNHCR) staff conducted the transfer operations and supplied resettlement packages.[55] The packages included food for 400 days and household essentials. Initially, UNHCR promised refugees five acres of land, but, given the lack of accurate cadastral surveys, widespread incidence of malaria, and the prevalence of land mines, the organization could not determine where refugees could safely resettle.[56] Instead, it provided cash grants to help returnees purchase land wherever they wanted to live.[57] Safe resettlement depended on mine removal and protection along the roads; therefore, once it became clear that demobilization efforts were irrevocably stalled, many peacekeepers were reassigned to resettlement operations and mine-clearance operations.[58]

---

[54] Ratner, 1995, p. 179.

[55] Doyle, 1995, p. 33.

[56] Samantha Power, *Chasing the Flame: One Man's Fight to Save the World*, New York: Penguin Books, 2008, p. 86.

[57] Dobbins, Jones, Crane, Rathmell, et al., 2005, p. 81.

[58] Power, 2008, p. 86.

Economic

At a conference in 1992, international donors pledged $880 million to assist recovery efforts.[59] Despite the strong international commitment, economic development measures had mixed results, in part due to the enormity of the need and to the unstable political environment. Although the economy had begun to grow under the SOC and the country was becoming increasingly self-sufficient, conditions in rural areas had scarcely improved since the early 1970s. Though there were nascent improvements under UNTAC, progress was slow.[60] During the early period of UNTAC, economic assistance was directed toward quick-impact rehabilitation efforts, such as small infrastructure repair and limited public health projects. International assistance was supposed to later fund long-term development programs, but few were ultimately funded because less than $100 million of the aid pledged was disbursed by the time of the election.[61] Donors were hesitant to distribute aid because the SOC's continued control of government administration meant that the CPP would likely benefit most from the assistance, thus undermining UNTAC's goal of maintaining political neutrality.[62] FUNCINPEC likewise believed that foreign assistance could provide the CPP with an advantage and, as a result, used its vote in the SNC to block a $75 million emergency loan from the World Bank.[63]

Political

By all measures, the elections were a technical success. UNTAC's education campaign about democracy convinced Cambodians that their ballots would be secret. Voters, excited about exercising their right to choose, were undeterred by the violence committed by the Khmer

---

[59] Dobbins, Jones, Crane, Rathmell, et al., 2005, p. 87.

[60] Doyle, 1995, p. 51.

[61] Daniel P. L. Chong, "UNTAC in Cambodia: A New Model for Humanitarian Aid in Failed States?" *Development and Change*, Vol. 33, No. 5, November 2002, pp. 957–978, p. 973.

[62] Doyle, 1995, p. 51.

[63] Dobbins, Jones, Crane, Rathmell, et al., 2005, p. 87.

Rouge and CPP in the run-up to the election and even by news of Khmer Rouge attacks on polling stations. Turnout was approximately 90 percent.[64]

Most observers thought that the CPP would win, as did the CPP. The CGDK had disintegrated into competing political factions, and Hun Sen used civil servants to campaign for the party.[65] Instead, Prince Sihanouk's FUNCINPEC came out on top, with 45 percent of the vote (58 seats), followed by the CPP with 38 percent (51 seats), the Buddhist Liberal Democratic Party with 4 percent (ten seats), and the Molinaka Party with 1 percent (one seat). The CPP alleged electoral misconduct and refused to recognize the election results unless the CPP was brought in as an equal coalition partner. Because the Paris Peace Accords had not specified how a government would be formed on the basis of election results, the CPP's demands could not be summarily dismissed.[66] Fearing that the CPP would break with the accords and ignite a civil war, and given that the entire army and government bureaucracy were under CPP control, UNTAC and FUNCINPEC caved in to CPP demands and created a power-sharing government. Afterward, to ensure inclusion in future governments, the CPP demanded a constitutional provision stipulating that government formation require approval of two-thirds of the National Assembly.[67]

After the election, the size of the government doubled. Prince Norodom Ranariddh, head of FUNCINPEC, and the CPP's Hun Sen became co–prime ministers. The 27 cabinet ministries were headed by 34 FUNCINPEC co-ministers, ministers, and vice ministers, paired with 33 from the CPP.[68] Provincial governorships were also shared.

---

[64] Doyle, 1995, p. 57.

[65] Sorpong Peou, "Hun Sen's Pre-Emptive Coup 1997: Causes and Consequences," in Derek da Cunha and John Funston, eds., *Southeast Asian Affairs: 1998*, Singapore: ISEAS, 1998, pp. 86–102.

[66] Jeffrey Gallup, "Cambodia's Electoral System: A Window of Opportunity for Reform," in Aurel Croissant, Gabriele Bruns, and Marei John, eds., *Electoral Politics in Southeast and East Asia*, Singapore: Friedrich Ebert Stiftung, 2002, pp. 25–73, p. 31.

[67] Gallup, 2002, p. 32.

[68] Peou, 1998.

Corruption grew in tandem with the government, and the bloated bureaucracy was highly inefficient.[69]

Institutional

The Khmer Rouge and CPP maintained their own forces throughout the UNTAC period. The CPP used the military and police forces under its control to harass and attack political opponents and intimidate their supporters. After the election, the CPP joined its forces with those of other non–Khmer Rouge factions to create the Royal Cambodian Armed Forces (RCAF). The defense ministry and armed forces suffered the same fate as other parts of the coalition government: A dual command structure emerged, and the unification of forces created redundancies that took years to correct.[70] Though officially combined, forces remained factionalized.[71] Even though the RCAF was significantly larger than Khmer Rouge forces, internal divisions hampered its ability to retake areas controlled by the Khmer Rouge.

Though UNTAC had intended to strengthen the rule of law in Cambodia, it made little headway; courts remained subordinate to the CPP-controlled Ministry of Justice.[72] The judicial system was staffed, for the most part, by unqualified CPP loyalists and was little more than a tool for imposing party control. Judicial independence was enshrined in the new constitution, and a commission of international legal experts drafted new laws. UNTAC drafted a limited penal-code document with approximately 40 offenses, under the assumption that the postelection government would promulgate a permanent penal code. Instead, no code was adopted, and the UNTAC "guidelines" document became the de facto penal code. Even though the right to a fair trial was included in the constitution, the incompetence, corrup-

---

[69] F. Brown and Timberman, 1998, p. 100.

[70] Peou, 1998.

[71] Grant Curtis, *Cambodia Reborn? The Transition to Democracy and Development*, Washington, D.C.: Brookings Institution, 1998, p. 35.

[72] Hughes, 1996, p. 36.

tion, and bias of the judges, coupled with an inadequately developed criminal code, worked against this promise.[73]

UNTAC was tasked with establishing supervisory control over Cambodia's civil administration and exercising direct control in five areas: foreign affairs, defense, public security, information, and finance. It was hoped that UNTAC could reduce the advantage that control of the SOC bureaucracy gave to the CPP and help create a neutral political environment before the elections.[74] UNTAC's civil administration staff of 218 was, however, inadequate to exert authority over the SOC's huge communist-style bureaucracy, estimated to be between 140,000 and 200,000 people.[75] The CPP, to ensure its advantage and maximize resources, let the government administration collapse in policy areas it deemed expendable and created secret parallel decisionmaking structures to work around UNTAC on issues about which it cared. Because the SOC continued to control government resources and personnel, UNTAC could do little more than negotiate with the CPP to gain its cooperation.

Government administration also suffered because corruption continued unabated under UNTAC. The SOC's patronage system remained in place throughout the UNTAC period. Public-sector employees expected that they could supplement their salaries with payoffs. When a cash crunch and inflation reduced civil-servant salaries by 75 percent between 1992 and 1993, the result was heightened corruption and absenteeism.[76]

---

[73] Asian Legal Resource Centre, "Civil and Political Rights, Including the Question of: Independence of the Judiciary, Administration of Justice, Impunity," written statement submitted to the UN Secretary-General, February 8, 2000.

[74] Doyle, 1995, p. 35.

[75] Power, 2008, p. 98; Widyono, 2008, p. 59.

[76] Dobbins, Jones, Crane, Rathmell, et al., 2005, p. 87.

Outcomes

For many observers, the continued conflict with the Khmer Rouge demonstrated UNTAC's failure to bring full and immediate peace to Cambodia. However, setting such a high standard of success obscures UNTAC's notable achievements: Battle deaths in 1989—before serious peace negotiations began—were around 1,000; after UNTAC was established, they dropped to 200 in 1991; and, from 1995 until the conflict with the Khmer Rouge ended in 1998, annual battle deaths did not exceed 25, except during a coup in 1997, in which they reached approximately 50 deaths.[77] Before UNTAC, Cambodia was, by any definition, still embroiled in civil war; afterward, it was not.

In terms of fulfilling UNTAC's political goals, like many post-conflict countries in which the civil war has ended through negotiated settlement rather than victory for one side, the postelection government was far from unified. In their positions as co-premiers, Hun Sen and Prince Ranariddh competed for support by spreading patronage and selling positions.[78] In 1996, the Khmer Rouge split, and both Ranariddh and Hun Sen tried to woo the Ieng Sary faction that was opposed to Pol Pot. Ranariddh finalized an alliance on June 4, 1997, but, before the balance of power "tipped in his rival's favor," Hun Sen launched a successful coup the next day.[79] FUNCINPEC was ousted from the government, and Hun Sen made his own deal with the Ieng Sary faction, welcoming its members back into society and folding its forces into the RCAF.

The international community condemned the coup and suspended foreign aid. To attract the resumption of aid, Hun Sen held elections in 1998, under conditions that met the bare minimum standard of

---

[77] Bethany Lacina and Nils Gleditsch, "Monitoring Trends in Global Combat: A New Dataset of Battle Deaths," *European Journal of Population*, Vol. 21, No. 2–3, June 2005, pp. 145–166.

[78] Discussion with a leader in Cambodia's international business community, Phnom Penh, February 3, 2009.

[79] Nate Thayer, "Pol Pot, I Presume," *Wall Street Journal*, August 1, 1997.

fairness.[80] The CPP won a majority but fell short of the two-thirds needed to form a government in accordance with the new constitution. The CPP and FUNCINPEC had to again share power. The scenario was repeated in 2003, but splits soon emerged within FUNCINPEC that Hun Sen used to his advantage. By 2006, he had bought the support of enough FUNCINPEC delegates to pass legislation lowering the threshold for forming a government to a 50-percent-plus-one majority.[81] Since that time, the CPP has ruled alone, and it has harassed and marginalized opposition groups. Yet, once its position was secured, the CPP began to pay more attention to governing and has made significant strides in fostering economic growth and improving education and infrastructure. In addition, Cambodia has been largely secure since 1999, when the Khmer Rouge effectively ceased to exist.

Local Attitudes

UNTAC was warmly welcomed by Cambodians who believed that it was their best chance to finally put an end to years of bloodshed. UNTAC personnel were thought of as "liberators" who would wrestle the Khmer Rouge into submission and keep the CPP from exercising dictatorial authority.[82] The mission's broad and ambitious mandate, coupled with UNTAC's impressive array of personnel, equipment, and cash, raised expectations to a level that guaranteed disappointment. Prior to UNTAC, Cambodians had been isolated from the rest of the world for nearly two decades, yet, quite suddenly, a parade of nations descended upon their country.[83] Cambodians dubbed UNTAC the "invasion of the white cars," referring to the ubiquitous Toyota Land Cruisers used by UN personnel; it felt like a "permanent circus coming

---

[80] Adrian Karatnycky, *Freedom in the World: The Annual Survey of Political Rights and Civil Liberties, 1999–2000*, New York: Freedom House, 2000, p. 112.

[81] Discussion with Cambodian political analyst, Phnom Penh, February 2, 2010.

[82] Caroline Hughes, *Dependent Communities: Aid and Politics in Cambodia and East Timor*, Ithaca, N.Y.: Southeast Asia Program, Cornell University, 2009a.

[83] Widyono, 2008, p.12.

to town."[84] Phnom Penh and some of the larger provincial capitals were suddenly abuzz with activity.

Yet, even before UNTAC was fully deployed, an event occurred that caused Cambodians to quickly revise their expectations downward. As former UNTAC peacekeeper Benny Widyono colorfully describes, "in what became known as the bamboo pole incident, the Khmer Rouge gave UNTAC the finger."[85] In May 1992, two months after their arrival, the head of UNTAC, Yasushi Akashi, and the head of UNTAC's military component, General John Sanderson, went to the Khmer Rouge stronghold of Pailin, from where they were to travel to the Thai border to meet with peacekeepers preparing for deployment to disarm Khmer Rouge fighters. On the way, they encountered a roadblock manned by a group of young Khmer Rouge soldiers who refused to remove the bamboo pole that obstructed passage. Instead of insisting on entering the zone and deploying UNTAC soldiers for protection (which the peace accords allowed), Akashi and Sanderson turned back. The incident was widely publicized and greatly embarrassed Akashi. Upon realizing that UNTAC was a "paper tiger," the Khmer Rouge soon announced that it would not disarm or allow UNTAC troops in its region, which, in turn, brought a halt to CPP cooperation with UNTAC.[86]

Hence, with one bamboo pole, some teenagers were able to prevent UNTAC from fulfilling the two most important goals of their mandate, or at least that was the view of many Cambodians. As one author concluded, "Disjuncture between UNTAC's outward signs of power and its obvious wealth, cars, helicopters, and so on—and its seeming impotence—was mystifying to many Cambodians."[87] Though UNTAC had only limited success, it continues to be appreciated for the relative peace that it established and for its contributions to

---

[84] Widyono, 2008, p. 13.

[85] Widyono, 2008, p. 77.

[86] Widyono, 2008, p. 77.

[87] Judy Ledgerwood as quoted in Hughes, 1996, p. 93.

Cambodian resettlement and reconstruction, the foundations of Cambodia's later economic growth.

Although opinions about UNTAC's achievement record are mixed, Cambodians have a strongly negative opinion of off-duty activities of UNTAC personnel. Cambodians believed that UN officials supported behavior that violated Cambodian mores. Several UN orders and statements seem to confirm this view or at least show that UN authorities were unwilling to get involved: UN personnel were allowed to visit brothels but not in uniform, nor could they park UN vehicles nearby. With regard to soliciting prostitution, the Special Representative said that this conduct of the peacekeepers was to be expected.[88] There were no restrictions on their freedom to intermingle with the host population. Prostitution flourished, and there were many complaints about rape, child abuse, and UNTAC personnel corrupting young Cambodians by using their power and money to solicit sexual favors.[89]

An accusation that is frequently made by Hun Sen and is a common response whenever Cambodians are asked about UNTAC is that UNTAC brought acquired immunodeficiency syndrome (AIDS) to Cambodia. Though it is doubtful that human immunodeficiency virus (HIV) or AIDS was first introduced by UNTAC, there is evidence that it spread quickly during the period of UNTAC and that many of the peacekeepers returned home with the Southeast Asian variant of HIV.[90] In this respect, UNTAC should serve as a cautionary tale for planners of nation-building operations: Though personnel behavior may not significantly affect a mission's operations, if not kept in check, it could seriously affect its legacy.

Geographical and Geopolitical

Without the international community's strong commitment to UNTAC and to Cambodia's development, it is unlikely that the coun-

---

[88] Hughes, 1996, p. 93.

[89] Hughes, 1996, p. 93.

[90] Chris Beyrer, "Burma and Cambodia: Human Rights, Social Disruption, and the Spread of HIV/AIDS," *Health and Human Rights*, Vol. 2, No. 4, 1998, pp. 84–97, p. 91.

try would have regular elections, an active civil society, and substantial improvements in literacy and public health, as it does today. The donor community financially supports these improvements and uses the pressure of the pocketbook to attempt to hold the government accountable and leverage concessions. These results are not, however, entirely self-sustaining, because the CPP has little reason to improve governance other than the possible loss of international assistance. It would seem that, given aid levels, Cambodia's dependence, and thus some level of government responsiveness to international pressures, will continue: Donors pledged $1.1 billion in aid for 2011, and, in 2011, foreign assistance accounted for 48 percent of the national budget.[91] There are changes on the horizon, however, that may undercut the international community's influence. Revenues from recent oil discoveries are expected to come on-line in 2012, and Chinese foreign direct investment is growing. Hun Sen has voiced his preference for forms of revenue with no strings attached, thereby indicating that he would behave differently if Cambodia were less dependent on aid.[92]

Cultural and Social

Respect for the royal family has remained strong and likely accounted for FUNCINPEC's surprise win in the first post–peace settlement election. Over time, as Sihanouk distanced himself from the party and Prince Ranariddh proved an inept party leader, FUNCINPEC lost much of its appeal. Although the current king, Norodom Sihamoni, does not inspire the same loyalty as did Sihanouk, the royal family remains a legitimating force, as shown by Hun Sen's continuing attempts to co-opt royal support.[93]

---

[91] Chhim Chhun, Chhoun Nareth, Em Sorany, Hing Vutha, Huon Chantrea, Joakim Ojendal, Keo Socheat, Khieng Sothy, Kim Sedara, Kim Sour, Koy Ra, Larry Strange, Lun Pide, Nang Phirun, Net Neath, Ros Bansok, Roth Vathana, Saing Chan Hang, Sok Sethea, and Sum Sreymom, *Annual Development Review 2011–12*, Phnom Penh: CDRI, February 2012, p. 5.

[92] Brian McCartan, "Cambodia Shrugs Off Aid Curb," *Asia Times*, August 23, 2011.

[93] Discussion with a U.S. official in Cambodia, Phnom Penh, February 1, 2010.

Xenophobia remains a salient feature of the political landscape. To discredit Hun Sen, the Sam Rainsy Party, Cambodia's main opposition party as of 2012, stokes anti-Vietnamese sentiments with accusations that the CPP willfully ignores Vietnamese land grabs.[94] Hun Sen uses a persistent border dispute with Thailand to stoke nationalist sentiment and garner greater support.

Only in recent years have Cambodians begun the process of transitional justice to address the crimes perpetrated by the Khmer Rouge. Most notably, the Cambodian government, under strong international pressure, and the United Nations jointly established the Extraordinary Chambers in the Courts of Cambodia (ECCC) to try Khmer Rouge leaders. Other than a show trial that occurred after the Vietnamese invasion, it is the first effort to hold the Khmer Rouge accountable. However, Hun Sen's government has repeatedly undermined the work of the ECCC.

Given the enormity of the Khmer Rouge's crimes, overwhelming public support for the tribunal might be expected, but, in reality, opinions are mixed and complex. Eighty-one percent of respondents in a 2010 survey believed that the ECCC will contribute to reconciliation, but justice and the rule of law were not considered personal or governmental priorities. Justice and rule of law ranked lowest out of a list of nine priorities, and 63 percent would rather spend money on something other than the Khmer Rouge tribunal.[95]

There are several reasons for the population's ambivalence and the lack of government support for the tribunal. First, the judicial reforms initiated by UNTAC largely failed to take hold, and Cambodians' lack of faith in their judicial system carries over to the tribunal. Some may prefer no trials to "substandard" trials.[96] Second, after two

---

[94] "Opposition Highs and Lows," *Phnom Penh Post*, July 14, 2011.

[95] Patrick Vinck, Phuong N. Pham, Mychelle Balthazard, and Sokhom Hean, *After the First Trial: A Population-Based Survey on Knowledge and Perception of Justice and the Extraordinary Chambers in the Courts of Cambodia*, Berkeley, Calif.: Human Rights Center, University of California Berkeley, June 2011, p. 3.

[96] Estelle Bockers, Nadine Stammel, and Christine Knaevelsrud, "Reconciliation in Cambodia: Thirty Years After the Terror of the Khmer Rouge Regime," *Torture*, Vol. 21, No. 2, 2011, pp. 71–83, p. 77.

decades of war, many older Cambodians have blood on their hands.[97] And finally, the CPP has rejected calls for a truth commission, fearing that it would implicate the party's leadership, most of whom were once Khmer Rouge members, including President Hun Sen.[98] Given the lack of enthusiasm on the part of the government and the mixed feelings of Cambodians, it is unlikely that actions aimed at addressing past human rights abuses will gain momentum, despite efforts of many domestic and international NGOs.

Economic

Many financial reforms that were introduced succeeded. Customs reforms and new tax measures raised government revenues. Sensible monetary policies slowed inflation and stabilized the exchange rate. In 1993, hyperinflation and food insecurity were avoided by UNTAC's placement of additional, imported rice on the market.

Since UNTAC ended in 1993, Cambodia has experienced impressive economic growth. Between 1994 and 2010, average annual GDP growth was 7.8 percent, lifting Cambodia's annual per capita income from $278 to $735.[99] Poverty fell from 39 percent in 1994 to 30 percent in 2007.[100] Trade and tourism have been the main drivers of growth. Between 1995 and 2009, trade increased at an annual average rate of 17 percent, with total trade reaching $10.2 billion per year. Yet, how far Cambodia has come is also a reflection of how undeveloped it was at the end of its civil war, and even earlier. Even though standards of living have improved, Cambodia ranks 139th of 187 countries on the Human Development Index (HDI),[101] and its GDP per capita ranks

---

[97] Discussion with Cambodian journalist, Washington, D.C., January 19, 2010; discussion with American Cambodia expert and journalist, Washington, D.C., January 18, 2010.

[98] Bockers, Stammel, and Knaevelsrud, 2011, p. 77.

[99] Chhun et al., 2012, p. 1.

[100] Chhun et al., 2012, p. 2.

[101] UN Development Programme, *Human Development Report 2011: Sustainability and Equity—A Better Future for All*, New York, 2011, p. 126.

only 185th of 226 countries.[102] Only 16 percent of Cambodians have access to a proper toilet.[103]

Cambodia ranks 164th among 183 countries on Transparency International's 2011 Corruption Perceptions Index.[104] Corruption restrains development by siphoning off potential tax revenues and depressing competition, which, in turn, further reduces tax revenues.[105] Hun Sen faces a conundrum: If he wants to broaden his popular support, he needs to combat corruption; however, if he interferes in patronage, he will lose current supporters and possibly risk splits within the party.[106] He has tried to solve the government's revenue crunch by exploiting Cambodia's natural resources, but this is not a long-term solution.[107] New oil revenue could ease the fiscal situation and allow Hun Sen to direct greater funding to public welfare and economic development without having to challenge Cambodia's entrenched patron-clientelism. However, the introduction of oil wealth will also likely reinforce the system that is already in place, leading to greater corruption.

Political

Although early observer accounts of UNTAC praised the election, later works are less generous, claiming that a fractured, inefficient government and six more years of much lower-level conflict were the true legacies of the operation. Although no one would argue that the CPP/FUNCINPEC government was effective—or even completely legitimate—during this early period of vulnerability and state weakness, having a power-sharing government was key to stabilizing the country. If the CPP had won a clear majority in the 1993 election,

---

[102] CIA, 2012b.

[103] Joel Brinkley, "Cambodia's Curse: Struggling to Shed the Khmer Rouge's Legacy," *Foreign Affairs*, March–April 2009.

[104] Transparency International, *Corruption Perceptions Index 2011*, 2011, p. 4.

[105] Discussion with UN development official, Phnom Penh, February 3, 2010.

[106] "Intrigue in Ruling CPP Detailed," *Phnom Penh Post*, July 13, 2011.

[107] Global Witness, *Cambodia's Family Trees: Illegal Logging and the Stripping of Public Assets*, Washington, D.C., June 2007.

Hun Sen could have used the continued threat of the Khmer Rouge to dampen political rights and extend state control—perhaps even declaring a state of emergency. If he had done so, it is unlikely that the international community would have reacted strongly because the elections would have demonstrated that he was more popular than his opponents. However, if FUNCINPEC had won a greater majority and had refused to share power, it is unlikely that it could have held off the Khmer Rouge unassisted. Without CPP forces, FUNCINPEC would have needed considerable time before it could stand up a force large enough to establish security. Both of these possibilities would have resulted in greater instability and reversed most of the political gains made under UNTAC.

With respect to the long-term impact of UNTAC, many critics claim that Cambodia is a democracy in name only and that elections are nothing more than a means of legitimizing a dictatorial regime.[108] Cambodia has held four national elections, yet it has been ruled by the same man—Hun Sen—for 27 years. But, even though elections in Cambodia have never provided government accountability to the extent that they should have, they may have strengthened government responsiveness to popular needs. Until 2003, the outcome of Cambodian elections was not certain, and parties could not afford to completely ignore the desires of constituents. By the time Hun Sen consolidated CPP dominance over the government, democratic elections had become the recognized method of legitimation, and Hun Sen had to at least keep up the pretense that they were free and fair.

Probably the main reason that elections have fostered somewhat better governance has been the personal insecurities and character of Hun Sen. He has continued to hold elections and to be attentive to (at least some) of the demands of the international community because the ostracism experienced by the PRK during its period in power made him sensitive to his international reputation. The domestic popularity of the CPP matters even more to Hun Sen, who only in recent years has been able to shed some of the stigma of his earlier depen-

---

[108] Joel Brinkley, *Cambodia's Curse: The Modern History of a Troubled Land*, New York: PublicAffairs, 2011.

dence on Vietnam. It is said that he looks carefully at election results to assess CPP popularity, identify underperforming representatives, and promote those who are popular.[109] Likewise, he directs projects and resources to areas where CPP vote share is at risk. Subjecting party cadres to electoral competition has helped him strengthen the party.[110] These efforts appear to have paid off: A 2010 survey showed that 76 percent of Cambodians believe that the country is going in the right direction.[111] Thus, even though Hun Sen biases the political system to ensure that the CPP wins, and therefore elections do not make him accountable to the electorate in the traditional manner, because of his sensitivity to the CPP's reputation, elections still play a role in improving governance and accountability.

Cambodia is experiencing a youth bulge that will rapidly change the Cambodian electorate. Sixty-three percent of the population is under 24 years of age.[112] Cambodian youth have been exposed to information provided by domestic and international NGOs and, as a result, have much greater expectations of the government than their elders had. Perhaps even more important is the fact that, unlike their parents, who grew up in an isolated society, Cambodian youth engage with the larger world through travel, independent media, and the Internet. They did not experience life under the Khmer Rouge, and they know little about the period.[113] Whereas their elders have tended to reward politicians who provide security, youth are concerned about jobs. The CPP is closely monitoring these demographic shifts, but, because the bulk of the CPP's resources are expended on patronage, it is unlikely that

---

[109] Discussion with U.S. official, Phnom Penh, February 1, 2010; discussion with senior UN adviser, Phnom Penh, February 4, 2010.

[110] Caroline Hughes, "Reconstructing Legitimate Political Authority Through Elections?" in Joakim Öjendal and Mona Lilja, eds., *Beyond Democracy in Cambodia: Political Reconstruction in a Post-Conflict Society*, Copenhagen: NIAS Press, 2009b, pp. 31–69, p. 49.

[111] This is down from a high of 82 percent reported in November 2008 (International Republican Institute [IRI], *Survey of Cambodian Public Opinion, July 31–August 26, 2009*, c. 2009).

[112] Discussion with UN official, Phnom Penh, February 3, 2010.

[113] Discussion with UN official, Phnom Penh, February 3, 2010; Bockers, Stammel, and Knaevelsrud, 2011, p. 79.

Hun Sen will be able to adequately respond to the demands of youth.[114] The CPP will either have to bear the risks of dismantling Cambodia's patronage system or face the wrath of young people at least at the ballot box.[115]

Institutional

After the first election, troops of the contending factions not only failed to reintegrate but also remained loyal to their party leaders and began to fight each other, as well as launch attacks against party opponents. These skirmishes evolved into street battles during the 1997 coup.[116] Eventually, CPP troops dominated the military, and Hun Sen was able to initiate some security sector reforms to weed out redundancies and positions previously belonging to FUNCINPEC. The number of generals was reduced from 1,876 to 147, the number of colonels from 5,000 to 304, and the number of divisions from 28 to 12.[117] Hun Sen has indulged corruption within the military, however, to maintain officer loyalty. Increasingly, the military has become engaged in criminal money-making activities.[118]

The Cambodian judicial system continues to be weak and ineffective. Human and capital resources are lacking. Court staff are underpaid and must provide their own supplies. The government assumes that court officials supplement their salaries with "fees" from litigants, and the police will usually not issue a warrant without financial incentives. Not surprisingly, cases in which little or no money is involved are often postponed in favor of more-lucrative contests.[119] Courts are not a check on executive authority and continue to accommodate inter-

---

[114] "Intrigue in Ruling CPP Detailed," 2011.

[115] Discussion with UN human rights official, February 11, 2010.

[116] Peou, 1998.

[117] Anga R. Timilsina, *Getting the Policies Right: The Prioritization and Sequencing of Policies in Post-Conflict Countries*, Santa Monica, Calif.: RAND Corporation, RGSD-222, 2007, p. 84.

[118] Nate Thayer, "U.N., Government Reports Cite Killings by Cambodian Military Officials," *Washington Post*, August 13, 1994.

[119] Un, 2009, pp. 76, 81.

ventions by state and party authorities. Hun Sen has recently taken to actively using the courts to suppress his opponents' freedoms of speech and assembly through defamation and disinformation suits.[120] In 2010, the government quickly passed long-awaited anticorruption laws without allowing for public scrutiny or debate. As a result, the laws have few protections for whistle-blowers and do not ensure the independence of the new anticorruption bodies that are supposed to root out illegal practices in the government and judiciary.[121]

Conclusions

What Local Factors Posed the Greatest Challenges?
The local factors within each category that were most important in shaping the environment in which nation-builders sought to promote an enduring peace included the following.

Geographical and Geopolitical
The geopolitical struggle among superpowers and interference by neighbors were the most-significant factors giving rise to the conflicts in Cambodia. Conflict resolution became possible when the priorities of external actors shifted.

Cultural and Social
The violence of the Khmer Rouge period grew out of the group's extreme version of traditional nationalist ideas and fears and socially deep-seated xenophobia. The nation-building efforts included only a limited attempt to overcome this legacy by fostering respect for human rights. Xenophobia remained strong in Cambodia, and political leaders continued to stoke nationalist sentiment to garner support. The government and perhaps also the population had limited appetite for transitional justice; external efforts in this area thus failed to gain traction.

---

[120]Human Rights Watch, *Human Rights Watch World Report 2011: Events of 2010*, New York: Seven Stories, 2011.

[121] Human Rights Watch, 2011.

Economic

Cambodia before the conflicts had a low level of development; afterward, it was an economic and infrastructural wasteland. The country lost one-fifth of its population, including almost all qualified professionals in every field. It lacked domestic capital for reconstruction and development, and the enormous needs swamped international commitments of support. Impressive growth has been achieved since the UN mission ended, though socioeconomic development remains low and the level of corruption is high.

Political

Cambodian politics have long been characterized by patronage relationships. The patrons have changed, but the political practices, by and large, have not. UNTAC sought to establish a functioning government of a more modern variety. Although UNTAC organized technically successful elections, the regime remained essentially authoritarian, and government effectiveness was hampered by a bloated bureaucracy that doubled in size under power-sharing arrangements.

Institutional

After the conflict, institutions, including security forces, a justice system, and a civil service, had to be created virtually from scratch, and government infrastructure was devastated. Nepotism was rampant in hiring for the new institutions. During UNTAC's tenure, little progress was made in these areas. UNTAC was given direct control over several domains of government, but its civil administration staff of little more than 200 was inadequate to exert much authority.

Were Local Factors Modified or Circumvented to Promote Enduring Peace?

In the decade following the UN-led intervention, peace was sustained, democratization and government effectiveness improved only slightly, and per capita GDP increased by 53.6 percent. Table 3.1 shows these outcomes, alongside key resources applied by nation-building interveners.

External pressures were principally responsible for Cambodia's civil war. Cambodian resistance to external interference, combined

Table 3.1
Postintervention Performance and Nation-Building Inputs in Cambodia

Performance Indicator	Year of Intervention (1991)	5 Years Later	10 Years Later
At peace?	—	Yes	Yes
Government effectiveness (10-point scale)	3.92	3.92	3.99
Freedom Index (10-point scale)	2.50	2.50	3.25
HDI (10-point scale)	NA	4.3	4.4
Cumulative growth in per capita GDP (in 1st 5 years and in 10 years after intervention) (%)	—	17.2	53.6
Nation-Building Input			
Peak military presence per capita, number of troops per 1,000 inhabitants	1.5		
Peak international civilian police presence per capita, number of police per 1,000 inhabitants	0.5		
Average annual per capita assistance in the first 5 years (constant 2010 US$)	38.36		

SOURCES: World Bank, "Worldwide Governance Indicators," undated (d), referenced August 2012; Freedom House, *Freedom in the World* reports, various years; UN Development Programme, "International Human Development Indicators: Do-It-Yourself Data Tables," undated; International Monetary Fund, "International Financial Statistics (IFS) Query Builder," undated; Dobbins, Jones, Crane, Chivvis, et al., 2008, Figures 9.2, 9.4, 9.9; UN Peace Operations, *Year in Review*, various years; World Bank, "World Development Indicators," undated (c).

NOTE: NA = not available.

with the population's customary deference to established authority, tended to magnify the impact of the resultant divisions between factions supported by one external party or the other. Once that support was removed, that same Cambodian deference to established authority seems to have reinforced the peace, rather than sustained the conflict. In this sense, a social factor facilitated the achievement of the primary goal of nation-building rather than needing to be overcome.

The UN intervention was among the first post–Cold War exercises in multinational nation-building. The interveners were granted exceptionally broad authority by the contending parties and the UN Security Council but, in the event, were never allowed to, or indeed capable of, exercising these plenary powers. By the standard of subsequent postconflict UN peacekeeping missions, this one was also exceptionally short-lived. Despite these limitations, the UN mission achieved its fundamental purpose, leaving behind a society at peace with itself and its neighbors, even though it did not achieve many of its initial, grander stated ambitions.

One of the three main contending factions, the Khmer Rouge, never implemented its agreed undertakings, and the UN proved unable to compel its compliance. Indeed, the UN mission never seriously tried. But, once denied external support, the Khmer Rouge faded away with remarkable rapidity.

UN-organized elections and a subsequent power-sharing agreement produced a politically inclusive coalition government. Years after the UN departure, this coalition collapsed, and one faction secured and has since retained control of the country. Democratic forms have been maintained and perhaps exercise some restraints over a basically authoritarian government.

Like many societies emerging from years of intense and prolonged conflict, Cambodia has since grown economically at a healthy rate, albeit from a low base. This growth has been sustained even as external assistance dropped after UNTAC's departure.

The success of the international community in bringing peace and some measure of economic improvement to Cambodia is mostly due to its modification of that country's geopolitical circumstances. In this particular case, it was less the end of the East-West competition than the more or less simultaneous rapprochement between Moscow and Beijing that significantly altered foreign interests in Cambodia.

Had the UN mission been sustained for a longer period, it is possible that the continuation of authoritarian government might have been interrupted. As it was, the rapid success of UNTAC in bringing peace and democratic forms—elections and a new constitution—to Cambodia gave the international community what proved to be an exaggerated sense of optimism about how much could be achieved quickly in the several postconflict stabilization and reconstruction missions that followed in the subsequent decade. In Cambodia, there proved few indigenous obstacles to peace once its geopolitical circumstances changed. This would not always be the case with other post–Cold War interventions.

CHAPTER FOUR

El Salvador

The peace agreement signed in January 1992 by the Salvadoran government and the Farabundo Martí National Liberation Front (Frente Farabundo Martí para la Liberación Nacional, or FMLN) in Chapultepec, Mexico, marked the end of a 12-year civil war that resulted in

Figure 4.1
Map of El Salvador

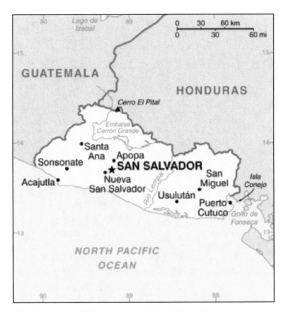

SOURCE: CIA, "El Salvador," *The World Factbook*, 2012d.

RAND *RR167-4.1*

80,000 people dead and another 70,000 severely wounded.[1] The provisions contained in this peace accord specifically aimed to address the core issues that had led to the conflict in the first place: a socioeconomic structure based on great inequalities between a small minority consisting of landowners and a large number of poor agricultural workers with little or no land of their own, and opposition to an authoritarian government supported by a powerful military.[2] The Chapultepec accord sought to compel political, social, and institutional change by redistributing land, democratizing political practices, and reforming the military and placing it under civilian control.

Such measures would transform El Salvador; implementation thus encountered strong resistance from those who stood to lose the most. Persistent mediation by international actors—in particular, the United Nations—played a key role in overcoming these obstacles, even as external powers pressed for quick implementation of the peace accords and the adoption of market-focused economic and financial policy changes to spur economic growth. Although El Salvador has now been at peace for 20 years and is politically stable—making it a model of successful UN-sponsored nation-building—the war has left disquieting legacies. In particular, rates of violent crime are very high, due in part to a failed reintegration process and widespread availability of wartime weapons.[3]

---

[1] Kevin Murray, *El Salvador: Peace on Trial*, Oxford, UK: Oxfam UK and Ireland, 1997, p. 14.

[2] Alvaro de Soto and Graciana del Castillo, "Obstacles to Peacebuilding," *Foreign Policy*, No. 94, Spring 1994, pp. 69–83, p. 70. For a detailed history of the negotiations that led to the Chapultepec accords, see Mark Levine, "Peacemaking in El Salvador," in Michael W. Doyle, Ian Johnstone, and Robert C. Orr, *Keeping the Peace: Multidimensional UN Operations in Cambodia and El Salvador*, New York: Cambridge University Press, 1997, pp. 227–254.

[3] Based on 2004–2009 data from Keith Krause, Robert Muggah, and Elisabeth Gilgen, eds., *Global Burden of Armed Violence 2011: Lethal Encounters*, Cambridge, UK: Cambridge University Press, 2011, p. 53.

Local Factors Before the Peace

El Salvador's civil war was ignited by a coup led by junior officers (the "Revolutionary Governing Junta") in October 1979, which opened an era of instability and increasing levels of violence during a succession of military governments. Left-wing guerrilla opposition groups united to create the FMLN and stepped up attacks against the military.[4] By 1990, the combatants had arrived at a military stalemate and separately requested mediation from the UN Secretary-General. This mediation resulted, after two years of negotiations, in the signing of the January 16, 1992, Chapultepec peace accord.

Geographical and Geopolitical

One of the smallest countries in Central America (see Figure 4.1), El Salvador is very densely populated, with 590 inhabitants per square mile. This density, as well as soil erosion and diminishing water supplies, has added pressure to the already-sensitive issue of landownership. The mountainous area in the north of the country is the poorest and was disproportionately affected by the fighting during the civil war.[5] Geographical factors made guerrilla fighting particularly difficult because the military could quickly reach any point in the country and rebels were unable to control territory other than small, mountainous areas.[6] The fact that the civil war nevertheless lasted 12 years and ended in a stalemate speaks at length to the incompetence of the Salvadoran army.

After the success of the July 1979 revolution in Nicaragua, the Revolutionary Governing Junta took power in November of that same

---

[4]   Charles T. Call, "Assessing El Salvador's Transition from Civil War to Peace," in Stephen John Stedman, Donald S. Rothchild, and Elizabeth M. Cousens, eds., *Ending Civil Wars: The Implementation of Peace Agreements*, Boulder, Colo.: Lynn Rienner, 2002, pp. 383–420, p. 385.

[5]   Murray, 1997, pp. 4–5; Edelberto Torres-Rivas, "Insurrection and Civil War in El Salvador," in Michael W. Doyle, Ian Johnstone, and Robert C. Orr, eds., *Keeping the Peace: Multidimensional UN Operations in Cambodia and El Salvador*, New York: Cambridge University Press, 1997, pp. 209–226, p. 221.

[6]   Torres-Rivas, 1997, p. 221.

year in an attempt to prevent El Salvador from experiencing a similar fate.[7] The United States provided the Salvadoran government with close to $6 billion in assistance over a period of ten years during the conflict. These funds were spent on improving the efficiency and accountability of the military, redistributing land, and democratization.[8] On the other side, the FMLN received support from the Soviet Union, Cuba, and Nicaragua, which, at the time, was ruled by the Sandinistas.[9]

Cultural and Social

Prewar socioeconomic indicators were generally very poor, with almost half of the population aged 15 years and older illiterate and life expectancy below 60 years old.[10] The civil war only made this situation worse; the government gave priority to military spending over spending on education and health care.[11] Near the end of the war in 1990, 56 percent of the population was living in poverty—5 percentage points more than in 1980.[12] The war also saw massive human rights violations, with government forces and their informally affiliated death squads targeting civilians suspected of supporting the FMLN. Overall, more than 40,000 civilians were killed during the war, mostly by the armed and paramilitary forces.[13] Victims could not expect any recourse from the

---

[7] Call, 2002, p. 385.

[8] Benjamin Schwarz, *American Counterinsurgency Doctrine and El Salvador: The Frustrations of Reform and the Illusions of Nation Building*, Santa Monica, Calif.: RAND Corporation, R-4042-USDP, 1991, pp. vii–viii, 16.

[9] Fen Osler Hampson, "The Pursuit of Human Rights: The United Nations in El Salvador," in William J. Durch, ed., *UN Peacekeeping, American Politics, and the Uncivil Wars of the 1990s*, New York: St. Martin's Press, 1996, pp. 69–102, p. 79.

[10] Graciana del Castillo, "Post-Conflict Reconstruction and the Challenge to International Organizations: The Case of El Salvador," *World Development*, Vol. 29, No. 12, December 2001, pp. 1967–1985, p. 1971.

[11] Del Castillo, 2001, p. 1972.

[12] Dobbins, Jones, Crane, Rathmell, et al., 2005, p. 50.

[13] Murray, 1997, p. 14. Another estimate gives 50,000 civilians killed by state forces (William Deane Stanley, "El Salvador: State-Building Before and After Democratisation, 1980–95," *Third World Quarterly*, Vol. 27, No. 1, 2006, pp. 101–114, p. 102).

government or judicial system because a 1987 amnesty law absolved these forces of all crimes committed before October 1987.

Land tenure is a key issue in El Salvador and is widely perceived to be one of the root causes of the civil war.[14] As of 1980, 1 percent of the population owned more than 70 percent of the land.[15] Concentration of landownership had been increasing for decades, with the average acreage for peasant households decreasing from 7.4 to 0.4 hectares between the end of the 19th century and the early 1970s.[16] The majority of Salvadoran society was composed of agricultural laborers, many of them without any land of their own: The number of landless peasants increased from about 30,000 in 1961 to 167,000 in 1975, when they represented more than 40 percent of the rural population.[17]

Shortly before and during the war, the U.S. Agency for International Development (USAID) attempted to promote a major land reform planned to benefit 80,000 peasant families. One key aim of this reform was to prevent further recruitment of peasants by the FMLN.[18] The involvement of the Armed Forces of El Salvador (Fuerza Armada de El Salvador, or FAES) in implementing the land reform, however, resulted in increased murder rates of civilians in the areas where it was active. The government also largely undermined the reform by failing to support the new landowners and their cooperatives, which struggled economically because of little access to credit and limited technical skills. This first attempt at land reform proved a failure, and disparities between rich and poor increased during the war.[19]

---

[14] Del Castillo, 2001, p. 1971.

[15] Schwarz, 1991, p. 44.

[16] Murray, 1997, p. 11.

[17] Tommie Sue Montgomery, *Revolution in El Salvador: From Civil Strife to Civil Peace*, Boulder, Colo.: Westview Press, 1995, p. 59; Graciana del Castillo, "The Arms-for-Land Deal in El Salvador," in Michael W. Doyle, Ian Johnstone, and Robert C. Orr, eds., *Keeping the Peace: Multidimensional UN Operations in Cambodia and El Salvador*, New York: Cambridge University Press, 1997, pp. 342–366, p. 344.

[18] Schwarz, 1991, p. 44.

[19] Schwarz, 1991, pp. 45–49; Murray, 1997, p. 24.

Economic

The Salvadoran economy experienced growth in the 1960s and 1970s, but the civil war reversed those gains.[20] Economic growth slowed greatly, averaging 1.3 percent during the 1980s.[21] Reconstruction needs at the end of the conflict were considerable, with the damage to the country's infrastructure amounting to more than $1.5 billion. Exports declined during the war, mainly because of an unfavorable global economic environment; the fact that the local currency, the *colón*, was overvalued only made this situation worse. The only sources of revenue that increased for El Salvador during the war were U.S. economic assistance and remittances of Salvadorans who had fled the country.[22]

As with land issues, the United States made some attempts to spur economic reforms. For example, USAID funded a Salvadoran Foundation for Economic and Social Development, which acted as a think tank for economic modernization. It organized seminars and provided technical assistance to encourage the development of more-modern sectors of the economy and more-diverse exports.[23]

Political

Since the 1930s, the political landscape in El Salvador had been largely dominated by the military, which tightly controlled the executive branch. Political opposition and social mobilization were severely repressed. Although the country had a constitution and elections after 1948, voting was a formality of no political consequence: Ruling regimes were invariably authoritarian.[24] By 1990, President Alfredo Cristiani, from the National Republican Alliance (Alianza Republicana Nacionalista, or ARENA) party, realized that, with the end of the Cold War and a scandal involving the murder of six Jesuit priests by a

---

[20] Del Castillo, 2001, p. 1971.

[21] "Economy: El Salvador," *Jane's Sentinel Security Assessment*, April 11, 2011.

[22] Stanley, 2006, p. 103. Remittances represented 5 percent of GDP in the late 1980s, more in the following years (del Castillo, 2001, p. 1972).

[23] Stanley, 2006, p. 108.

[24] Call, 2002, pp. 384–385.

military unit, U.S. military aid would be less forthcoming.[25] This coincided with the military failure—but political success—of an FMLN offensive on the capital, San Salvador, which convinced both parties that a military victory was unlikely and opened the way to negotiations.

Institutional

During the war, the United States provided training, equipment, and intelligence to the FAES. However, the FAES suffered from problems with morale and proficiency, and the U.S. contribution to training can be characterized as, at best, a mixed success.[26] Even with precise intelligence on FMLN positions, the FAES was reluctant to launch attacks.[27]

One reason for these problems is to be found in the *tanda* system, which created special bonds among members of the same officer-training cohort by ensuring that they were all commissioned and promoted together regardless of individual competence. Members of the same *tanda* were careful to protect each other from investigation or prosecution.[28] Another reason lies in recruitment methods, which aimed at increasing the number of soldiers without great regard for skills or training. Forced recruitment practices were widespread, and recruits were subjected to abuse.[29] U.S. efforts to improve respect for human rights among FAES personnel were unsuccessful.[30] Corruption and false

---

[25] The housekeeper of the Jesuits and her daughter were also killed in the attack (Call, 2002, pp. 387–388).

[26] Michael Childress, *The Effectiveness of U.S. Training Efforts in Internal Defense and Development: The Cases of El Salvador and Honduras*, Santa Monica, Calif.: RAND Corporation, MR-250-USDP, 1995, pp. 27–43. See also Schwarz, 1991, pp. 17–22.

[27] Stanley, 2006, p. 102.

[28] Schwarz, 1991, pp. vi, 18.

[29] Murray, 1997, p. 14.

[30] Stanley, 2006, p. 102. One author even noted, "It is precisely the young, aggressive, U.S.-trained officers who are most intoxicated by the extreme right's vision and most resentful of America's influence over the conduct of the civil war, and who commit many of the worst atrocities" (Schwarz, 1991, p. vii).

accounting (through the addition of "ghost soldiers" to units, which enabled officers to obtain extra pay and supplies) were widespread.[31]

Some early attempts to improve El Salvador's criminal justice system were initiated with U.S. support during the war, following the assassination of Archbishop Oscar Romero and six U.S. citizens between 1980 and 1982. However, faced with a lack of political will on the part of the government, the USAID-led Administration of Justice project was unable to undertake comprehensive reform and had to focus on providing technical assistance. The justice system remained ineffective and flawed, although this early experience may, in retrospect, have laid the groundwork for new attitudes and facilitated—albeit to a small extent—the later acceptance and implementation of more-radical reforms.[32]

Nation-Building Efforts

The U.S. attempts to help make Salvadoran institutions more accountable and promote land reform laid the groundwork for reforms that were needed to sign a peace agreement between the warring parties. The 1992 peace accord's key measures included a land-for-arms exchange, military reform, and the creation of a National Civilian Police (Policia Nacional Civil, or PNC). These were implemented under the close scrutiny of the United Nations, the United States, and El Salvador's "Four Friends" (Spain, Colombia, Mexico, and Venezuela). The United Nations, through the UN Observer Mission in El Salvador (ONUSAL) played a key role in overseeing the implementation of the peace agreement. Its constant "good offices" helped build confidence between parties. The commitment of the United States to support the peace process proved to be key because it provided assurance to the different parties that they would receive substantial financial help to implement the

---

[31] Schwarz, 1991, p. vi.

[32] Charles T. Call, "Democratisation, War and State-Building: Constructing the Rule of Law in El Salvador," *Journal of Latin American Studies*, Vol. 35, No. 4, November 2003, pp. 827–862, p. 850.

accord. By June 1992, the United States had provided $200 million to El Salvador—one-quarter of the total pledged by all donors.[33] International involvement in nation-building was phased out after 1996. The UN Mission in El Salvador (Misión de las Naciones Unidas en El Salvador, or MINUSAL), which had succeeded ONUSAL, closed its office in December of that year, leaving behind a small staff that reported directly to UN Secretary-General's Special Envoy Álvaro de Soto.[34] By then, most of the provisions of the peace accord had been implemented.

Geographical and Geopolitical

The Chapultepec agreement was, to a large extent, the product of a new geopolitical context, at both the regional and global levels. The end of the Cold War and the electoral defeat of the Sandinistas in Nicaragua in 1990 provided motivations for both parties to enter negotiations because they realized that external support would soon decrease or disappear. The UN Security Council, which had been paralyzed by the contest between the United States and the Soviet Union, was finally in a position to provide the Salvadoran government and the FMLN with the good offices and institutional support they needed to negotiate a peace agreement and carry out a peacebuilding process.

Cultural and Social

One million Salvadorans fled their homeland, mainly to the United States, during the war. Many of those who remained were displaced internally toward the southwest of the country, especially the capital, San Salvador. A smaller number of Salvadorans fled to Honduras, Guatemala, Nicaragua, and Mexico, of whom 32,000 returned after the war.[35] In the late 1990s, tighter restrictions on immigration to the United States and an increase in deportations resulted in the return of many Salvadorans, including young gang members who opened

---

[33] Elisabeth Jean Wood, *Forging Democracy from Below: Insurgent Transitions in South Africa and El Salvador*, Cambridge, UK: Cambridge University Press, 2000, p. 94–95.

[34] Murray, 1997, p. 23.

[35] Murray, 1997, p. 4; Call, 2002, p. 386.

local chapters of American gangs—the transnational *maras*—which would prove particularly difficult for Salvadoran security institutions to suppress.[36]

Reintegration programs for former combatants included vocational training, packages of tools, credits for small businesses, and university scholarships.[37] The most critical program was to be the land-transfer program (known as the Programa de Transferencia de Tierras, or PTT), generally described as a land-for-arms exchange. Its dual purposes were to provide an economic opportunity for reintegration of ex-combatants and to address the issue of land reform. Former combatants, as well as those who occupied land during the war, could purchase land with the help of government loans. This program left some key details undefined, including the size of the plots of land to be transferred, the number of beneficiaries, and the amount of government loans to be granted.[38]

The land-transfer process was slowed by what appears to have been a lack of government commitment and the FMLN's difficulties in establishing a list of beneficiaries. The United Nations had to intervene early on in the process when tensions mounted between the government and peasant organizations. It sent its Under-Secretary-General for Peace Operations, Marrack Goulding, to engage in discussions with all parties and rescheduled the implementation of the agreement. The process threatened to break down again in mid-1992: The FMLN stopped demobilizing on the grounds that the land-transfer program was not moving. The United Nations stepped in, eventually clearing up important points of contention, such as the number of beneficiaries and the amount of land each could claim.[39]

---

[36] Ana Arana, "How the Street Gangs Took Central America," *Foreign Affairs*, Vol. 83, No. 3, May–June 2005, p. 135.

[37] Call, 2002, p. 395.

[38] Timothy A. Wilkins, "The El Salvador Peace Accords: Using International and Domestic Law Norms to Build Peace," in Michael W. Doyle, Ian Johnstone, and Robert C. Orr, eds., *Keeping the Peace: Multidimensional UN Operations in Cambodia and El Salvador*, New York: Cambridge University Press, 1997, pp. 255–281, p. 275.

[39] Wood, 2000, pp. 92–100.

The implementation of the land-for-arms program was made more difficult by different donor policies. The World Bank initially refused to support the program on the grounds that it violated its "equity principle," according to which every Salvadoran, not just former combatants, should benefit from a land-redistribution program.[40] The UN position was that some parts of the population had special needs following the conflict and that failure to address the demands of ex-combatants could endanger the peace if these were not addressed. A UN official, reflecting on the episode, concluded,

> That early grim experience ultimately convinced the IMF [International Monetary Fund], the World Bank, and others to start working more closely together in matters of human security in subsequent operations in Angola, Guatemala, and the Balkans. The Bretton Woods institutions finally came to accept that economic reconstruction is not "development as usual" and became more sensitive to the specific needs and idiosyncrasies of countries affected by conflict.[41]

Economic

The costs of implementing the Chapultepec accord were largely overlooked during the peace process, probably so as not to create additional obstacles to the negotiation.[42] The overall National Reconstruction Plan, which included, among other measures, the reconstruction of infrastructure, reintegration of combatants, the land-transfer program, creation of a civilian police, and institutional reform, ended up costing an estimated $2 billion, at a time when the country was not only recovering from the damage that war inflicted on its economy but was also

---

[40] Graciana del Castillo, "The Political Economy of Peace," *Project Syndicate*, January 12, 2012.

[41] Del Castillo, 2012.

[42] Wilkins, 1997, p. 274. Wood (2000, p. 95) notes,

> According to [a] senior UN official [close to the peace negotiations], no attempt had been made during the negotiations to estimate the agreement's financial implications, a process that would probably have impeded the parties from reaching an agreement by the end of 1991.

facing falling world market prices for coffee, El Salvador's most important export.[43] El Salvador also struggled to meet its obligations under a structural adjustment program, which imposed some important limitations on public spending. These challenges led de Soto and Senior UN Economic Officer Graciana del Castillo to argue in 1994 that the United Nations–supported peace-program and the IMF and World Bank structural adjustment programs were "on a collision course."[44]

External assistance proved critical for paying for peacebuilding programs. Foreign assistance reached $400 million per year, with the United States and the Inter-American Development Bank (IDB) the largest bilateral and multilateral donors, respectively.[45]

The peace process did little to address El Salvador's economic issues beyond the land-for-arms program. Government economic policy was not part of the peace negotiations.[46] Most economic issues were to be discussed by all interested parties—government, business, unions—in a Socio-Economic Forum, but labor protests in 1993 led to the suspension of the forum, which was never reactivated.[47]

Political

The FMLN was allowed to register as a political party in December 1992, after certification by the United Nations that it had completely disarmed. Six months later, however, an arms cache exploded in neighboring Nicaragua, revealing that the FMLN still held weapons. The FMLN subsequently listed additional arms caches to prove its commitment to the peace accord and to regain some of the credibility lost in

---

[43] Del Castillo, 2001, p. 1975; de Soto and del Castillo, 1994, p. 70–71; Wood, 2000, p. 95.

[44] De Soto and del Castillo, 1994, p. 70.

[45] James K. Boyce, "External Assistance and the Peace Process in El Salvador," *World Development*, Vol. 23, No. 12, December 1995, pp. 2101–2116, pp. 2101–2102.

[46] Jenny Pearce, "Peace-Building in the Periphery: Lessons from Central America," *Third World Quarterly*, Vol. 20, No. 1, February 1999, pp. 51–68, p. 57.

[47] Stanley, 2006, p. 109; Ricardo Córdova Macías, "Demilitarizing and Democratizing Salvadoran Politics," in Margarita S. Studemeister, ed., *El Salvador: Implementation of the Peace Accords*, Washington, D.C.: U.S. Institute of Peace, Peaceworks 38, January 2001, pp. 27–32, p. 31.

this episode.[48] It participated as a political party in the presidential, legislative, and municipal elections of 1994, coming in second in the presidential and legislative elections and winning only 15 out of 251 municipalities. Former President Cristiani's political party, ARENA, was the winner of all three elections. Importantly, these elections took place without violence, and, in subsequent elections, alternation in power between ARENA and FMLN has proven peaceful.[49]

El Salvador also underwent electoral reform, with a new electoral code enacted in 1993 and the creation of a Supreme Electoral Court (Tribunal Supremo Electoral, or TSE). Substantial irregularities were still reported in the first round of the 1994 presidential elections: Some voters found that their names were not on the lists, leading the United Nations and newly elected President Armando Calderón Sol (ARENA) to push for further electoral reforms.[50] In December 1995, the National Assembly adopted a National Voter Registry. The United Nations was, however, less successful at improving the functioning of the TSE, which it publicly declared in 1995 to be unsatisfactory. Political practices were slower to change than electoral rules; Salvadoran political life remained marred by corruption and patronage in the postconflict period. This resulted in low involvement of the population in elections, with voter participation rates around 50 percent in the late 1990s.[51]

Institutional

Reforming El Salvador's military was a core element of the country's nation-building process. The FAES had been in charge of both external and internal security through the tight control it exercised over the National Guard, the police, paramilitary forces, and intelligence forces.[52] Challenging the control of the military over the security forces was no small endeavor; the government was adamant that the military

---

[48] Wood, 2000, p. 96–97; Córdova Macías, 2001, p. 29.

[49] Montgomery, 1995, p. 265; Stanley, 2006, p. 111; del Castillo, 2012.

[50] Montgomery, 1995, pp. 263–265.

[51] Call, 2003, p. 861; Córdova Macías, 2001, p. 30.

[52] Dobbins, Jones, Crane, Rathmell, et al., 2005, p. 47.

should keep some degree of strength to remain a national symbol and an expression of sovereignty.[53] It was agreed in the Chapultepec accord that the military would be reduced in size, its mission redefined, and its ranks purged—key measures that took place under the leadership of the U.S. military group (MILGROUP) in El Salvador. The military would also be placed under the control of civilian authorities, thereby putting an end to 60 years of military dominance of the political system.

The size of the armed forces was halved between January 1992 and February 1993 to 31,000.[54] The mandate of the armed forces was constitutionally limited to responding to external threats. The Ad Hoc Commission on Purification of the Armed Forces and the Commission on the Truth for El Salvador were set up to identify those members of the armed forces who had committed gross human rights abuses during the war. The ad hoc commission vetted all military officers based on their past records with regard to human rights and respect for the law, their competence, and their prospects for integrating well in postconflict El Salvador. Its conclusions could lead to the transfer or discharge of officers but not to their judicial prosecution.[55] The ad hoc commission eventually named 102 officers, including some high-ranking officials, who—after some reluctance—left the military.[56] This result was achieved thanks to the pressure exerted by international donors, with the United States making a contribution of $11 million in aid contingent upon the Salvadoran government supporting the implementation of the commission's conclusions.[57]

The truth commission established that about 85 percent of wartime human rights violations had been committed by government forces, 10 percent by paramilitaries and death squads, and 5 percent by

---

[53] Wilkins, 1997, p. 262.

[54] Córdova Macías, 2001, p. 27.

[55] Wilkins, 1997, p. 264.

[56] Stanley, 2006, p. 110.

[57] Call, 2003, p. 836.

the FMLN.[58] In March 1993, it published a list of individuals whom it determined had committed grave human rights violations.[59] That same month, the National Assembly approved an amnesty law for wartime crimes, which resulted in none of the individuals identified being prosecuted and none of the victims receiving any compensation.[60]

Directly linked to the limitation of the military's mandate to external security was the creation of the PNC. The former police force was dissolved along with the National Guard and Treasury Police. Out of the PNC's target number of 5,900 agents and officers, 60 percent were to be civilians who had not been involved on either side of the fighting in the civil war; 20 percent of the force was to come from the former police force; and 20 percent was to be former FMLN.[61] The United Nations played an important role in monitoring the PNC at its beginnings. ONUSAL's CIVPOL mission oversaw the transition, playing a law enforcement role when security gaps arose and training the new force. Technical experts from El Salvador, Spain, and the United States contributed to setting up the National Public Security Academy that would train PNC members. The U.S. Justice Department's International Criminal Investigative Training Assistance Program (ICITAP) sent instructors, while ONUSAL oversaw admission to the academy and coordinated bilateral assistance.[62]

---

[58] Joaquín M. Chávez, "Perspectives on Demobilisation, Reintegration and Weapons Control in the El Salvador Peace Process," in Cate Buchanan, ed., *Reflections on Guns, Fighters and Armed Violence in Peace Processes*, Geneva: HD Centre for Humanitarian Dialogue, 2008, pp. 13–18, pp. 16–17.

[59] For a critique of the truth commission process, see Call, 2003, p. 852.

[60] Ian Johnstone, "Rights and Reconciliation in El Salvador," in Michael W. Doyle, Ian Johnstone, and Robert C. Orr, eds., *Keeping the Peace: Multidimensional UN Operations in Cambodia and El Salvador*, New York: Cambridge University Press, 1997, pp. 312–341, p. 326; Call, 2003, p. 851.

[61] Stanley, 2006, p. 111. When the FMLN proved unable to bring enough recruits to fill in its quota, the share of civilians increased.

[62] William Deane Stanley, "Building New Police Forces in El Salvador and Guatemala: Learning and Counter-Learning," *International Peacekeeping*, Vol. 6, No. 4, 1999, pp. 113–134, pp. 113–114; David H. McCormick, "From Peacekeeping to Peacebuilding: Restructuring Military and Police Institutions in El Salvador," in Michael W. Doyle, Ian Johnstone,

Financial difficulties arose early on because international donors felt that the government was not committed to the process and accordingly had little motivation to fund a reform they suspected was doomed to failure.[63] The government, for instance, failed to provide funding for basic equipment for the PNC.[64] Here again, Goulding's intervention and the provision of more flexibility to the initial implementation schedule helped keep the reform of the police on track and rebuild confidence with donors.[65] Another difficulty arose in June 1993, when Oscar Peña, who formerly led the narcotics unit of the old police force, was nominated deputy director of the PNC, a nomination perceived as a possible first step back toward the methods of the previous era. The United States suspended its provision of vehicles and equipment until Peña resigned, a process that took almost a year.[66]

The justice system was also the focus of important reforms. Postconflict measures included increasing independence of judges, ensuring that the justice system would receive regular and substantial funding from the state, and reforming the National Council on the Judiciary.[67] The United States provided $15 million over a five-year period, with a special focus on training judges.[68] Several legal texts were adopted, including a new criminal procedure code and a new penal code, and a National Counsel for the Defense of Human Rights was created. The supreme court was reformed so as to make it less politicized—an objective that was only partly reached.[69]

This set of reforms, too, experienced financial difficulties. The courts received the lion's share of government funds devoted to justice

---

and Robert C. Orr, eds., *Keeping the Peace: Multidimensional UN Operations in Cambodia and El Salvador*, New York: Cambridge University Press, 1997, pp. 282–311, pp. 298–299.

[63] Wood, 2000, pp. 95–96.

[64] Boyce, 1995, p. 2107; Stanley, 1999, pp. 116–117.

[65] Wood, 2000, p. 93.

[66] Boyce, 1995, p. 2112.

[67] Wilkins, 1997, p. 270–271.

[68] Pearce, 1999, p. 59.

[69] Call, 2003, p. 853.

system reform, while the public ministry, attorney general's office, and other institutions were underresourced, resulting in underqualified and undertrained staff at the precise moment when prosecutors were supposed to take over investigations and procedures previously under the responsibility of police and judges.[70] International donors stepped in again, with the United Nations Development Programme (UNDP) and other donors becoming involved in training prosecutors.

Outcomes

The nation-building process in El Salvador can be considered a success on many counts. The country has not reverted to war; it has remained democratic; and it has enjoyed solid economic growth as its economy has been restructured. Some serious issues remain, however. The reintegration program has not proven effective, and El Salvador is battling high crime rates that caused more violent deaths in the 1990s than occurred during the war.[71] The inability of successive governments to curb crime has led some parts of the Salvadoran population to question the efficiency of the postwar institutions.

Local Attitudes

Postconflict institutional changes were generally well received by the population. In 1995, 49 percent of respondents ranked the conduct of the PNC higher than the former national police; 18 percent ranked it lower. The fact that these institutions experienced progress does not mean, however, that they are considered satisfactory. As of 2010, only 31 percent of respondents had "a lot" or "some" confidence in the police, while 21 percent had no confidence at all.[72] The most-trusted institu-

---

[70] Call, 2003, p. 855.

[71] Mo Hume, "El Salvador: The Limits of a Violent Peace," in Michael C. Pugh, Neil Cooper, and Mandy Turner, eds., *Whose Peace? Critical Perspectives on the Political Economy of Peacebuilding*, Basingstoke, UK: Palgrave Macmillan, 2008, pp. 318–336, p. 319.

[72] Forty-eight percent of respondents had "little confidence" in the police (Latinobarómetro, "Análisis de resultados en línea," data set from various years, accessed February 2012).

tions as of December 2010 were the military and the Catholic Church, ahead of local politicians and the media.[73] This shows very little change from a 1998 poll, according to which the army and church were the institutions that "best defend human rights," with the supreme court ranking at the bottom.[74]

Rising crime rates in the 1990s and 2000s largely account for this disaffection toward the judiciary and, to a lesser extent, the police. A 1998 survey shows that "weak laws" were largely considered responsible for the crime wave. Alongside increasing incidence of crime came calls for a more authoritarian political leader, in the hope that he or she would be tougher on crime.[75] Support for democracy reached a peak in 1998, with more than 80 percent of respondents judging that "Democracy is preferable to any other kind of government," but this figure fell to 35 percent in 2001. This percentage has since fluctuated widely; it had rebounded to 64 percent as of 2010. Between 2005 and 2008, the percentage of respondents agreeing with the statement "Under some circumstances, an authoritarian government can be preferable to a democratic one" increased from 5 to 29 percent and was at 21 percent as of 2010.[76]

Geographical and Geopolitical

With the end of the Cold War, the ideological and geopolitical tensions that had polarized Central America largely evaporated, allowing politically motivated violence to be brought to a rapid and enduring halt, only to be replaced by a region-wide violent-crime wave. From the Andes to the southern border of the United States, the narcotics trade has fueled virulent organized crime and gang-related violence that El Salvador, emerging from its own civil war, has been particularly poorly equipped to combat. Other countries in the region recovering from years of civil war, such as Guatemala and Nicaragua, have shared

---

[73] "El Salvador (El Salvador), World Armies," *Jane's World Armies*, May 16, 2011.

[74] Call, 2003, p. 858.

[75] Call, 2003, pp. 856–859.

[76] Latinobarómetro, 2012.

a similar experience of weapon availability, incomplete reintegration of former combatants, and difficult economic recovery. Cross-border criminality has been and remains a key issue for the region, with a 2012 UN Office on Drugs and Crime report on transnational crime suggesting that "Central America . . . has never really recovered from the civil wars that ended in the 1990s."[77]

Cultural and Social

Land reform was a key change in the Salvadoran social landscape and was completed by the end of 1997. A 1999 estimate gives the number of properties redistributed at 3,305, to a total of 36,100 former combatants and civilians. New owners have had to face many challenges. Increases in property prices due to heightened demand, agricultural crises, lack of technical assistance, and lack of credit have eroded the ability of these new landowners to make a living in spite of the considerable financial assistance provided by international donors.[78] Additionally, hundreds of thousands of Salvadorans have not been able to acquire any land.[79]

The land-reform program has not fulfilled its expected reintegration role for former combatants. The program was based on the assumption that, because almost all former combatants were of rural origin, they would want to work in the agricultural sector and had the skills to do so. In many instances, these assumptions proved unfounded. Perhaps a more varied choice of government- or donor-funded opportunities should have been offered to former combatants, rather than limiting them mostly to the agricultural sector.[80]

Overall, reintegration proved unsuccessful, with former combatants having a difficult time finding economic opportunities. Only about one-quarter of the 42,000 estimated former combatants bene-

---

[77] UN Office on Drugs and Crime, *Transnational Organized Crime in Central America and the Caribbean: A Threat Assessment*, Vienna, 2012, p. 15.

[78] Chávez, 2008, pp. 15–16.

[79] Mitchell A. Seligson, "Thirty Years of Transformation in the Agrarian Sector of El Salvador, 1961–1991," *Latin American Research Review*, Vol. 30, No. 3, 1995, pp. 43–74, p. 71.

[80] Del Castillo, 1997, p. 359.

fited from the reintegration program.[81] Combined with the availability of weapons, this contributed to El Salvador experiencing a 300-percent increase in violent crime in the first nine months of 1993.[82] Beyond the lack of reintegration opportunities for former combatants, other key explanatory factors include the role that the 12 years of war have played in creating a "culture of violence"; the reform of the police system, which replaced experienced police officers (who had networks of informers) with brand-new recruits; the "security gap" created by the transition from the old police force to the new one; the large availability of weapons after the war; and the "recycling" of right-wing death squads into criminal groups.[83] In some instances, the population has taken law enforcement into its own hands and created antigang militias. One of them, Mano Blanco, bears the same name as a death squad from the civil war era that killed thousands.[84]

Economic

Since the end of the war, El Salvador's economic performance has markedly improved. Heightened confidence in the country's budget management led to an influx of capital and an ability to renegotiate external debt.[85] The poverty rate decreased from 66 percent before the peace accord to 38 percent in 2012. El Salvador was less dependent on aid than some other postconflict countries: In 1992, aid as a percentage of national income reached 7 percent and fell rapidly afterward—compared with, for instance, 80 percent for Mozambique, which reached a peace accord around the same time.[86]

---

[81] Chávez, 2008, p. 15; Call, 2002, p. 395.

[82] According to ONUSAL's statistics (Call, 2003, p. 839).

[83] Juan Luis Londoño de la Cuesta and Rodrigo Guerrero, *Violencia en América Latina: Epidemiología y costos*, Washington, D.C.: Banco Interamericano de Desarrollo, Oficina del Economista Jefe, August 1999, p. 27; Call, 2003, p. 843; Hume, 2008, p. 324; Stanley, 1999, p. 119.

[84] Hume, 2008, p. 329.

[85] Del Castillo, 2001, p. 1976.

[86] Del Castillo, 2012.

The liberalization of the economy, which included the privatization of some state services, such as the pension system, telecommunications, and water services, as well as the replacement in 2001 of the *colón* with the U.S. dollar, have met with criticism.[87] Agricultural and manufacturing sectors suffered most from the changes while the financial sector, transportation, construction, and commerce sectors largely benefited. The considerable amount of remittances from Salvadorans abroad has, in part, cushioned the population from the shock of structural adjustment.[88]

Political
Electoral participation increased markedly during the 2004 presidential election.[89] Although corruption and patronage have not been eradicated, political parties and civil society organizations have reached some degree of institutionalization that contrasts with the personalism that existed previously.[90]

Institutional
El Salvador's institutional capacity compares favorably with that of other postconflict countries. In 2006, out of 35 postconflict countries and areas analyzed by the United Nations, El Salvador had the highest score for "government efficiency," "regulatory quality," and "voice and accountability."[91] As for political stability and lack of political violence,

---

[87] Hume, 2008, p. 321.

[88] Pearce, 1999, p. 57; Stanley, 2006, p. 112.

[89] Stanley, 2006, p. 111.

[90] Call, 2003, p. 861.

[91] UN Department of Economic and Social Affairs and UNDP, *The Challenges of Restoring Governance in Crisis and Post-Conflict Countries*, Seventh Global Forum on Reinventing Government: Building Trust in Government, Vienna, ST/ESA/PAD/SER.E/101, June 26–29, 2007, pp. 12–13. The "voice and accountability criteria" broadly cover freedom of expression and association, as well as free media.

El Salvador ranked third;[92] it also came third for rule of law[93] and fourth for "control of corruption." It is worth noting, however, that its institutional capacity remains largely below that of OECD countries, scoring, for instance, 45.9 for "government efficiency" when the OECD average is 88.[94]

The military has been reduced in size, but conflicting assessments prevail with regard to the political role it still plays: While some see the military fading "into political irrelevance,"[95] others warn that it is gaining in importance, especially as it is being called on by the government to assist in fighting gangs. In the context of El Salvador's Mano Dura (Iron Fist) antigang policy, the military has provided specialized antigang units, the Grupos Territoriales Antipandilleros—a major first break with the constitutional prohibition for the military to engage in internal policing. This policy, however, has enjoyed wide public support from a population exasperated by high levels of violence and has been expanded in 2009 and 2010.[96]

Certain key elements of police reform are generally seen as a success.[97] Although issues of corruption and abuse have not been entirely solved, they are not nearly as widespread as they were with the previ-

---

[92] This ranking does not include levels of criminal (as opposed to political) violence.

[93] *Rule of law* is defined as the

> perceptions of the extent to which agents have confidence in and abide by the rules of society, and in particular the quality of contract enforcement, property rights, the police, and the courts, as well as the likelihood of crime and violence. (Aart Kraay, Daniel Kaufmann, and Massimo Mastruzzi, *The Worldwide Governance Indicators: Methodology and Analytical Issues*, Washington, D.C.: World Bank, 2010, p. 4)

[94] UN Department of Economic and Social Affairs and UNDP, 2007, pp. 11–13.

[95] Stanley, 2006, p. 110.

[96] Hume, 2008, p. 327; "El Salvador (El Salvador), World Armies," 2011. On the results achieved by the Mano Dura policy, see, for instance, Dennis Rodgers, Robert Muggah, and Chris Stevenson, *Gangs of Central America: Causes, Costs, and Interventions*, Geneva: Small Arms Survey, Graduate Institute of International and Development Studies, Occasional Paper 23, May 2009, p. 14; and Arana, 2005, p. 103.

[97] Call, 2003, p. 847. This author notes that, "Of six experts and former US and UN officials asked in personal interviews in Jan.–Feb. 2002 to name the most successful police reforms of the past decade, El Salvador was the only country to be named by all six."

ous police force. Some officers accused of these crimes have been prosecuted, and a purge in the late 1990s led to the dismissal of 2,700 PNC officers and administrative personnel.[98] The force is also much better trained and educated than its predecessor.[99] Other elements have proven less successful. The main complaint with regard to the PNC has been its inefficiency in combating crime, resulting in a marked difference in how the PNC is judged by external observers (relatively positively) and by the Salvadoran population (often negatively).[100]

The judicial system has experienced progress in terms of case-management efficiency, conviction rates, modernization, and citizen access to justice, but progress has been slow. Ten years after the peace accords, judges were rarely replaced when issues of professional ethics arose, and the justice system was still prone to corruption, as well as politicization.[101]

Conclusions

What Local Factors Posed the Greatest Challenges?

The local factors within each category that were most important in shaping the environment in which nation-builders sought to promote an enduring peace included the following.

Geographical and Geopolitical

A key factor that gave rise to and perpetuated the conflict in El Salvador was superpower support for opposing sides in the conflict, in the context of broader superpower contestation in Central America generally. The prospect of their backers withdrawing that support in the post–Cold War geopolitical environment motivated both sides to sue for peace. As a result, the conflict was brought to an enduring end.

---

[98] Call, 2003, p. 844; Stanley, 2006, p. 111.

[99] Stanley, 1999, p. 118.

[100] Hume, 2008, p. 326; Call, 2003, p. 830.

[101] Call (2003, pp. 853–860) notes that "The justice reforms *pluralized* the courts more than *depoliticising* them."

Cultural and Social

Struggles over land tenure in this small, underdeveloped, and densely populated country and extreme and increasing concentration of land-ownership figured significantly in causing the conflict. Land reform after the conflict was focused on providing reintegration opportunities for ex-combatants. The reform program was completed five years after the conflict, but it benefited only a small slice of the rural population. And, more broadly, reintegration efforts had limited effect. Although the persistence of these factors—inequitable landownership and lack of economic opportunity—did not cause a renewal of the conflict, together with the wide availability of weapons after the war, it did lead to a transfer of the dynamics of violence to the criminal sphere.

Economic

The civil war slowed economic growth to a crawl and created a huge need for reconstruction. External assistance financed implementation of the peace agreement but did little to address El Salvador's underlying economic problems. Nevertheless, since the end of the civil war 20 years ago, the country's economic performance has markedly improved, and poverty has been reduced.

Political

El Salvador had a long history of authoritarianism before and during the conflict. Afterward, the United Nations organized elections in which political parties representing both warring sides participated. Political practices changed slowly, and corruption and patronage remained widespread. But United Nations–supported electoral reforms gradually improved the functioning of some democratic mechanisms, and, over time, political parties and civil society organizations became institutionalized.

Institutional

The Salvadoran military and police had a history of incompetence, abusiveness, and involvement in politics inconsistent with democratic norms. Professionalization and depoliticization of the military and building of a new national police force were thus key elements of the nation-building effort. Despite difficulties in implementation, marked improvements were achieved in these areas over time, and, overall, El Salvador's government efficiency rates much better than that of many postconflict countries.

Were Local Factors Modified or Circumvented to Promote Enduring Peace?

Ten years after the end of its civil war, El Salvador remained at peace, its democracy had been consolidated, the efficiency of its government had increased only slightly, and it had made some socioeconomic gains. Table 4.1 shows these outcomes, alongside key resources applied by nation-building interveners.

Table 4.1
Postintervention Performance and Nation-Building Inputs in El Salvador

Performance Indicator	Year of Intervention (1992)	5 Years Later	10 Years Later
At peace?	—	Yes	Yes
Government effectiveness (10-point scale)	4.28	4.58	4.64
Freedom Index (10-point scale)	7.00	7.75	7.75
HDI (10-point scale)	5.80	6.20	6.50
Cumulative growth in per capita GDP (in 1st 5 years and in 10 years after intervention) (%)	—	8.6	20.6
Nation-Building Input			
Peak military presence per capita, number of troops per 1,000 inhabitants	0.1		
Peak international civilian police presence per capita, number of police per 1,000 inhabitants	0.06		
Average annual per capita assistance in the first 5 years (constant 2010 US$)	79.57		

SOURCES: World Bank, undated (d); Freedom House, various years; UNDP, undated; IMF, undated; Dobbins, Jones, Crane, Chivvis, et al., 2008, Figures 9.2, 9.4, 9.9; UN Peace Operations, various years; World Bank, undated (c).

Although external influences may not have sparked El Salvador's civil war, they certainly helped sustain it for more than a decade and then were decisive in ending it. External actors funded and advised both sides in the civil war, external mediation brought it to a close, and external pressures forced some changes in the internal factors that gave rise to the conflict. That mediation helped bring about a mutual accommodation among the contending armed factions, resulting in arrangements that have allowed them to peacefully share and alternate the exercise of power.

The factors that perpetuated the conflict were thus resolved definitively once the geopolitical environment changed, while the deeper causes of the conflict, such as peasant landlessness, were modified more slowly and to a more limited extent. Important improvements contributing to securing peace were achieved, such as externally promoted and supported military and police reforms, even though those reform processes were not fast or free from difficulties.

As a result, El Salvador is better governed and more prosperous than at any time in its history. Unfortunately, it is also more violent. In part, this is a product of the war and its aftermath. The civil conflict bred a culture of violence, the peace left many armed young men with little livelihood free from crime, and the reforms left a weakened security establishment.

CHAPTER FIVE

Bosnia and Herzegovina

Prior to its 1991 declaration of independence, Bosnia had been a reasonably harmonious multiethnic republic in the midst of a rather less harmonious multiethnic state (see Figure 5.1). Its leaders had no particular desire to secede from Yugoslavia, but, once Slovenia and Croatia

Figure 5.1
Map of Bosnia and Herzegovina

SOURCE: CIA, "Bosnia and Herzegovina," *The World Factbook*, 2012a.
RAND *RR167-5.1*

proclaimed their independence in June 1991,[1] Bosnia faced a choice between remaining within a Yugoslav state dominated by Serbia or following the other two republics out. When Bosnia chose the latter course, its Serb population, encouraged by the government in Belgrade, revolted.

From 1992 to 1995, the Bosnian Serb army, supported by Serbia, captured majority Serb–populated Bosnian territory and purged from it many Bosnian Muslims and Croats. Its strategy was aimed at creating a contiguous Bosnian Serb state bordering on Serbia with an ethnically homogenous Serb population. Bosnian Croat and Muslim[2] armies and militias fought an initially losing and ultimately stalemated battle against the Serb advance.[3]

After three years of unsuccessful diplomacy and an ineffectual UN peacekeeping mission, the United States and its allies, backed by limited North Atlantic Treaty Organization (NATO) airstrikes and the threat of further NATO action, forced the belligerents to the negotiating table. The result was the General Framework Agreement for Peace in Bosnia and Herzegovina, commonly known as the Dayton Peace Accords, signed in December 1995, which left the belligerent leaderships in power but ended the violence by effecting a compromise: Bosnian territorial integrity but with a very high degree of autonomy for the country's warring ethnic groups. The Dayton Accords ratified the concept of three distinct "peoples" and created two political and territorial so-called "entities" within the Bosnian state, the Muslim-

---

[1] Slovenia's decision to secede led to a very brief conflict between Slovenian forces and the Yugoslav National Army, but, otherwise, Slovenian secession was peaceful. In Croatia, however, the declaration of independence led to a four-year war between Croat forces and the substantial Serb minority there.

[2] Bosnian Muslims are often referred to as "Bosniaks."

[3] Sabrina P. Ramet, *Thinking About Yugoslavia: Scholarly Debates About the Yugoslav Breakup and the Wars in Bosnia and Kosovo*, Cambridge, UK: Cambridge University Press, 2005; Norman Cigar, *Genocide in Bosnia: The Politics of "Ethnic Cleansing,"* College Station, Texas: Texas A&M University Press, 2000; Renéo Lukic and Allen Lynch, *Europe from the Balkans to the Urals: The Disintegration of Yugoslavia and the Soviet Union*, Oxford, UK: Oxford University Press, 1996; Laura Silber and Allan Little, *Yugoslavia: Death of a Nation*, New York: TV Books, 1996.

and Croat-dominated Federation of Bosnia and Herzegovina, which was itself subdivided into cantons (most of which are dominated by either Muslims or Croats), and the Serb-dominated Republika Srpska.

A major effort to stabilize, democratize, and reconstruct Bosnia ensued. The United States and its European allies proved highly successful at altering the geopolitical environment that had sparked and sustained the war, but they had less success in overcoming the internal ethnic divisions and antagonisms that provided fuel for the war and that the war greatly intensified.

Local Factors Before the Peace

During the Cold War, the Republic of Bosnia and Herzegovina had been one of six republics that made up the federal state of Yugoslavia.[4] The 1992–1995 war in Bosnia was the direct consequence of the political collapse of Yugoslavia and the irredentist ambitions of the leaderships in Serbia and Croatia. Contributing causes included increasing ethnic polarization in the period leading up to the outbreak of violence, and fears of political domination by other ethnic groups as the post–World War II era's enforced ethnic balancing of political power disintegrated. Growing economic problems beginning in the 1980s contributed as well—in particular, by creating incentives for the better-off republics, Slovenia and Croatia, to shed the financial burden of being in the same state with the poorer areas of Yugoslavia. Although not causes of the war, the institutional and physical legacies of the uniquely Yugoslav socialist economic system greatly complicated postwar reconstruction.

Bosnia had no modern history as an independent, sovereign state, and the war was fought over the very question of whether or not it should exist as such. It emerged from the war with three mutually antagonistic, ethnically defined de facto administrations: parallel Bosnian Muslim and Croat administrative structures within the Federa-

---

[4] These were Bosnia-Herzegovina, Croatia, Macedonia, Montenegro, Serbia, and Slovenia. There were also two autonomous regions within Serbia—Kosovo and Vojvodina—that had representation at the federal level. The state's official name was the Socialist Federal Republic of Yugoslavia.

tion of Bosnia and Herzegovina, and a Bosnian Serb structure within Republika Srpska. Overlaying these three administrations was a weak central government established under the terms of the Dayton agreement, in which positions and political power were apportioned on an ethnic basis.

Geographical and Geopolitical

The newly independent Bosnia was an effectively landlocked state,[5] with hilly and heavily wooded terrain that had facilitated smuggling and irregular warfare during the conflict. Bosnia was bordered by two neighbors more powerful than itself, Serbia and Croatia,[6] both hostile to its existence during the conflict and, at best, grudgingly accepting of it at the time of the peace. During the conflict, what remained of Yugoslavia, under Serb domination, was unwilling to see the Bosnian Serbs submerged in a Muslim-dominated state; the leadership of the new state of Croatia felt similarly regarding the Bosnian Croat minority. Serbia and Croatia were also at odds with each other up until the time the Dayton Accords were signed because Belgrade had supported the efforts of the Serb minority in Croatia to carve out areas of Croatia populated principally by Serbs.

The Dayton Accords divided Bosnia by validating the creation of the two entities. Although essential to securing a negotiated peace, this arrangement had important consequences for the efforts of foreign nation-builders to create an effective government for the whole of Bosnia. It also complicated efforts to ameliorate the social divisions that the war had exacerbated.

---

[5] Bosnia technically has access to the Adriatic Sea at the small town of Neum, which does not have a port suitable for shipping. Bosnia has an important river port in the North, at Brčko.

[6] Montenegro also borders Bosnia to the east.

Cultural and Social

The view that the Bosnian conflict was the consequence of "ancient" ethnic hatreds has been widely criticized.[7] Bosnia's ethnic groups had a long history of peaceful coexistence, and many Bosnians were proud that their society was relatively cosmopolitan. Under Yugoslav leader Marshal Josip Broz Tito, ethnic nationalism had been suppressed, and all three of Bosnia's ethnic groups spoke mutually understandable versions of Serbo-Croatian. Both the Latin and Cyrillic alphabets were widely used. Nevertheless, the conflict was initiated and conducted along ethnic lines.

Beginning in the late 1980s, political-economic factors within Yugoslavia generated tensions among ethnic groups—largely as a result of financial transfers from one republic to another. Elites in Serbia and Croatia, for example, were resentful of transfers to less prosperous Bosnia, as well as even poorer areas of Yugoslavia. Slovenia and Croatia, the most developed of the Yugoslav republics, resented the degree to which Serbia, the largest and most powerful of the republics, was able increasingly to gain control of important state assets once Tito died. The interspersion of the various ethnic groups in Bosnia, Croatia, and Serbia made a peaceful dissolution of the Yugoslav state highly problematic.[8] In Bosnia, no ethnic group was a majority; Muslims were the largest group, and Croats the smallest.

The war, which caused at least 100,000 deaths, greatly intensified existing ethnic divisions. Atrocities committed on all sides resulted in a postwar environment in which ethnic hatreds were very strong. The peace settlement forced Bosnian citizens to choose an ethnic identity if they were to vote or otherwise participate in public life. Many individuals and families fled their homes as a result of ethnic cleansing or to escape violence during the war. This further intensified ethnic polarization and created a huge resettlement challenge after the conflict. By the

---

[7] For example, Susan Woodward, "Bosnia and Herzegovina: How Not to End Civil War," in Barbara F. Walter and Jack Snyder, eds., *Civil Wars, Insecurity, and Intervention*, New York: Columbia University Press, 1999, pp. 73–115.

[8] Noel Malcolm, *Bosnia: A Short History*, New York: New York University Press, 1994, pp. 203–209.

war's end, the Bosnian Serb population was almost entirely separated physically and socially from the Bosnian Muslim and Croat populations.[9] A fragmented educational system also resulted, with each ethnic group using different textbooks and curricula. These course materials perpetuated ethnic intolerance, conflicting views of the war, and divergent versions of Bosnian history. Media outlets were "ethnicized" as a result of the war and would serve as mouthpieces for nationalists seeking to reinforce ethnic insecurities. And differences among the forms of Serbo-Croatian spoken and written by the three groups were purposefully magnified to create three purportedly distinct languages.

Economic

Bosnia's prewar level of economic development was low by European standards but higher than that of most other countries that have recently experienced civil wars. It industrialized after World War II and, by 1990, was in the world's middle-income category. Bosnia also had a good system of higher education, and, by the 1980s, most young people were literate. Ten percent of high school graduates were enrolled full time in universities.[10]

Although industrialized, Bosnia's economy was based on markets not integrated into the global economy. The main industries were metallurgy, mining, and basic manufactures,[11] with some weapon production.[12] Almost all of Bosnia's socially owned enterprises were saddled with debts. Socialist methods of allocating resources had resulted in major inefficiencies, including, for example, the largest aluminum plant

---

[9] UNHCR, *The State of the World's Refugees 2000: Fifty Years of Humanitarian Action*, Geneva, January 1, 2000, pp. 230–232.

[10] John R. Lampe, *Yugoslavia as History: Twice There Was a Country*, Cambridge, UK: Cambridge University Press, 1996, p. 340.

[11] Neven Andjelic, *Bosnia-Herzegovina: The End of a Legacy*, London: Frank Cass, 2003, p. 31.

[12] World Bank, European Commission, and European Bank for Reconstruction and Development (EBRD), *Bosnia and Herzegovina: Toward Economic Recovery*, Washington, D.C.: World Bank, 1996.

in Europe, which had to import its bauxite from Africa.[13] Other factories in Bosnia included arms manufacturers, the locations of which had been selected based on military rather than economic criteria and which, in any case, provided a less-than-ideal postconflict industrial base.[14] Significant administrative and institutional barriers to private investment remained, and Bosnia had no commercial banking sector.[15]

The war largely destroyed the economy but not the attitudes that went with the prewar economic system. Industrial production ground to a near halt.[16] Unemployment immediately after the war topped 70 percent.[17] The World Bank estimated that the war had destroyed roughly half of the country's capital stock, some $15 billion to $20 billion in damage. There was also significant loss of manpower due to death and displacement, and many college-educated people had fled the country.[18]

The war also expanded and entrenched criminal networks. The arms embargo imposed by the international community had encouraged the expansion of the traditional black markets by leaving all three sides no alternative for obtaining military supplies except through cross-border smuggling channels.[19] In addition, smuggling and other criminal activities were often the source of war financing; looting, theft, kidnapping for ransom, and trafficking in drugs and people all helped sustain wartime paramilitary organizations. At the start of the war, given its sharp military disadvantage, the government in Sarajevo

---

[13] Malcolm, 1994, p. 210.

[14] Susan Woodward, *Balkan Tragedy: Chaos and Dissolution After the Cold War*, Washington, D.C.: Brookings Institution, 1995.

[15] DFID, *Bosnia and Herzegovina*, London, Country Strategy Paper, 2000, p. 6.

[16] EBRD, "Bosnia and Herzegovina Economic Overview," web page, date unknown; World Bank, European Commission, and EBRD, 1996.

[17] IMF, *Bosnia and Herzegovina: Selected Issues*, Washington, D.C., Staff Country Report 98/69, August 1998.

[18] World Bank, European Commission, and EBRD, 1996; discussion with World Bank official, by telephone to Sarajevo, September 4, 2009.

[19] Peter Andreas, "The Clandestine Political Economy of War and Peace in Bosnia," *International Studies Quarterly*, Vol. 48, No. 1, March 2004, pp. 29–52.

was heavily dependent on irregular combatants with criminal ties as it developed a more professional regular military force.[20] Many of the paramilitary groups waging the war, such as the Serb "Tigers" led by Željko "Arkan" Ražnatović, took advantage of the conflict to rape and pillage.[21]

The criminal power structures consolidated during the war remained intact in the postwar era and, in many cases, expanded their criminal activities. Bosnia became a major transit point for illicit trafficking to Western Europe, and the proceeds of illegal activities were then often used to finance political parties and patronage networks— networks that grew all the more significant in the absence of a functioning postwar state.[22] The postwar political system, especially the nationalist (that is to say, ethnically based) parties that were born from the wartime political-military power structures, thus became inextricably intertwined with organized criminal networks, complicating the process of political reform.[23] The fact that many of the political elites profited directly from criminal activities gave them little incentive to fight organized crime or to establish rule of law. In general, endemic corruption provided both a means for maintaining political support and a reason to do so.

Political

Bosnia had been granted an assembly briefly by the Habsburgs from 1908 to 1918, and Yugoslavia was a constitutional monarchy for a short period following World War I. Two generations of Bosnians prior to the war, however, had had very limited experience with self-governance or democracy beyond pseudo-democratic practices at the local level. Yugoslavia was a single-party state, under what was some-

---

[20] Andreas, 2004, pp. 32–35.

[21] Timothy Donais, *The Political Economy of Peacebuilding in Post-Dayton Bosnia*, London: Routledge, 2005, p. 69.

[22] Michael Pugh, "Rubbing Salt into War Wounds: Shadow Economies and Peacebuilding in Bosnia and Kosovo," *Problems of Post-Communism*, Vol. 51, No. 3, May–June 2004, pp. 53–60.

[23] Donais, 2005, p. 66.

times described as "decentralized totalitarianism."[24] State security services actively enforced the system, although, within the communist world, Yugoslav citizens were generally better off when it came to personal freedoms than their counterparts in Warsaw Pact countries, enjoying, for example, greater opportunities for foreign travel.[25] Bosnia held democratic elections in 1990, prior to the outbreak of war, but this did not make Bosnia an established democracy.

The peculiarities of Yugoslavia's political-economic system would prove significant in the postconflict environment. By contrast with other communist systems, in which the directors of a firm were responsible to the state and, by extension, the Communist party, firms in Yugoslavia were supposed to be managed by the workers.[26] Workers thus ostensibly controlled their own fate and made decisions that were sensitive to market signals. In reality, however, the lack of central control meant that the local party elite or *nomenklatura* was able to establish patronage networks that, in many cases, survived the war and became a fundamental part of the postwar political and economic landscape. Ironically, Bosnia's more "liberal" socialist economic model was more difficult to shed than the more-centralized systems that characterized most other Central and Eastern European societies.

Institutional

The Yugoslav bureaucracy, including Bosnia's, had been well developed, though corrupt.[27] Bosnia emerged from the war with a complex, bloated institutional architecture. It had nominal but weak federal-level institutions created by the Dayton Accords, including a three-person presidency and a parliament; two entity-level governments, with their own presidents, parliaments, and court systems; multiple

---

[24] Andjelic, 2003, p. 27.

[25] Lampe, 1996, p. 265 and following.

[26] K. Gligorov, "The Economic System of Yugoslavia," in George Macesich, ed., *Essays on the Yugoslav Economic Model*, New York: Praeger, 1989, pp. 1–11; Josip Obradovic and William N. Dunn, eds., *Worker's Self-Management and Organizational Power in Yugoslavia*, Pittsburgh, Pa.: University Center for International Studies, University of Pittsburgh, 1978.

[27] Pugh, 2004.

cantonal governments in the Federation of Bosnia and Herzegovina; municipality[28] governments throughout the country; and other local governments. Although the Croatian minority did not have its own entity government, it did have its own army during the conflict and a proto-administration to support it, and it strongly resisted dismantling that administration. Creating the new national institutions called for by the Dayton Accords would be a major aspect of the postwar reconstruction effort.

Nation-Building Efforts

In the aftermath of the Dayton Accords, Bosnia became the focus of the largest of the late 20th-century international nation-building efforts. Led by the United States and the European Union, international efforts sought both to change the geopolitical circumstances that had given rise to the war and to build a functional, self-sufficient Bosnian state.

Dayton provided for an international civilian and military effort to enforce the peace and help reconstruct the country.[29] NATO forces (first, the Implementation Force [IFOR], then the Stabilization Force [SFOR]) were deployed, and a civilian Office of the High Representative (OHR) was established to coordinate the nonmilitary aspects of implementing the peace agreement.[30]

The international community had three basic types of tools at its disposal to build a functioning Bosnian state. First, it had the authority under the Dayton Accords to implement the peace agreement, and the parties to the agreement were formally required to cooperate in this effort. The presence of NATO forces was supposed to bolster the inter-

---

[28] *Municipality*, or *opstina*, is a territorial designation that may encompass multiple towns or villages.

[29] On Dayton, see Derek H. Chollet, *The Road to the Dayton Accords: A Study of American Statecraft*, New York: Palgrave Macmillan, 2005; and Richard C. Holbrooke, *To End a War*, New York: Modern Library, 1999.

[30] For more on the organization of the international effort, see Dobbins, McGinn, et al., 2003, pp. 87–109.

national community's leverage for implementing the civilian aspects of the Dayton agreement. Even with the NATO presence, persuasion and negotiation proved initially to be weak methods for achieving implementation. As a result, the High Representative and his international backers created in 1997 the so-called "Bonn Powers," which authorized the High Representative to intervene directly in Bosnian politics, dismissing obstructionist officials, overturning legislation that worked against the Dayton Accords, and making new laws by fiat. Second, there were the incentives of NATO and EU integration, which, as time progressed and NATO forces were drawn down, became increasingly important. Third, there were financial incentives, such as development aid and economic support.

The High Representative, chosen by and accountable to a self-selected group of European and North American states that constituted itself as the Peace Implementation Council (PIC), was the main actor on all civilian aspects of implementing the peace agreement and was supposed to coordinate all nonmilitary international actors in Bosnia. The PIC was led by a smaller steering group of major donor states. NATO deployed and directed the peacekeeping force. The United Nations and later European Union deployed CIVPOL monitors and promoted police reform. Cultural and social matters, along with the conduct of elections and the reform of political parties, were the responsibility of the Organization for Security and Co-operation in Europe (OSCE). Economic development fell largely to bilateral donors, of which the United States was the largest, the European Commission, and the World Bank. The UNHCR was responsible for facilitating the return or resettlement of hundreds of thousands of refugees and displaced persons.

Geographical and Geopolitical

The Dayton Accords marked both the end of a war and the starting point for a major effort to reorder Balkan geopolitics. The United States and its allies employed military force, political persuasion, economic incentives, criminal prosecutions, and the prospect of NATO and EU membership to tamp down hypernationalism and build regional cooperation. They sidelined or imprisoned obstructionist leaders, halted ethnic cleansing in Kosovo, and intervened to head off civil war in Macedonia. They provided moral and tangible support to democratic reformist elements, consolidating nascent democracies throughout the region, promoting a peaceful political transition in Croatia on President Franjo Tudjman's death, and encouraging the popular uprising that unseated Serbian President Slobodan Milošević. Very substantial resources were pumped into efforts to build a new regional infrastructure and integrate the Balkan economies with each other and the rest of Europe. Sweeping political, economic, military, and legal reforms were required of all countries of the region on the path to NATO and EU membership.

The Dayton Accords also set in motion a regional disarmament process. Croatia and Serbia partially disarmed. The OSCE created a Department of Regional Stabilization and implemented an arms control regime based on the Treaty on Conventional Armed Forces in Europe. It included verification, inspections, and communication measures. Seminars, training programs, and courses were also organized to bring formerly warring factions together, and there was a parallel effort to "democratize" the armed forces and introduce a code of military conduct.[31]

Cultural and Social

Starting in 1999, the OHR endeavored to encourage refugee return in an effort to rebuild trust among ethnic groups. Refugee return was a right under Dayton, and promoting it was intended to recreate the multiethnic Bosnian state that had existed under Tito.[32] It was also expected to bolster moderate political parties. The first High Representative, Carl Bildt, initially moved slowly on refugee return, fearing, not without reason, that, in the ethnically charged postwar atmosphere, rapid refugee return could reignite violence. As a result, ethnic segregation actually worsened in the early postwar period as remaining

---

[31] International Crisis Group, *Is Dayton Failing? Bosnia Four Years After the Peace Agreement*, Europe Report 80, October 28, 1999, p. 7.

[32] OHR, "The General Framework Agreement: Annex 7," December 14, 1995.

minorities migrated to areas where they felt more secure.[33] Cognizant of slow progress, and under media and other criticism of the slow pace at which Bosnia was returning to its prewar self, efforts to increase returns intensified in 1999, starting with the High Representative's imposition of new property legislation and continuing with related efforts over the next few years.

International actors also took immediate and direct action against the nationalist (i.e., ethnically aligned) media outlets that continued to foment conflict and encourage rejection of Dayton. In May 1997, the PIC directed the High Representative to suspend media that threatened the Dayton Accords. In October 1997, SFOR took control of Serb radio in the Republika Srpska to put an end to anti-Dayton broadcasting. International efforts to support the development of nonnationalist radio and TV stations ensued and would continue over the course of the next decade.

Efforts to build civil society and democratic culture to underpin Bosnia's democratic institutions were more limited. The OSCE and international development agencies were the main actors on the ground. Within the OHR, responsibility for democratization and interethnic issues fell under the responsibility of the third in command—a sign of its perceived lack of importance relative to more-strictly political matters.

Work on strengthening civil society began in 1998, although it was partially an ad hoc means of building local structures through which to channel international aid directly to the grass roots, circumventing governing elites.[34] Over the course of the next decade, more than 7,000 NGOs were registered, although this figure exaggerates the number of active organizations.[35] Moreover, not all the NGOs became forces for the development of liberal democracy. The new NGOs were often linked with nationalist political forces and thus did not consti-

---

[33] Roberto Belloni, *State Building and International Intervention in Bosnia*, London: Routledge, 2007, p. 23.

[34] Adam Fagan, "Civil Society in Bosnia Ten Years After Dayton," *International Peacekeeping*, Vol. 12, No. 3, 2005, pp. 406–419.

[35] Fagan, 2005.

tute an independent check on the state, let alone a wellspring of social capital.

At the same time, some effort was made to address the problem of an educational system split along ethnic lines, although, at first, most of the international focus was on rebuilding schools rather than on changing curricula or confronting the issue of children being segregated by ethnicity. The OSCE established a department dedicated to education reform in 2002. As the political situation began to deteriorate again in 2005, the problem of the ethnically divided educational system began to receive more attention, although some would argue that it was too late.

Economic

The devastation of the war, combined with the legacies of Bosnia's communist past, meant that international authorities would have to simultaneously restructure and rebuild the Bosnian economy to generate the growth needed to underpin peace. Bosnia received the world's highest level of international aid per capita for several years after Dayton.[36] Initial efforts focused on rebuilding destroyed infrastructure, with some €4 billion in aid spent in the first five years.[37] To ensure price stability, a currency board was established, with international staff in management roles.

Distributing economic aid, however, was complicated by the fact that Bosnia lacked a functioning central government, compelling donors to work with local officials, many of whom were extreme nationalists. Consequently, there was a persistent risk that aid that was intended to weaken the appeal of the nationalists would end up in their pockets.[38] At the same time, cutting off aid to nationalist-dominated

[36] Laurie Effron and F. Stephen O'Brien, *Bosnia and Herzegovina: Post Conflict Reconstruction and the Transition to a Market Economy*, Washington, D.C.: World Bank, 2004.

[37] DFID, 2000, p. 5.

[38] Belloni, 2007, p. 100.

regions risked making their situations worse while also further strengthening malign forces.[39]

Beginning roughly in 2000, as levels of aid began to decline, the international focus shifted from economic assistance to broader economic development strategies. Efforts at postcommunist transformation accelerated, with international lenders intensifying their focus on privatization and restructuring. Even before his arrival in 2002, High Representative Paddy Ashdown took the view that sluggish economic growth was one of the main obstacles to lasting peace. He made "jobs and justice" a centerpiece of his tenure, including a "bulldozer initiative" aimed at clearing out legislation that inhibited private-sector growth.[40] After he left in 2006, however, these efforts were not fully sustained.

Economic reform and development efforts were boosted by a broader regional initiative that began after the Kosovo conflict. The multiyear Stability Pact for South Eastern Europe was conceived as akin to a Marshall Plan for the Balkans: Generous aid was designed to enhance economic growth, address a wide range of postconflict and democratization goals, and further the integration of the region into the European Union and NATO. A coordinator was appointed to ensure an effective regional approach. Participants came together in Sarajevo in July 1999 to set the pact in motion, with more than 100 donors pledging $2.1 billion in aid for the first year.[41] Under the Stability Pact, international donors committed €2.4 billion in March 2000 and an additional €3 billion in October 2001 for projects to be implemented by two or more countries in order to strengthen regional cooperation.[42]

---

[39] Francine Friedman, *Bosnia and Herzegovina: A Polity on the Brink*, London: Routledge, 2004, pp. 104–106.

[40] See Mark Landler, "Newcomer Charges Bosnia Business Barricades," *New York Times*, June 25, 2003.

[41] Andrew Cain, "Rebuilt Sarajevo Hosts Balkans Summit: U.S. at Odds with Allies over Kosovo Aid," *Washington Times*, July 30, 1999, p. A20.

[42] "Achievements and Chronology," *Stability Pact for South Eastern Europe*, undated, referenced August 2012.

Political

Although some observers hoped that peace would lead to a rapid decline in the popularity of wartime ethnic group leaders, it did not. The war's nationalist protagonists retained political power and emerged victorious in all the early elections—the 1996 national elections, the 1997 municipal elections, and the 2000 municipal elections. Nationalist success at the polls was, in part, attributable to the power networks established during and prior to the war, often funded by criminal activities. It was also a reflection of the fact that many individuals believed that the nationalists were their best defense against reprisals from other groups. Needless to say, many nationalists obstructed implementation of the peace agreement and—in the case of some Serb nationalists—continued to speak out in favor of secession.

The prevalence of ethnically based power structures was particularly problematic for international actors, who were forced to work with these groups in order to make progress on reconstruction, development, and other issues. By working with them, the international actors strengthened them, delaying and complicating efforts to establish state-level institutions that were inimical to these groups but that Bosnia needed to become a functioning state.[43]

International actors would consequently shift their strategy in two major ways in the first five years. In 1997, the PIC authorized the High Representative to intervene more aggressively in Bosnian politics, creating the Bonn powers that would be used extensively over the course of the next eight years in attempts to undercut nationalist strength. For example, in 1999, the High Representative sacked 22 municipal and cantonal officials from all three ethnic groups on the ground that they had obstructed Dayton implementation.[44] NATO was simultaneously encouraged to take a more liberal interpretation of its mandate and support Dayton implementation more actively.

---

[43] Marcus Cox, *State Building and Post-Conflict Reconstruction: Lessons from Bosnia*, Geneva: Centre for Applied Studies in International Negotiations, January 2001.

[44] Sumantra Bose, "The Bosnian State a Decade After Dayton," *International Peacekeeping*, Vol. 12, No. 3, Autumn 2005, pp. 322–335.

With Serbia deflated after the 1999 Kosovo war, Bosnian Croat groups became increasingly the main threat to Dayton. As a result, in 2000, when the Croat nationalist party (the Croatian Democratic Union, or Hrvatska Demokratska Zajednica, [HDZ]) set up its own minigovernment, dubbed an "intercantonal council," the High Representative removed the president of the HDZ from his position in the joint presidency of Bosnia. Authorities also went after the HDZ's financial base, raiding the party-controlled Hercegovacka Banka with the help of SFOR.

The High Representative also used the Bonn powers to force greater centralization—for example, by establishing common license plates, the Bosnian Border Service, and the State Investigation and Protection Agency; instituting defense-sector reform; forging agreement on the Bosnian flag and other national symbols; and creating a value-added tax.[45] Ashdown was especially quick to wield the Bonn powers, removing several Bosnian Serb officials and exercising the powers some 447 times between 2002 and 2006.[46]

One particularly effective means of removing obstructive political figures was international prosecution for war crimes. The International Criminal Tribunal for the Former Yugoslavia (ICTY) was created by the UN Security Council in 1993, at a time when the international community was as yet unwilling to intervene forcefully enough to compel an end to the conflict. Even after the Dayton Accords, the United States and its allies were initially hesitant to employ the now-abundant forces at their disposal in Bosnia to seize individuals who had been indicted for war crimes and transport them to the court in the Hague. Over time, however, more-aggressive efforts were made to round up indictees, which, at a minimum, drove them underground and made it more difficult for them to play active political roles. Eventually, under great international pressure, the governments of Croatia and Serbia also cooperated in arresting indictees and handing them over for prosecution.

---

[45] International Crisis Group, *Ensuring Bosnia's Future: A New International Engagement Strategy*, Europe Report 180, February 15, 2007b, p. 5.

[46] International Crisis Group, 2007b, p. 27.

Although useful in removing some spoilers, international war-crime prosecutions did little to promote reconciliation among Croat, Serb, and Muslim populations within Bosnia and its neighbors. Indeed, the publicity attendant on the trials seemed, in the short term at least, to stimulate renewed nationalist sentiment in each of the three communities. The judicial process necessarily focused on the wartime records of individuals involved, not their postwar behavior. As a result, several political leaders who, in the aftermath of the war, had cooperated with the international community's efforts in the Balkans were removed and transported to the Hague for trial. The process also turned out to be expensive, costing around $2.5 billion through 2013,[47] far more than the aid that has been spent improving the domestic judicial systems in Bosnia and the other affected states. With the captures of Radovan Karadžić and Ratko Mladić after many years on the run, these trials continue as of late 2012 and are not due to end until 2014, 19 years after the war in Bosnia ended.

Institutional

The political institutions called for by the Dayton Accords were difficult to implement. State-level institutions stipulated in the accords remained hollow in the first five years after Dayton. Real power resided at the entity level. Although the three-person presidency, the parliament, and the council of ministers existed, competencies were limited: These institutions rarely conducted business in the first five years after Dayton.

The problems created by a lack of state-level institutions became more serious as time went on and Bosnia attempted to move toward membership in NATO and the European Union. Some progress was made between 2000 and 2004, and, in 2005, a major effort to overhaul state institutions was undertaken. Aims included replacing the tripartite presidency with a single figure and abolishing so-called entity

---

[47] "In the Dock, but for What? Enthusiasm Is Flagging for Spectacular Trials to Punish War Crimes and Human-Rights Abuses," *Economist*, November 25, 2010, reported a figure of about $2 billion. The ICTY budget for 2010 through 2013, reported on its website (ICTY, "The Cost of Justice," undated, accessed November 2012), is more than $500 million.

voting, which gave the entities effective veto powers over central government decisionmaking. After an initial success in building a loose coalition around these constitutional reforms, however, the process died in the 11th hour when parties failed to come up with the necessary votes in their own ranks.[48] The failure marked the start of a period of increased tension and mounting difficulty for Bosnia. Afterward, efforts to strengthen the institutions of state government were blocked by the entities, more than once bringing Bosnia back to political crisis.

Entities thus remained the main locus of governance, but there was progress on building state-level institutions in a few areas. One such area was defense. Defense reform had the potential benefit of reducing the chances of a return to civil war by integrating the armed forces under a single command-and-control structure and strengthening civilian oversight. In the immediate postwar period, the issue was considered off-limits. In 2003, however, recognizing the inherent insecurity that the ethnically segregated defense forces created for the country, Ashdown seized the opportunity provided by the discoveries that factories in Republika Srpska had been refurbishing engines for Iraqi fighter jets and that the Bosnian Serb Army had been spying on NATO, to initiate a significant reform program under NATO auspices. Defense reform, not included in Dayton, involved integrating the forces into a single national army, further professionalizing the army, and preparing Bosnia for membership in NATO's Partnership for Peace.

There was less progress on police reform, which was important because police officers were the security forces in closest proximity to the population.[49] In practice, police reform meant unifying ethnically divided police forces under a central authority. The slow pace at which reform had progressed by 2004 led Ashdown to establish a Police Restructuring Commission, tasked with proposing a single structure

---

[48] International Crisis Group, 2007b, p. 9.

[49] See Tija Memisevic, "EU Conditionality in Bosnia and Herzegovina: Police Reform and the Legacy of War Crimes," in Judy Batt and Jelena Obradovic-Wochnik, eds., *War Crimes, Conditionality and EU Integration in the Western Balkans*, Paris: Institute for Security Studies, European Union, Chaillot Paper 116, June 2009, pp. 49–66.

for Bosnia's police, unified under the central government. Despite pressure from both Ashdown and EU foreign policy chief Javier Solana, however, the reform proposals were blocked by the Republika Srpska leadership, which claimed that they amounted to an infringement on Serb "sovereignty."[50]

Work on building the rule of law was limited. Several years passed before the links between organized crime and the nationalist leaderships became fully evident, and, by that time, crime had become entrenched and even endemic in some areas. Nevertheless, beginning in 2000, the High Representative started making more-systematic efforts to reform the justice system and tackle organized crime and corruption. High Representative Wolfgang Petritsch established a state court of Bosnia in 2000 and appointed judges. In 2002, Ashdown bolstered the court's independence by providing external funding for its proceedings. Ashdown also appointed international judges and prosecutors and imposed a new criminal code.[51] The deployment of the EU Police Mission in January 2003 and the EU's later insistence on police reform as a requirement for signing a Stabilization and Association Agreement were also intended to improve the rule of law.

Efforts to target criminals directly also increased. At first, NATO had refused to participate in anticrime efforts on the grounds that they were not within the military mandate. Dealing with criminals was left to the UN International Police Task Force. The more the links between war criminals and ordinary criminality became clear, however, the more difficult it was for NATO to resist pressure to use its powers to interdict criminals. SFOR and then EU Force (EUFOR), the international military force that succeeded NATO, both undertook efforts to disrupt criminal networks.[52]

---

[50] International Crisis Group, *Bosnia's Stalled Police Reform: No Progress, No EU*, Europe Report 164, September 6, 2005b.

[51] International Crisis Group, 2007b, p. 12.

[52] See Ursula C. Schroeder and Cornelius Friesendorf, "State-Building and Organized Crime: Implementing the International Law Enforcement Agenda in Bosnia," *Journal of International Relations and Development*, Vol. 12, 2009, pp. 137–167.

Outcomes

Bosnia has been at peace for more than 15 years but is not yet a fully functional, self-sufficient state. The geopolitical factors that produced the conflict in the early 1990s have been significantly modified, but the ethnic divisions that gave shape to the conflict and were exacerbated by it largely remain, as do the dysfunctional governance arrangements embodied in the peace agreement.

Local Attitudes

Polling data have shown, paradoxically, that, although citizens were pessimistic about the direction in which the country was going, they were relatively optimistic about Bosnia's long-term future. Polls conducted by the International Republican Institute (IRI) between 2005 and 2008 consistently showed that more than 50 percent of the population was pessimistic about the general direction in which Bosnia was headed, with only 30 percent or less optimistic. The same polling, however, found that 60 percent of Bosnians were optimistic about the country's long-term prospects. All ethnic groups were pessimistic about the economic situation.[53]

The attitude of the Bosnian population toward the OHR has been mixed and has varied according to ethnic group. Although consistent, comprehensive longitudinal data are not available, in general, confidence in the OHR rose during Ashdown's tenure from 2002 to 2005, although Bosniaks' confidence in the OHR during this period was roughly double that of Serbs and Croats. These trends continued through 2006 and 2007, with a slight increase in overall support in 2008.[54] As of June 2008, 72 percent of Bosniaks still believed that the OHR should impose legislation, as compared with 44 percent of

---

[53] Unpublished IRI polling data provided to the authors.

[54] UNDP, *Early Warning System: Annual Report 2002*, May 20, 2003; UNDP, *Early Warning System: Annual Report 2003*, 2004; UNDP, *Early Warning System: Annual Report 2004*, June 24, 2005; UNDP, *Early Warning System: Annual Report 2005*, May 17, 2006; UNDP, *Early Warning System: Annual Report 2006*, May 17, 2007; UNDP, *Early Warning System: Annual Report 2007*, May 6, 2008; UNDP, *Early Warning System: Annual Report 2008*, April 22, 2009.

Croats and 25 percent of Serbs. Interestingly, 64 percent of respondents in the Republika Srpska said that maintaining "sovereignty" was more important to them than prosperity for Bosnia as a whole. Seventy-five percent of Serbs wanted the United States to hand over leadership in Bosnia to the Europeans.[55]

Most local elites agreed that the international effort had been necessary to bring the violence to an end while admitting that the constitution Dayton provided was not working. Some said that the international community should have done more, earlier on, to ensure minority returns (i.e., the return of displaced persons to areas where they would be ethnic minorities). Others faulted early elections and willingness to tolerate nationalist politicians. Some felt that international aid, although generous, had been arbitrary, badly coordinated, and not linked to local needs.

Representatives of civil society have emphasized that too much aid went into sustaining operational costs of NGOs and that not enough attention was paid to building a longer-term financial foundation for civil society. Many, especially (though not exclusively) Serbs, emphasized the shortcomings of the United States in understanding the nature of Bosnian society and the ethnic issue in particular. Some pointed to the divisions within the international community, including between the United States and Europe, both during the war and afterward, as a problem. Many lamented widespread corruption and expressed disappointment that the international community had not used its powers more effectively to build the rule of law and break down corrupt networks.[56]

Geographical and Geopolitical

The regional dynamics that gave rise to the war were successfully managed through coordinated diplomacy among the international powers and the integration of some regional states into broader institutional structures, the European Union and NATO in particular. Although

---

[55] Unpublished IRI polling data provided to the authors.

[56] The views described in this and the preceding paragraph were expressed to the author in discussions with Bosnian elites in Sarajevo.

the situation in Bosnia was potentially explosive after Kosovo's declaration of independence in February 2008, the region in general was much more stable than in 1995. The arms-control regime was widely considered successful. Three of these states became NATO members (Albania, Croatia, and Montenegro), Croatia will join the European Union in 2013, and others are on the road to EU membership. As the regional context shifted, neighboring countries came to play constructive or neutral roles in Bosnia's stabilization, rather than negative ones.

Cultural and Social

The international community's efforts to rebuild interethnic trust and foster democratic culture were mostly unsuccessful. Minority returns remained far from complete, a factor that may have contributed to peace even as it hardened ethnic segregation. Although reliable figures will not be available until a postwar census is finally conducted, rough calculations suggest that minority returns were low. The UNHCR recorded 467,000 minority and 559,403 majority returns by mid-2009,[57] of a total number of displaced persons estimated to be 2.4 million. But the 467,000 figure likely overstates the real number of minority returnees because it does not take into account how many returnees stayed after returning and how many sold their restituted property and moved elsewhere.

Practical barriers to minority returns remain, including lack of employment opportunities, lack of funds for reconstruction of homes and necessary infrastructure, and lack of access to social services.[58] Many displaced minorities are no longer seeking to return home, especially Muslims who once lived in Serb areas. Anecdotal evidence indi-

---

[57] Majority returns calculated from total returnees of 1,026,993.

[58] OHR, *34th Report of the High Representative for Implementation of the Peace Agreement on Bosnia and Herzegovina to the Secretary-General of the United Nations*, November 21, 2008, ¶ 63.

cates significant improvements in particular areas along the interentity boundary line, but the overall picture is not positive.[59]

Reforms of education and the media have not fared well. Curricula and textbooks are still ethnically segregated. Theoretically "multi-ethnic" schools often have different hours for different ethnic groups. It is possible the postwar generation of Bosnians may prove more nationalistic than their parents. This generation has no real memory of the years before the war, when interethnic marriages were not uncommon and truly integrated communities the norm in urban areas.[60] Freedom House ranks the Bosnian media as "partly free," and some media outlets continue to amplify the messages of nationalist leaders, working against rather than in favor of reconciliation and political normalization.[61]

Efforts to build democracy and stability by investing in civil society have produced limited results. The NGOs established by the international community have ultimately been neither responsible to nor sustained by Bosnians themselves, a fact that has made them less likely to play a role in democratizing Bosnian political culture.[62] When efforts have been made to shift the funding for NGOs away from the international community, most of those that have survived have become closely linked with political parties.[63] Civil society is nascent at best.[64]

---

[59] For a positive picture of interethnic relations in the town of Doboj, see European Stability Initiative, *A Bosnian Fortress: Return, Energy and the Future of Bosnia*, Berlin, December 19, 2007.

[60] On schools, see Valery Perry, "Democratization in Brcko and Bosnia," in Michael A. Innes, ed., *Bosnian Security After Dayton: New Perspectives*, London: Routledge, 2006, pp. 51–70; Aida Cerkez-Robinson, "Bosnia's Ethnic Divisions Are Evident in Schools," Associated Press, August 23, 2009.

[61] International Crisis Group, 2007b, p. 12.

[62] Belloni, 2007, pp. 109–112.

[63] Fagan, 2005.

[64] Belloni, 2007, p. 121.

Economic

Peace and generous external assistance produced exceptionally high growth rates through the late 1990s. As aid flows dried up, Bosnia was able to sustain respectable growth rates, comparable to those in its neighborhood. Its economy remains hobbled, however, by high levels of corruption and patronage-driven inefficiencies.

Despite initially high annual growth rates, the economy had recovered to only 60 percent of its prewar level by 1999.[65] Inflation was low, and the currency board had helped enable the development of domestic capital markets, which were comparatively strong. Ten years after Dayton, Bosnia's GDP had tripled, and its exports had risen tenfold.[66] By 2011, more than 15 years after Dayton, Bosnia's per capita GDP had risen to a level below that of Macedonia, which had been the least developed of the constituent republics at the time Yugoslavia broke apart (see Figure 5.2).[67]

Bosnia's economic situation still leaves much to be desired. A decade after Dayton, income was still less than it had been in 1989, a level to which it had yet to return by 2011.[68] Bosnia's rate of convergence toward EU norms has also been slower than that of other aspirants for EU membership.[69] The IMF estimated unemployment to be 23 percent in 2008, with low overall labor-force participation rates.[70] The poverty rate had fallen from 18 percent in 2004 to 14 percent in 2007, although this was still significantly greater than in Serbia.

---

[65] Effron and O'Brien, 2004.

[66] IMF, *Bosnia and Herzegovina: 2005 Article IV Consultation—Staff Report, Staff Supplement, Public Information Notice on the Executive Board Discussion, and Statement by the Executive Director for Bosnia and Herzegovina*, Washington, D.C., Country Report 05/199, June 2005.

[67] CIA, "Macedonia," *The World Factbook*, 2012e.

[68] EBRD, "Bosnia and Herzegovina Country Assessment," undated, accessed August 2012.

[69] IMF, *Bosnia and Herzegovina: 2008 Article IV Consultation—Staff Report; Public Information Notice on the Executive Board Discussion; and Statement by the Executive Director for Bosnia and Herzegovina*, Washington, D.C., Country Report 08/327, October 2008, p. 4.

[70] Milan Cuc, "Bosnia and Herzegovina: On the Road to EU Accession," *IMF Survey Magazine: Countries and Regions*, November 12, 2008.

Figure 5.2
Bosnia's per Capita Gross Domestic Product Based on Purchasing Power Parity (current international $) Compared with That of Some Neighbors, 2011

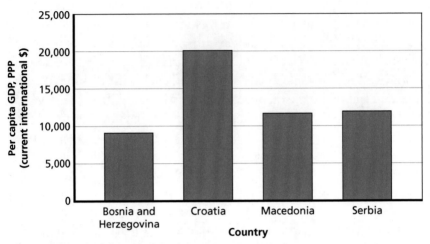

SOURCE: World Bank, undated (c).
NOTE: PPP = purchasing power parity. An international dollar has the same purchasing power over gross national income (GNI) as a U.S. dollar has in the United States.
RAND RR167-5.2

Despite OHR and EU efforts to improve the rule of law, organized crime is still pervasive, with implications for political reform efforts, as well as economic growth and the integration of Bosnia into the subregional and regional economies. However, between 2003 and 2006, the situation improved with regard to trafficking; smuggling of weapons, cigarettes, fuel, alcohol, and other goods had declined, as did human trafficking.[71] Bosnia nevertheless remains a very corrupt country, where political elites capture a large portion of the national revenue.[72]

---

[71] Schroeder and Friesendorf, 2009, pp. 148–149.

[72] James H. Anderson and Cheryl Williamson Gray, *Anticorruption in Transition 3: Who Is Succeeding and Why?* Washington, D.C.: World Bank, 2006, p. 9.

Political

The Dayton Accords accommodated the nationalist political forces in the country in order to bring peace and in the hope that peace, in turn, would bring about a moderation of politics. This accommodation, however, proved difficult to reverse. Nationalists have continued to block progress on establishing institutions and a functioning government at the national level. According to the World Bank, Bosnia's government effectiveness score was in the bottom quartile globally in 2011 (from 1995 to 2005, Bosnia had made gains in this area, but, by 2011, its score had dropped below the 2005 level). Strikingly, this made it the lowest in the region, behind both Kosovo and Albania.[73]

The situation has not improved since. Republika Srpska leader Milorad Dodik continues to strongly resist any centralizing moves and periodically threatens to secede. The European Union, which, in 2004, took over NATO's peacekeeping responsibilities, is poorly positioned to forcefully prevent such a move, by reason of both its internal divisions and waning force presence. Its political and economic leverage, on the other hand, remains considerable and has so far been enough to forestall any such move to break the country apart.

Institutional

Overall, Bosnia's political institutions developed somewhat in the 15 years after Dayton, but many gaps remain, especially in state-level institutions. Power continued to reside largely at the entity level, and, in 2011, the state was without a government (i.e., ministers) for nearly a year, leading many observers to fear the possibility of a slide toward a more serious crisis. Without stronger state-level institutions, Bosnia's path to membership in NATO and the European Union has been very

---

[73] With a score of −0.73 (scores range from −2.5 to 2.5, with higher numbers indicating better governance effectiveness), Bosnia had a percentile rank of 27.3 percent, while Kosovo and Albania, with respective scores of −0.6 and −0.27, had percentile ranks of 32.5 percent and 45.5 percent, respectively. The measurements are in a broad band, and the low end of Kosovo's range is below the low end for Bosnia (Daniel Kaufmann, Aart Kraay, and Massimo Mastruzzi, *Governance Matters VII: Aggregate and Individual Governance Indicators, 1996–2007*, Washington, D.C.: World Bank, World Bank Institute, Global Programs Division, and Development Research Group, Macroeconomics and Growth Team, 2008).

difficult. Not only does the lack of unified representation make negotiations nearly impossible; many of the reforms needed for membership in these structures require state-level legislation. The international community's progressive weakening of the OHR before any indigenous replacement emerged has only heightened this vacuum of power at the state level.

By 2006, the military was under civilian control, and Bosnia had a ministry of defense—one of the few genuine competencies of the central government. Conscription was abolished, and a professional military force of 10,000 was created.[74] Units were ethnically integrated only down to the brigade level, however. Battalions remained mono-ethnic and located in their respective entities. Police reform remained an area of contention and limited progress.

Conclusions

What Local Factors Posed the Greatest Challenges?
The local factors within each category that were most important in shaping the environment in which nation-builders sought to promote an enduring peace included the following.

Geographical and Geopolitical
The support of Bosnia's neighbors, Serbia and Croatia, for their ethnic brethren within Bosnia was the crucial factor that gave rise to and perpetuated the conflict. U.S. and European pressure focused directly on ending that support and culminated in a peace agreement signed by leaders of all three countries. The agreement also, however, ratified Bosnia's ethnic fractures and embedded them in its political system. Bosnia's neighbors were eventually brought around to playing a constructive or neutral role in the country's affairs.

---

[74] Derek Chappell, "NATO and the Defence Reform Commission: Partners for Progress," *SETimes*, June 2, 2006.

Cultural and Social

Whether or not the war in Bosnia was *caused* by ethnic hatred is a matter of dispute, but it was clearly initiated and fought on ethnic lines, and the war greatly intensified ethnic social and physical divisions. The physical divisions were, to some extent, addressed through programs to help refugees and internally displaced persons return to their homes, but externally driven efforts to rebuild ethnic trust were largely unsuccessful.

Economic

Economic deterioration in the former Yugoslavia is considered by some to have been a contributing cause of the conflict. By war's end, the Bosnian economy was shattered, and, at the same time, it was saddled with the legacy of an inefficient socialist economic system. War profiteering contributed to the expansion and entrenchment of criminal groups with transnational ties and linked to political patronage networks, which inhibited both economic and political reforms. To reinforce the peace, foreign donors spent huge sums on rebuilding infrastructure and worked to create new monetary and financial systems. Generous external assistance fed high growth rates in the early postconflict years; the rates then settled down to regional norms. But the prospects for further economic advancement remained hobbled by corruption and patronage-driven inefficiencies.

Political

The particular nature of the prewar socialist system in the former Yugoslavia encouraged the development of patronage networks, and, in Bosnia, these were reinforced during the conflict, became linked with ethnically oriented political parties, and helped support those nationalist parties' victories in successive postconflict elections. Nation-building efforts countered the most-egregious nationalist political behaviors but did not dismantle the power structures behind them. The accommodation of nationalist political forces in the structure of the peace agreement proved difficult to reverse. These forces, which some fear could once again pull Bosnia apart, have so far been held sufficiently in check by the long international presence in Bosnia and continuing international counterpressures and incentives even as that presence has waned.

Institutional

Bosnia was not nearly as bereft of bureaucratic capabilities as many postconflict countries, but implementing the institutional scheme laid out in the peace agreement was highly problematic, and political crises repeatedly erupted over interveners' efforts to construct statewide institutions of government. Progress was eventually made in ethnically integrating (to the brigade level) and professionalizing the military and in some other state institutional development, but many gaps remained. Without stronger and more-authoritative state-level (as opposed to entity-level) institutions, prospects for integrating into the European Union and NATO—which could help maintain incentives and pressures for holding Bosnia together—would remain dim.

Were Local Factors Modified or Circumvented to Promote Enduring Peace?

Fifteen years after the Dayton Accords, peace had been sustained, improvements in governance and democratization were registered, and impressive economic growth (from a level of wartime devastation) had been achieved. But Bosnia remained a ward of the international community—as time wore on, more specifically of the European Union. Table 5.1 shows these outcomes, alongside key resources applied by nation-building interveners.

Stabilizing the Balkans was a major foreign policy preoccupation of the U.S. and European powers throughout the 1990s and into the first few years of the next century. Dayton was the pivot on which these efforts turned. Prior to Dayton, the United States and Europe were disunited, their policies in conflict, and their actions ineffectual. Thereafter, they acted in concert and largely succeeded in reordering relations with and among all the Balkan states.

In Bosnia, it proved easier to deal with the regional factors that precipitated the conflict than the social fault lines along which the conflict was fought and that it exacerbated. In addition, physical reconstruction proved easier than creating unified governance structures.

Table 5.1
Postintervention Performance and Nation-Building Inputs in Bosnia

Performance Indicator	Year of Intervention (1995)	5 Years Later	10 Years Later
At peace?	—	Yes	Yes
Government effectiveness (10-point scale)	3.24	4.60	5.19[a]
Freedom Index (10-point scale)	2.50	4.75	6.25
HDI (10-point scale)	NA	NA	7.20
Cumulative growth in per capita GDP (in 1st 5 years and in 10 years after intervention) (%)	—	155.2	213.7
Nation-Building Input			
Peak military presence per capita, number of troops per 1,000 inhabitants	17.5		
Peak international civilian police presence per capita, number of police per 1,000 inhabitants	0.59		
Average annual per capita assistance in the first 5 years (constant 2010 US$)	384		

SOURCES: World Bank, undated (d); Freedom House, various years; UNDP, undated; IMF, undated; Dobbins, Jones, Crane, Chivvis, et al., 2008, Figures 9.2, 9.4, 9.9; UN Peace Operations, various years; World Bank, undated (c).

[a] As noted in the text, as of 2011, Bosnia's government effectiveness score had dropped below its 2005 level.

Once Croatia and Serbia had become stabilizing or at least neutral rather than radicalizing forces for Bosnia, the likelihood of renewed conflict diminished greatly. But the compromise agreement that ended the war left Bosnia with a dysfunctional constitutional structure, while persistent ethnic antagonisms and a political system that reinforces them have so far doomed any effort to amend it for the better. At the same time, the economic devastation the war wrought was largely reversed, but factors inhibiting economic advancement—such as corruption and a pervasive patronage system—had not been resolved.

Bosnia is no longer economically dependent but remains without the capacity to govern itself unaided. Nation-building in the literal sense of creating a single national identity based on a common historical narrative and sense of values has made little progress. Efforts to build institutions have achieved somewhat more, in that most public services are performed by governmental institutions to at least regional norms of competence, but only with the international community continuing to push forward institutional development. This is a small price to pay, however, for a state and a region at peace and continuing to slowly converge toward European norms of governance and behavior in the international system.

CHAPTER SIX

East Timor

In September 1999, the international community deployed the first of a succession of peacekeeping missions whose task was to prepare East Timor for independence from Indonesia. First came an Australian-led, UN-mandated force, followed a month later by the UN Transitional

Figure 6.1
Map of East Timor

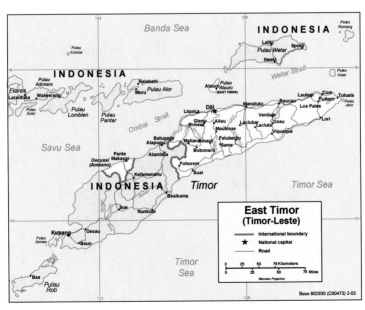

SOURCE: CIA, "Timor-Leste," *The World Factbook*, 2012g.
RAND *RR167-6.1*

Administration in East Timor (UNTAET). The UN mandate in East Timor was exceptionally broad. It included "overall responsibility for the administration of East Timor" and gave the mission the power to "exercise all legislative and executive authority, including the administration of justice."[1] UNTAET was also charged with enforcing law and order and setting up a new administration.[2] Other key tasks for UNTAET included repatriating the 250,000 refugees who had fled to West Timor, kick-starting the economy, establishing a currency, securing East Timor's oil wealth in negotiations with Australia, supporting a reconciliation process, and establishing political institutions.

This very broad mandate soon raised concerns from East Timorese that they did not have sufficient ownership of their own nation-building process. As local demands for greater political empowerment arose, the United Nations tried to find ways to address them without compromising its mandate to quickly build efficient institutions. The United Nations never really succeeded in resolving this tension, and, when UNTAET closed its doors in 2002, the mission was accused of both leaving too early and not having empowered local actors soon enough, the former of which certainly proved correct.

After the country's assumption of sovereignty in 2002 and the transfer of most of UNTAET's responsibilities to the East Timorese government, nation-building efforts continued. East Timor has experienced repeated civil unrest and serious political crises in 2002, 2006, and 2008, including a 2008 assassination attempt against the president. International peacekeeping forces returned in 2006, and UN CIVPOL remained in significant numbers as of early 2012. Despite several elections, some economic growth, and the development of a fledgling democracy, the country remains politically and economically fragile.

---

[1]   UN Security Council, Resolution 1272 (1999), October 25, 1999, ¶ 1.

[2]   UN Security Council, 1999, ¶¶ 2(a), 2(b).

Local Factors Before the Peace

East Timor had been a Portuguese colony from the 16th century onward. In 1975, in the aftermath of Portugal's own revolution, Indonesia seized and annexed East Timor. In 1999, acting under international pressure, Indonesia permitted a United Nations–supervised referendum on independence. The results were overwhelmingly in favor of separation. This result triggered a wave of violence organized by pro-Indonesian militia supported by Indonesia's military.[3]

The May 5, 1999, agreement setting the referendum in train had stipulated that Indonesia would "be responsible for maintaining peace and security in East Timor in order to ensure that the popular consultation is carried out in a fair and peaceful way in an atmosphere free of intimidation, violence or interference from any side."[4] The militias that perpetrated much of the postreferendum violence, however, were trained and supplied by the Indonesian military and operated out of its barracks.[5] Indonesia was dealing at the time with other restive regions, including Aceh, the Moluccas, and Irian Jaya, and the Indonesian military's actions in East Timor may have been intended to deter pro-independence movements elsewhere.

In September 1999, the Indonesian government, caught in the midst of the Asian financial crisis and under mounting international pressure, agreed to withdraw its forces from East Timor and to allow the deployment of an Australian-led peacekeeping force operating with a UN Security Council mandate, which gave way a month later to the UN mission.

---

[3] Michael G. Smith and Moreen Dee, "East Timor," in William J. Durch, ed., *Twenty-First-Century Peace Operations*, Washington, D.C.: U.S. Institute of Peace and Henry L. Stimson Center, 2006, pp. 389–466, pp. 395–396.

[4] UN General Assembly Security Council, *Question of East Timor: Report of the Secretary-General*, S/1999/513, May 5, 1999, Annex I.

[5] See Clinton Fernandes, *Reluctant Saviour: Australia, Indonesia, and the Independence of East Timor*, Carlton North, Vic.: Scribe Publications, 2004, Chapter Three; and Hamish McDonald, D. Ball, G. van Klinken, D. Bouurshier, D. Kammen, and R. Tanter, *Masters of Terror: Indonesia's Military and Violence in East Timor in 1999*, Canberra: Strategic and Defence Studies Centre, Australian National University, 2002 (cited in Damien Kingsbury, *East Timor: The Price of Liberty*, Houndmills, UK: Palgrave Macmillan, 2009, p. 71).

Geographical and Geopolitical

East Timor's social and political complexity is rooted in its geography (see Figure 6.1). The mountainous island territory's location between Australia, Southeast Asia, and the Pacific resulted in its population being split between two distinct language groupings, more than a dozen languages, and dozens more dialects. The collision between the Australian tectonic plate and Southeast Asia has created very broken terrain that has generally kept communities apart.[6]

Geopolitical factors have also played an important role in the political evolution of East Timor. Most Western powers initially chose not to challenge Indonesia's occupation of East Timor in 1975 because East Timor was seen as one of the "dominoes" that could fall into China's orbit if a communist movement prevailed there. Scholars still debate whether East Timor's pro-independence group Frente Revolucionária de Timor-Leste Independente (FRETILIN) was a Marxist organization or whether it became one at a later stage;[7] in any case, this concern led the United States, the United Kingdom, and Australia to acquiesce to the annexation.[8] With the end of the Cold War, however, Western powers increasingly sided in favor of East Timor's self-determination.[9] The death of Indonesia's President Suharto in 1998 and the consequences of the Asian financial crisis for Indonesia—which both increased Indonesian susceptibility to mounting international pressures and made East Timor an increasingly unwelcome financial burden—created the political space for a reexamination of East Timor's status.

Cultural and Social

The island of Timor was first inhabited by people coming from Papua, Malay groups, and migrants from various small Pacific islands. Over

---

[6]   Kingsbury, 2009, p. 26.

[7]   Kingsbury, 2009, p. 52.

[8]   Dobbins, Jones, Crane, Rathmell, et al., 2005, p. 151; Kingsbury, 2009, p. 48.

[9]   Dobbins, Jones, Crane, Rathmell, et al., 2005, pp. 151–152; see also Tim Huxley, *Disintegrating Indonesia? Implications for Regional Security*, Oxford, UK: Oxford University Press, 2002, p. 34.

the centuries, an influx of traders from China and India; missionaries, explorers, and colonizers from Europe; and soldiers from Indonesia resulted in a complex society divided along linguistic, regional, and political lines.[10] The linguistic diversity in particular complicated the development of a cohesive national polity and identity and continues to contribute to the country's political divisions.

The 1999 postreferendum violence resulted in the destruction of more than 70 percent of East Timor's infrastructure and 1,000–2,000 deaths. This violence, however, is overshadowed by the abuses that took place during the 24 years of Indonesian occupation, which included torture, executions, and mass starvation during Indonesia's program of resettlement. Overall, it is estimated that between one-third and one-quarter of East Timorese lost their lives during the occupation.[11]

Economic

While Indonesia was struggling with the economic consequences of the Asian financial crisis, the World Bank in particular raised the issue of the cost involved in maintaining Indonesia's presence in East Timor, especially at a time when various austerity measures had to be considered.[12] East Timor was Indonesia's poorest province and accordingly received more per capita support than the rest of the country—a cost that became increasingly difficult for Jakarta to justify to its own population.[13] Indonesia's domestic context was also radically changed. Deeply affected by the economic crisis, its middle class had become more amenable politically to new views toward the East Timor issue. Along with mounting international pressure, these factors convinced Indonesian President B. J. Habibie to allow a referendum enabling

---

[10] Kingsbury, 2009, p. 26.

[11] Derrick Silove, "Conflict in East Timor: Genocide or Expansionist Occupation?" *Human Rights Review*, Vol. 1, No. 3, April–June 2000, pp. 62–79, p. 67.

[12] Kingsbury, 2009, p. 66.

[13] Smith and Dee, 2006, p. 395.

East Timorese to choose between integration into Indonesia and independence.[14]

Following the referendum results in favor of independence, economic considerations were also crucial to halting the violence. The United States threatened to withhold World Bank funding for Indonesia unless it accepted having international peacekeepers deploy to East Timor. The IMF, too, suspended a visit to Indonesia to discuss the financial crisis. In the context of a severe economic crisis, Indonesia relented and acquiesced to the deployment of international peacekeepers.[15]

The economic situation in East Timor itself was dire. Even before the postreferendum violence, East Timor's per capita GDP was less than half of Indonesia's; more than 30 percent of the population lived below the absolute poverty level.[16] The 1999 violence resulted in the destruction of half of the livestock and much of the infrastructure—including 95 percent of commercial and retail buildings; all banks in the capital city, Dili; and all communication lines outside of it.[17] The formal economy had ceased to function.

Political

In the 1960s and early 1970s, East Timor's various linguistic communities clustered around three broad political groupings: the Associação Popular Democrática Timorense (APODETI), which favored the integration of East Timor as an autonomous province within Indonesia; the União Democrática Timorense (UDT), which pressed for continued links with Portugal; and the pro-independence FRETILIN.[18]

---

[14] Suzanne Katzenstein, "Hybrid Tribunals: Searching for Justice in East Timor," *Harvard Human Rights Journal*, Vol. 16, 2003, pp. 245–278, p. 248.

[15] Kingsbury, 2009, p. 74.

[16] Kingsbury, 2009, p. 78.

[17] Dobbins, Jones, Crane, Rathmell, et al., 2005, p. 157; Richard Caplan, *International Governance of War-Torn Territories: Rule and Reconstruction*, New York: Oxford University Press, 2005, p. 138. See also World Bank, *East Timor: Building a Nation—A Framework for Reconstruction and Development*, Governance Background Paper, November 1999, Annex I.

[18] Kingsbury, 2009, pp. 44–46.

After the end of Portuguese rule in 1975 (brought on by Portugal's own revolution and democratic transition), disagreements between these different parties over East Timor's political future evolved into a civil war. In December 1975, Indonesia invaded East Timor, engaging FRETILIN in battles and gradually gaining control over the territory. In May 1976, a regional assembly of pro-Indonesian parties invited Indonesia to annex East Timor.[19] FRETILIN, along with the United Nations, contested this annexation, and the group's military wing, FALINTIL, engaged for the next 24 years in an armed struggle against Indonesian occupation. The August 1999 referendum that eventually took place under UN supervision saw a voter turnout of 98 percent of all registered voters, 78.5 percent of whom chose independence.[20]

Institutional

Indonesia's abrupt and violent exit from East Timor left the territory with no functioning public institutions or institutional capacity. Along with the anti-independence militias, the territory's entire administrative apparatus left the territory, so that, even if there had been no destruction of the infrastructure, there would still have been little local human resource capacity remaining to provide government services.[21]

Nation-Building Efforts

Nation-building in East Timor started with a civilian UN Mission in East Timor (UNAMET), which organized the August 1999 referen-

---

[19] Kingsbury, 2009, pp. 44–46.

[20] Simon Chesterman, "East Timor," in Mats R. Berdal and Spyros Economides, eds., *United Nations Interventionism, 1991–2004*, Cambridge, UK: Cambridge University Press, 2007, pp. 192–216, p. 194. East Timor's population was asked to vote on the following questions: "Do you accept the proposed special autonomy status for East Timor within the unitary state of the Republic of Indonesia? Or, Do you reject the proposed special autonomy for East Timor, leading to East Timor's separation from Indonesia?" (see Smith and Dee, 2006, p. 397).

[21] Kingsbury, 2009, p. 78.

dum. Following the vote for independence and the ensuing violence, most of the UNAMET staff was evacuated. On September 20, 1999, after the militias had already perpetrated the worst atrocities, Indonesia agreed to allow and the United Nations mandated an Australian-led force, International Force for East Timor (INTERFET), to restore order. This was quickly followed by the UN peacekeeping mission, UNTAET, with a mandate to temporarily administer the territory and assist it in its transition toward independence.

Geographical and Geopolitical

East Timor has been heavily influenced by its more-powerful neighbors, most notably Indonesia but also Australia. Its original attempt at independence was snuffed out by Indonesia in 1975; its opportunity to decide on independence 24 years later was granted by Indonesia as a result of pressure from even more-powerful states. The resultant violence was stimulated and supported by Indonesia. International peacekeepers led by Australia were permitted to deploy by Indonesia, again under external pressures, and Indonesia's subsequent hands-off behavior vastly eased the international community's efforts to pacify and build an East Timor state.

Australia led military interventions under UN mandates in 1999 and again in 2002. Australia also provided the core of the subsequent UN peacekeeping operations. Australia was simultaneously engaged, however, in a dispute with East Timor over revenue sharing from oil reserves from the Timor Sea. Indonesia had granted Australia significant concessions in this area in exchange for recognizing its annexation of East Timor—an arrangement that became null and void when East Timor separated from Indonesia. At stake were significant revenues from proven oil fields that were geographically located within East Timor's seabed boundaries and would be vital for East Timor's economic development. The UN administration, while not fully settling this dispute, was able to negotiate with Australia a commitment for a steady source of revenue for East Timor, which proved crucial in its economic recovery.[22]

---

[22] Dobbins, Jones, Crane, Rathmell, et al., 2005, p. 173.

Cultural and Social

The UN mission was mandated to ensure that all those responsible for violence be brought to justice and to take all necessary steps to repatriate refugees[23]—tasks regarded as essential for social reconciliation.[24] A fundamental tension existed between these two objectives, however, because many refugees were former militia members who feared prosecution if they returned. Further, among those susceptible to indictment were influential leaders whose cooperation was politically necessary to make the repatriation process a success. The United Nations eventually chose to prioritize refugee return and reconciliation over a vigorous prosecution policy.[25] With many East Timorese dissatisfied with the progress made by the UN Serious Crimes Unit, which was responsible for prosecutions, UNTAET established in 2001 a Commission for Reception, Truth and Reconciliation.[26]

Language politics also had a significant impact on UNTAET's nation-building efforts. The choice by East Timor's elite to designate Portuguese—which only 5 percent of the population spoke—as an official language was particularly controversial. The preferred choice of a majority was Bahasa Indonesia, whose use was more widespread in the country, but this was rejected by the Portuguese speakers, ironically enough, as the "colonial" language. This decision has done little to encourage East Timorese unity.[27]

---

[23] The violence of September 1999 created circa 250,000 refugees.

[24] UN Security Council, 1999, Articles 10 and 16.

[25] Calin Trenkov-Wermuth, *United Nations Justice: Legal and Judicial Reform in Governance Operations*, Shibuya-ku, Japan: UN University Press, 2010, p. 111. See also Sylvia de Bertodano, "East Timor: Trials and Tribulations," in Cesare Romano, André Nollkaemper, and Jann K. Kleffner, eds., *Internationalized Criminal Courts and Tribunals: Sierra Leone, East Timor, Kosovo, and Cambodia*, Oxford, UK: Oxford University Press, 2004, pp. 79–98, pp. 82–83.

[26] Chesterman, 2007, p. 207; UNTAET, *On the Establishment of a Commission for Reception, Truth and Reconciliation in East Timor*, UNTAET/REG/2001/10, July 13, 2001b.

[27] Kingsbury, 2009, p. 93.

Economic

When UNTAET began its mission in October 1999, it became responsible for governing one of the poorest places in Asia. The UN mission's
assessed contribution budget of close to US$1.28 billion for the transi-
tion period represented about 70 percent of total international contributions. The remainder came from bilateral agencies and NGOs; the
UN Trust Fund; the Trust Fund for East Timor; and nonhumanitarian projects by UN agencies.[28] A World Bank assessment found coordination among these different funding sources to be inadequate and
concluded that donors' different modalities for aid disbursement "created barriers to national ownership of the reconstruction planning process in the initial period, and prevented the integration of all funding
sources into the national budget."[29]

Other international institutions—in particular, the IMF—played
key roles in East Timor's economic reconstruction. The IMF supported
UNTAET's establishment of a Central Payments Office tasked with
helping clear payments, transfer funds, and more generally fulfill the
tasks of a central bank.[30] The IMF was also instrumental in introducing
the U.S. dollar as East Timor's new currency in January 2000, based
on an assessment that it would be unwise to create a national currency
while the financial market was not functioning and the appropriate
institutional and legal frameworks were not yet in place.[31] The adoption of the dollar initially increased inflation, leading to more poverty
for most East Timorese, but eventually had a stabilizing effect on the
economy.[32] Other key tasks the IMF undertook in East Timor included
establishing a fiscal framework, designing a tax system, establishing a

---

[28] Klaus Rohland and Sarah Cliffe, *The East Timor Reconstruction Program: Successes, Problems and Tradeoffs*, Washington, D.C.: IBRD, 2002, p. 7.

[29] Rohland and Cliffe, 2002, p. ii.

[30] UNTAET, *On the Establishment of a Central Payments Office of East Timor*, UNTAET/
REG/2000/6, January 22, 2000a.

[31] Dobbins, Jones, Crane, Rathmell, et al., 2005, p. 175.

[32] Kingsbury, 2009, p. 88; CountryWatch, *East Timor: 2012 Country Review*, Houston,
Texas, 2012, p. 71.

Central Fiscal Authority, budgeting expenditures, and providing technical assistance for the design of a macroeconomic policy framework.[33]

Political

After the violence of 1999, national unity became a recurring theme in East Timorese politics. FALINTIL leader Xanana Gusmão created a new political entity, the National Council of Maubere Resistance (Conselho Nacional da Resistência Maubere, or CNRM, later the National Council of Timorese Resistance or Conselho Nacional de Resistência Timorense [CNRT]), which aimed at crossing over party lines. In July 2001, an overwhelming majority of East Timor's registered political parties—14 out of a total of 16—signed a Pact of National Unity supporting the principle of nonviolence and affirming their respect for the results of the upcoming Constituent Assembly elections. The political balance, however, soon proved most favorable to FRETILIN, which won 55 of the 88 seats in the Constituent Assembly in August 2001, in spite of electoral rules designed precisely to prevent the clear domination of one party. A decision was made soon after to turn the Constituent Assembly, which was charged with creating a new constitution, into the first legislature, so as to avoid having new elections. This decision created resentment among FRETILIN's political opposition, which would have to wait until 2007 for the next elections.[34] In later elections, FRETILIN's share of the vote has diminished, and there has been alternation of power.

The constitution was adopted on March 9, 2002. Though supporting constitution-making was not part of its initial mandate, UNTAET played an important role in the process, setting up rules for the Constituent Assembly's election, voting procedures in the assembly for adoption of the constitution, and the procedures for popular consultations. UNTAET did not, however, give any guidelines regarding

---

[33] Dobbins, Jones, Crane, Rathmell, et al., 2005, p. 175.

[34] Sven Gunnar Simonsen, "The Authoritarian Temptation in East Timor: Nationbuilding and the Need for Inclusive Governance," *Asian Survey*, Vol. 46, No. 4, July–August 2006, pp. 575–596, pp. 579–582; Philipp Dann and Zaid Al-Ali, "The International *Pouvoir Constituant*: Constitution-Making Under External Influence in Iraq, Sudan and East Timor," *Max Planck Yearbook of United Nations Law*, Vol. 10, 2006, pp. 423–463, p. 432.

the contents of the constitution.[35] The FRETILIN majority within the assembly largely dictated the substance of the constitution, while the popular consultations that were supposed to mitigate this influence mostly failed to play that role.[36]

Institutional

The United Nations had to both govern East Timor and prepare it for a more or less self-sufficient independence. This at least provided the UN mission a clearer objective than its counterpart mission in Kosovo, which was responsible for governing that territory without any international agreement on its ultimate status.

The United Nations nevertheless encountered an almost immediate tension in East Timor between administering the territory and transferring authority to local, almost entirely unprepared hands.[37] In December 1999, Special Representative of the Secretary-General (SRSG) Sérgio Vieira de Mello established and chaired a 15-member National Consultative Council (NCC), including four members from UNTAET.[38] The NCC's purely consultative nature, however, did little to quell local desires for political empowerment and increasingly vocal calls for greater and more-direct political participation.[39] The SRSG's response was to announce in April 2000 the appointment of Timorese

---

[35] Dann and Al-Ali, 2006, p. 433, note that "There seems to have been hardly any direct international influence on the Constitutional Assembly's proceedings." See also Louis Aucoin and Michele Brandt, "East Timor's Constitutional Passage to Independence," in Laurel Miller and Louis Aucoin, eds., *Framing the State in Times of Transition: Case Studies in Constitution Making*, Washington, D.C.: U.S. Institute of Peace Press, 2010, pp. 245–274.

[36] Dann and Al-Ali, 2006, pp. 432–434.

[37] See UN Security Council, 1999; Article 1 vested UNTAET with the power to "exercise all legislative and executive authority, including the administration of justice," while Article 8 stressed the need for UNTAET to "consult and cooperate closely with the East Timorese . . . with a view to the development of local democratic institutions . . . and the transfer to these institutions of its administrative and public service functions." On this tension, see also Caplan, 2005, and Chesterman, 2007.

[38] UNTAET, *On the Establishment of the National Consultative Council*, UNTAET/ REG/1999/2, December 2, 1999.

[39] Chesterman, 2007, p. 200. See also UNTAET, *On the Establishment of a National Council*, UNTAET/REG/2000/24, July 14, 2000c.

deputy district administrators, who would work alongside the 13 UN district administrators; the opening of NCC proceedings to local NGOs and FALINTIL; and the establishment of district advisory councils, which would be more representative of East Timorese society than was feasible in the NCC.[40]

These changes did not prove sufficient. In May 2000, José Ramos-Horta, who would later become East Timor's foreign minister and subsequently its president, officially requested from UN Secretary-General Kofi Annan that UNTAET replace all district administrators with local leaders.[41] Vieira de Mello responded to these demands by considering two options: a "technocratic model," which would see East Timorese entirely staff the administration and yield a fully national civil service by the time of independence, and a "political model," which would allow East Timorese to hold ministerial portfolios in the interim government. Eventually choosing the political model, UNTAET established in July 2000 a National Council, whose initial 33 and eventual 36 members included representatives from a broad selection of civil society, interest groups, and organizations.[42] Although members were exclusively East Timorese, the SRSG retained the prerogative of appointing them.[43] He also established a Cabinet of the Transitional Government in East Timor on the same day,[44] assigning four portfolios to international staff and four portfolios (internal administration, infrastructure, economic affairs, and social affairs) to East Timorese.[45]

UNTAET moved more quickly to inject East Timorese staff into the justice system than into the institutions in charge of civil and

---

[40] Sérgio Vieira de Mello, press briefing, Dili, April 5, 2000 (cited in Chesterman, 2007, p. 200).

[41] Caplan, 2005, p. 98.

[42] UNTAET, 2000c.

[43] Chesterman, 2007, p. 200.

[44] UNTAET, *On the Establishment of the Cabinet of the Transitional Government in East Timor*, UNTAET/REG/2000/23, July 14, 2000b.

[45] Eventually, he expanded it to five portfolios for locals when José Ramos-Horta was made cabinet member for foreign affairs (Chesterman, 2007, p. 202).

political affairs.[46] Given the minimal qualifications of local candidates for legal and judicial positions, UNTAET devised a three-step training program consisting of a one-week quick-impact course prior to the appointment, job training while in office, and association with a mentor. Even though most prospective local jurists had not had sufficient time to acquire adequate skills, UNTAET handed over complete control over the judiciary to the East Timorese, as well as complete jurisdiction over ordinary crimes, in January 2000, two months after it had started its mission.[47]

Linguistic division remained a key issue. The choice of Portuguese as the official language, one that 95 percent of the population could not speak, made justice reform and specifically access to the justice system challenging. As a consequence of its language policy, East Timor's elite lobbied for more Portuguese speakers in UNTAET, irrespective of their other qualifications, resulting at times in the hiring of inadequately skilled personnel.[48] The Timorese-administered Ministry of Justice had a preference for appointments from Lusophone countries; it turned down public defenders and judges from English-speaking countries simply because of the language they spoke. This meant that important positions went unfilled and that key institutions, such as the court of appeals, were unable to function for an extended period of time.[49]

UNTAET was slow to establish a local military, the FALINTIL-Forças de Defesa de Timor Leste (F-FDTL), which was constituted

---

[46] Joel C. Beauvais, "Benevolent Despotism: A Critique of U.N. State-Building in East Timor," *New York University Journal of International Law and Politics*, Vol. 33, Summer 2001, pp. 1101–1178, p. 1149.

[47] Trenkov-Wermuth, 2010, p. 106. See also Katzenstein, 2003, p. 254. It should be noted, however, that the Serious Crimes Unit and the special panels remained primarily UN entities.

[48] Kingsbury, 2009, pp. 92–94.

[49] Trenkov-Wermuth, 2010, p. 113; see also David Cohen, "Seeking Justice on the Cheap: Is the East Timor Tribunal Really a Model for the Future?" *Asia Pacific Issues*, Vol. 61, August 2002; Katzenstein, 2003, p. 269.

only in January 2001.[50] This force included 650 former FALINTIL fighters, while another 1,300 entered the FALINTIL Reinsertion Assistance Program, which provided them with tools, grants, and training to promote their demobilization and reintegration into civilian society.[51] UNTAET's Australian contingent was the primary provider of training for the F-FDTL, while the United States supplied equipment. A rift quickly appeared between former FALINTIL members, who had fought against Indonesia and pro-Indonesian militia, and new recruits. The first category of soldiers came mostly from the east of the country, while new recruits came from the west—an important source of tensions in a country where regional divides are strong markers of political and social identity.

A further division existed between the F-FDTL and the new police, the National Police of East Timor (Policia Nacional de Timor-Leste, or PNTL). The PNTL were recruited and trained by UN CIVPOL, with Australia providing, after 2004, management and technical assistance with British funding.[52] The perception that the police were receiving more donor attention than the army was a source of tension between the two institutions, which were also supporting competing factions of the FALINTIL.[53] The police were perceived as a "Westerner" institution (that is dominated by people from the west of the country), while the army was mainly "Easterner."[54] The inability of international donors to alter these perceptions, both within the

---

[50] UNTAET, *On the Establishment of a Defence Force for East Timor*, UNTAET/REG/2001/1, January 31, 2001a.

[51] Caplan, 2005, p. 155.

[52] Ludovic Hood, "Security Sector Reform in East Timor, 1999–2004," *International Peacekeeping*, Vol. 13, No. 1, 2006, pp. 60–77, p. 64. The Australian police program benefited from UK funding until 2009 (see Andrew Goldsmith and Sinclair Dinnen, "Transnational Police Building: Critical Lessons from Timor-Leste and Solomon Islands," *Third World Quarterly*, Vol. 28, No. 6, 2007, pp. 1091–1109, p. 1098).

[53] Hood, 2006, p. 73; Nicolas Lemay-Hébert, "UNPOL and Police Reform in Timor-Leste: Accomplishments and Setbacks," *International Peacekeeping*, Vol. 16, No. 3, 2009, pp. 393–406, p. 395.

[54] International Crisis Group, *Handing Back Responsibility to Timor-Leste's Police*, December 3, 2009b, p. 3, note 14.

F-FDTL and between the military and the police, eventually led to a major political and institutional crisis that brought the country to the brink of collapse in 2006.

Outcomes

In addition to sporadic outbreaks of violence, such as riots in December 2002 and incidents surrounding the 2007 elections, East Timor experienced two major crises. The first led to a collapse of state authority in 2006 as a result of a dispute between the military and the government over the firing of 600 soldiers. This decision led to an outbreak of violence between the police and former soldiers and deteriorated into general lawlessness. The violence was brought under control only by the reinsertion of international forces and the initiation of a new UN peacekeeping mission that remained in place in early 2012 with some 1,200 UN CIVPOL still deployed.

A second serious breach of security, which occurred in February 2008, involved the successful attack by rebel leader (and escaped prisoner) Alfredo Reinado and his gang against President Ramos-Horta and Prime Minister Gusmão in their homes, resulting in the former being severely injured.[55]

Local Attitudes
Although the UN presence had been broadly welcomed by East Timor's political elite, popular frustrations over the economic situation and resentment against foreigners who seemed removed from the everyday hardships of the local community made the UN's large, white, four-wheel-drive vehicles a popular target for attacks, such as rock throwing or dart firing. East Timorese politicians blamed INTERFET for a dramatic prison break in 2006, and a FRETILIN-led political campaign accused Australian soldiers of having taken sides in the violence of 2006.[56]

---

[55] Kingsbury, 2009, p. 189. Reinado and one of his men were killed in the attacks.

[56] See Kingsbury, 2009, pp. 86, 152.

Geographical and Geopolitical

Although Australia's intervention initially made Australia popular with the Timorese, the inability of the two countries to come to an agreement over oil fields soon resulted in a deterioration of this relationship. The dispute was partially resolved in 2006 when the two countries signed the Treaty on Certain Maritime Arrangements in the Timor Sea, agreeing to split revenues on a 50-50 basis and to defer other disputed matters for 50 years.[57]

From the time of independence, East Timor and Indonesia have made constant efforts to put the past behind them and build peaceful relations. Indonesia's president attended East Timor's independence ceremony in 2002. East Timor did not seek the arrest of the high-ranking Indonesian military officers who had been indicted by the UN tribunal. And the two countries reached agreements on the issues of Indonesian government assets in East Timor and the status of the Indonesian military cemetery in Dili. Indonesia supports East Timor's entry into ASEAN, and, as of 2009, Indonesia was the largest trading partner of East Timor for imports and the fourth for exports.[58] There have been some tensions along the Indonesia–East Timor border, where both countries are concerned with population movements and smuggling, but they have cooperated with the United Nations to address the issue and increase security in this area. The two countries signed a defense agreement in August 2011 to improve cooperation between their armed forces under the aegis of the Timor Leste–Indonesia Defense Joint Committee.[59]

---

[57] Australia and the Democratic Republic of Timor-Leste, "Treaty Between Australia and the Democratic Republic of Timor-Leste on Certain Maritime Arrangements in the Timor Sea," *Australian Treaty Series*, Sydney, January 12, 2006.

[58] "External Affairs (Indonesia): External Affairs," *Jane's Sentinel Security Assessment: Southeast Asia*, November 28, 2011; "External Affairs (East Timor): External Affairs," *Jane's Sentinel Security Assessment: Southeast Asia*, September 5, 2001; East Timor Ministry of Finance, *External Trade Statistics: Annual Report 2009*, Dili, 2009, pp. 9, 20.

[59] "External Affairs (Indonesia)," 2011.

Cultural and Social

Most perpetrators of the 1999 violence were never prosecuted. This reflected both President Gusmão's desire to build a good relationship with Indonesia rather than damage it through high-level indictments, and the importance of "forgiveness" in East Timorese culture.[60] The United Nations itself stood at a distance from the process it had helped set up; in 2003, it failed to support the indictment by its own prosecutors of Indonesian General Wiranto, who headed the Indonesian armed forces in 1999, and of seven other prominent individuals, including East Timor's former governor Abílio Soares. President Gusmão also opposed these indictments.[61]

By the time East Timor became independent on May 20, 2002, close to 220,000 of the 250,000 East Timorese refugees who had fled to West Timor had returned home. The UNHCR no longer considered the remaining 30,000 East Timorese in West Timor to be refugees.[62] The 2006 crisis, however, led to ethnic-based community violence—particularly Westerners against Easterners—and spurred another refugee crisis that displaced internally tens of thousands of East Timorese.[63] All eventually returned to their homes and received $4,000 in compensation,[64] but this violence demonstrated that tensions among East Timor's various social groups still have the potential to erupt.

Economic

During the three years of East Timor's transition toward independence, economic activity recovered quickly, and inflation fell from 140 percent in late 1999 to 7 percent in early 2003. The drawdown of the international presence in East Timor after 2002, however, negatively

---

[60] Trenkov-Wermuth, 2010, p. 164.

[61] Trenkov-Wermuth, 2010, p. 112.

[62] UNHCR, "East Timorese Refugee Saga Comes to an End," Geneva, December 30, 2002.

[63] Jane Perlez, "In East Timor, Refugees Born of Chaos, Carnage and Fear," *New York Times*, May 29, 2006.

[64] Kingsbury, 2009, p. 207.

affected economic growth.[65] A more serious challenge to economic recovery was the civil unrest of 2006, which resulted in a severe contraction of the economy by 5.8 percent.[66]

After 2007, however, economic growth rebounded again as a result of improved security and public spending. Despite a decline of exports due to the global economic crisis, East Timor's economy grew by 5 percent in 2009, in part as a result of government spending that supported domestic demand. Such spending was made possible by East Timor's significant fiscal surplus due to revenue from large offshore petroleum resources; the surplus increased from 46 percent of nonoil GDP in 2004 to close to 400 percent of nonoil GDP in 2008 as a result of the rise in oil prices.

In spite of a budget surplus and no public debt, the country remains one of the least developed states in the world, with close to 50 percent of its population living in poverty.[67] Economic pressures present a threat to the country's stability because of high unemployment rates and dependence on oil. The country also remains heavily dependent on international assistance to feed its population.[68]

Political

Less than one year after UNTAET was created, local demands for greater political involvement led the UN mission to change its Office of Governance and Public Administration into the East Timor Transitional Authority and to establish a co-administration model, which remained in place until 2002.[69] This co-governance approach, however, failed to satisfy the East Timorese, and, in December 2000, cabinet ministers threatened to resign on the grounds that UNTAET failed to share decisionmaking power and did not provide them with adequate

---

[65] Dobbins, Jones, Crane, Rathmell, et al., 2005, p. 175.

[66] CountryWatch, 2012, p. 71.

[67] CountryWatch, 2012, p. 71.

[68] Kristen Blandford, "Profile 2011: Timor-Leste," Washington, D.C.: Fund for Peace, Country Profile CCPPR11TL, December 15, 2011.

[69] Caplan, 2005, pp. 99–100. See also Beauvais, 2001.

resources to carry out their mandate.[70] Such threats were frequently used—as was, in one instance, an actual resignation (later reversed) by Gusmão—as a means of pressuring UNTAET, which East Timorese argued was exceeding its mandated authority.

The SRSG responded to these claims by announcing in March 2001 the scheduling of elections for a Constituent Assembly five months later. A Council of Ministers composed exclusively of East Timorese was also established in September 2001.[71] Both bodies, however, remained subject to the authority of the SRSG. The Constituent Assembly was transformed into East Timor's first legislature when it voted to adopt a constitution in January 2002. Gusmão won the first presidential election in April 2002 with 82.7 percent of the vote. East Timor became fully independent on May 20, 2002.[72] Although UNTAET and subsequent UN missions helped the country transition from a postcolonial and postoccupation territory to a parliamentary democracy, the state remains "extremely fragile," according to the Failed State Index, where it ranks 23rd, right behind North Korea.[73]

Institutional

Indonesia's violent exit from East Timor left the territory with no functioning public institutions or institutional capacity. It is in this context that UNTAET was presented with the tasks of helping build an effective administration, police force, justice system, and national army. Ten years after independence, East Timorese political institutions are functioning. Despite political tensions, the country has held several

---

[70] Caplan, 2005, p. 116; in a letter to Vieira de Mello, the ministers wrote that "The East Timorese Cabinet members are caricatures of ministers in a government of a banana republic. They have no power, no duties, nor resources to function adequately" (cited in Caplan, 2005, p. 116). See also Mark Dodd, "Give Us a Free Hand or We Quit, E. Timor Leaders Say," *Sydney Morning Herald*, December 5, 2000.

[71] UNTAET, *On the Establishment of the Council of Ministers*, UNTAET/REG/2001/28, September 19, 2001c.

[72] Caplan, 2005, pp. 117–118.

[73] J. J. Messner, Nate Haken, Joelle Burbank, Kristen Blandford, Annie Janus, Melody Knight, and Kendall Lawrence, *The Failed States Index 2011*, Washington, D.C.: Fund for Peace, CR-11-14-FS, June 20, 2011.

presidential and legislative elections, and it has experienced democratic transitions of power.[74] Some serious governance issues remain, however, including corruption. In June 2012, for example, a former minister of justice received a five-year jail sentence for corruption, and the country ranks 143rd out of 182 countries in Transparency International's Corruption Perceptions Index.[75] A 2006 World Bank study reported both lack of equipment and capacity within the parliament and recommended a better separation in practice between the legislative and executive branches.[76]

The 2006 crisis brought about the institutional collapse of the police force, and, despite reform attempts over several years, it has not yet fully recovered. As of early 2012, the police force was still receiving international assistance to build its operational capability but remained an institution prone to politicization. Division of tasks between the police and the army is not clearly established, which has the potential to create more tensions in the future.[77] The prison system has not fared much better: A mass prison breakout in August 2002 was followed by another four years later, during which 56 prisoners managed to escape, including the rebel leader involved in the attacks against Ramos-Horta and Gusmão.

Although earlier political empowerment of East Timorese in certain areas may have been desirable, UNTAET's proactive "Timorization" of the justice system created some serious challenges. The lack of qualified local staff meant that key posts could not be filled quickly, leading to significant delays in trials and to prisoners being held in pretrial detention for longer periods than legally allowed. The appointed jurists and other justice system personnel were, for the most part,

---

[74] U.S. Department of State, "Timor-Leste (10/11/11)," Background Note, October 11, 2011b.

[75] "Internal Affairs (East Timor): Internal Affairs," *Jane's Sentinel Security Assessment: Southeast Asia*, July 11, 2012; Transparency International, 2011.

[76] Shabbir Cheema, Bertrand de Speville, Terhi Nieminen-Mäkynen, David Mattiske, and Peter Blunt, *Strengthening Accountability and Transparency in Timor-Leste*, Dili: United Nations Office in Timor-Leste, January 27, 2006, pp. 25–26.

[77] Lemay-Hébert, 2009, p. 401.

underqualified for their positions, leading frequently to the incorrect application of the law and an inability to provide effective defense. The decision to hand over judicial administration to East Timorese early allowed local actors to block important appointments of English-speaking jurists on a transitional basis and use funds for political purposes related to linguistic cleavages. Better use of funds and more-qualified appointees would have helped alleviate many of the issues that affected the justice system.[78] Delays in trials and lack of access to defense counsel were blamed for the mass jailbreak of August 2002, during which more than half of East Timor's prison population escaped.[79]

East Timor's World Bank score for government effectiveness has consistently decreased since 2006, placing it in the 10th percentile among all countries in 2010.[80] The fact that East Timor is essentially a "rentier" state highly dependent on oil revenue suggests that it is particularly at risk for revenue confiscation by the ruling elite and the entrenchment of patronage networks.[81]

Conclusions

What Local Factors Posed the Greatest Challenges?

The local factors within each category that were most important in shaping the environment in which nation-builders sought to promote an enduring peace included the following.

Geographical and Geopolitical

External dynamics—regime change in Portugal and Cold War politics—were crucial factors paving the way for Indonesia's annexation of East Timor in the mid-1970s and thus giving rise to the long

---

[78] Trenkov-Wermuth, 2010, p. 137.

[79] Simon Chesterman, *Justice Under International Administration: Kosovo, East Timor and Afghanistan*, Vienna: International Peace Institute, September 14, 2002. See also Jill Jolliffe, "Jail Breakout over Delays," *Age*, August 17, 2002.

[80] World Bank, undated (d).

[81] Peter Blunt, "The Political Economy of Accountability in Timor-Leste: Implications for Public Policy," *Public Administration and Development*, Vol. 29, 2009, pp. 89–100, p. 93.

struggle for independence and ultimately the violence of 1999. Once the geopolitical context changed and the question of independence was settled, the specific factors that precipitated conflict did not threaten to renew it, and space was created for nation-building interveners to try to build an East Timorese state.

Cultural and Social

The brutality of the Indonesian occupation had a dramatic impact on East Timorese society. The United Nations was mandated to ensure that those responsible for violence be brought to justice, on the assumption that justice was necessary for reconciliation. But most perpetrators were never prosecuted, largely because of President Gusmão's desire to build a good relationship with Indonesia and the importance of "forgiveness" in East Timorese culture. Good relations have been developed between East Timor and Indonesia, its former antagonist in the conflict, though this progress has been driven mostly by domestic actors rather than external actors engaged in promoting enduring peace.

Economic

Already very poor before the conflict, East Timor's economy and infrastructure were devastated during it. The United Nations had direct responsibility for the country's economic reconstruction during the postconflict period of transition to independence, and other international institutions also participated in creating new monetary and fiscal systems for the country. Exploitation of petroleum resources in recent years has enabled a rise in public spending and created a budget surplus, but socioeconomic development still remains low in East Timor, and economic pressures, such as high unemployment, could threaten the country's stability.

Political

Before 1999, political groups in East Timor organized around their differing stances on the preferred status of the territory. Afterward, the party that had consistently sought independence and contested Indonesian annexation (FRETILIN) became dominant in the first parliament and in the constitution-making process. Later, it performed less well in elections, and there has been some alternation of power in the country. Despite significant advances in democratization, the country continues to be dogged by political instability and civil unrest.

Institutional

East Timor was practically an institutional blank slate when UNTAET arrived. The UN mission tried to build institutional capacity while directly administering the territory during the transitional period. It cannot be considered to have been entirely successful, but the challenges that the mission faced were great. Limited progress in creating effective and professional new security institutions has been an important weakness in East Timor's institutional development. Rifts within and between the military and police (based on regional and political identity divides) have contributed to the persistence of instability in the country and the risk of future conflict.

Were Local Factors Modified or Circumvented to Promote Enduring Peace?

Ten years after the arrival of international forces, East Timor was at peace, democratization had advanced significantly, and per capita GDP had expanded by 42.7 percent, but government effectiveness remained weak, and the country was still in the low human development category despite having oil and gas resources. Given that the territory had no government and no history of self-government when international forces arrived, governance can be considered to have improved from that point. Although democratization has advanced, there was some regression between the fifth and tenth years after the arrival of the United Nations. Table 6.1 shows these outcomes, alongside key resources applied by nation-building interveners.

East Timorese society remains poor, largely illiterate, and badly divided along ethnic, geographic, and class lines but, at least in some respects, less so than when international forces arrived in 1999. Such conditions change only slowly. What did change dramatically, in 1999 and thereafter, was East Timor's geopolitical situation.

Indonesia seized East Timor in 1976 with international backing and agreed to give it up in 1999 under international pressure. The Indonesian Army's decision to support and give sanctuary to anti-independence militias initiated the postreferendum violence, and its withdrawal of that support enabled the subsequent international peacekeeping effort led and sustained by East Timor's other important neighbor, Australia.

Geopolitics was thus responsible for East Timor's transfer from Portuguese to Indonesian control in 1976. Geopolitics was largely responsible for that society's opportunity to choose independence in 1999, as it was for the Indonesian Army–inspired violence that ensued and then for the international intervention that followed. Given Indo-

Table 6.1
Postintervention Performance and Nation-Building Inputs in East Timor

Performance Indicator	Year of Intervention (1999)	5 Years Later	10 Years Later
At peace?	—	Yes	Yes
Government effectiveness (10-point scale)	NA	3.43	3.43
Freedom Index (10-point scale)	1.00[a]	7.00	6.25
HDI (10-point scale)	4.00	4.50	4.90
Cumulative growth in per capita GDP (in 1st 5 years and in 10 years after intervention) (%)	—	17.8	42.7
Nation-Building Input			
Peak military presence per capita, number of troops per 1,000 inhabitants	9.8		
Peak international civilian police presence per capita, number of police per 1,000 inhabitants	1.56		
Average annual per capita assistance in the first 5 years (constant 2010 US$)	361		

SOURCES: World Bank, undated (d); Freedom House, various years; UNDP, undated; IMF, undated; Dobbins, Jones, Crane, Chivvis, et al., 2008, Figures 9.2, 9.4, 9.9; UN Peace Operations, various years; World Bank, undated (c).

[a] Freedom House has no separate rating for East Timor in the pre-intervention context. Given that the society had suffered massive repression in the period immediately prior to the arrival of international forces, we have suggested a rating of 1 (the lowest) for the condition at the time of intervention.

nesia's hands-off attitude once international forces were deployed, at no point did peacekeepers need to seriously worry about a resumption of the conflict they had come to end, that between pro- and anti-independence forces. Rather, they had to focus on the task of preventing the emergence of an essentially new conflict among competing claimants for power and influence within the newly independent country. Even against this benign external environment, however, the international community faced a major challenge in preparing this small, impoverished, and long-abused society to govern itself for the first time in its history.

International authorities reestablished a semblance of law and order, brokered an understanding with Australia on revenue sharing from disputed oil fields, stabilized the economy and introduced a currency, ran successful elections, established institutions for local political participation, and managed to bring the territory to independence. However, the fragile security situation in the country has required a continued international peacekeeping presence. International forces were too quickly drawn down after independence and had to be reintroduced following the breakdown of order in 2006. It was not until March 2011 that the United Nations officially handed policing responsibilities back to the East Timorese authorities, yet, in January 2012, close to 1,200 UN CIVPOL officers were still deployed in the country. The UN mission concluded operations at the end of December 2012.[82]

---

[82] UN Integrated Mission in Timor-Leste, "Closure of UNMIT," c. 2012.

CHAPTER SEVEN

Sierra Leone

The civil war in Sierra Leone began in 1991 with an invasion of armed rebels coming from and supported by one of the contending factions in neighboring Liberia. In its final report published in 2004, the Sierra Leone Truth and Reconciliation Commission also cited poor gover-

Figure 7.1
Map of Sierra Leone

SOURCE: CIA, "Sierra Leone," *The World Factbook*, 2012f.

RAND *RR167-7.1*

nance, rampant corruption, denial of human rights, and disregard for democracy and the rule of law as key contributing factors to the war. A year earlier, Sierra Leone's National Recovery Strategy Assessment cited the same factors, along with economic deterioration and sub-regional instability.[1] After the end of the war in 2002, Sierra Leone received considerable attention from international donors, especially its former colonial ruler the United Kingdom.[2] Nation-building efforts have attempted to address the roots of the conflict by improving governance, strengthening state institutions, regulating the mining industry, providing opportunities for the young, and reforming Sierra Leone's armed forces. During more than a decade of nation-building, international donors have achieved mixed results, prompting them to redirect their efforts or change their strategies. Overall progress in Sierra Leone remains tenuous in spite of marked achievements because patronage and corruption prove hard to eradicate and the country remains extremely fragile economically.

Local Factors Before the Peace

Sierra Leone has significant commercially exploitable deposits of diamonds, bauxite, rutile, and gold. It is also endowed with forests, agricultural land, and fisheries. Sierra Leone has been politically unstable. And, like many other African states, Sierra Leone was governed by long-standing rulers who utilized patronage to stay in power. By the 1970s, the country had become what William Reno describes as a

---

[1] Karen Moore, Chris Squire, and Foday MacBailey, *Sierra Leone National Recovery Strategy Assessment*, Freetown: Government of Sierra Leone, December 24, 2003, pp. 2–5; Adrian Horn and Funmi Olonisakin, "United Kingdom–Led Security Sector Reform in Sierra Leone," *Civil Wars*, Vol. 8, No. 2, 2006, pp. 109–123, p. 110; Brian Thomson, *Sierra Leone: Reform or Relapse? Conflict and Governance Reform*, London: Chatham House, June 2007, p. 2.

[2] For more details on the UN and UK roles in the postconflict reconstruction of Sierra Leone, see Dobbins, Jones, Crane, Rathmell, et al., 2005, pp. 129–149; and Dobbins, Jones, Crane, Chivvis, et al., 2008, pp. 25–48.

"shadow state":[3] Government institutions were ineffective, focused on providing funds for ministers and employees. Sierra Leone was largely a failed state before the advent of the civil war.[4] The war only exacerbated those factors that helped precipitate it: Easily accessible and poorly regulated diamond resources fueled the conflict, the rebel movement Revolutionary United Front (RUF) attracted dissatisfied ethnic groups, and the economy deteriorated because of the war.

Geographical and Geopolitical

Sierra Leone's proximity to Liberia and the porosity of its borders have made the country vulnerable to spillovers from its neighbor's crises (see Figure 7.1).[5] The war in Sierra Leone started with a small group of RUF rebels, supported by the leader of the National Patriotic Front of Liberia (NPFL), Charles Taylor, that crossed the southern border between Liberia and Sierra Leone. One of Charles Taylor's motives for supporting the RUF was the prospect of taking advantage of Sierra Leone's considerable diamond resources to help him fund the NPFL.[6] Sierra Leone mainly has alluvial diamonds, which means that almost anyone with very limited equipment can potentially become a diamond miner.[7] Ease of extraction, combined with the fact that the size of diamonds makes them easy to smuggle, facilitated the use of diamonds to fund

---

[3] William Reno, *Corruption and State Politics in Sierra Leone*, Cambridge, UK: Cambridge University Press, 1995, p. 1.

[4] Thomson, 2007, p. 2; Kwaku Nuamah and I. William Zartman, *Case Study: Intervention in Sierra Leone*, case study prepared for the conference on Intervention in Internal Conflict, Center for International and Security Studies at Maryland, University of Maryland, December 7, 2001.

[5] John L. Hirsch, *Sierra Leone: Diamonds and the Struggle for Democracy*, Boulder, Colo.: Lynne Rienner, 2001, p. 24; Moore, Squire, and MacBailey, 2003, p. 9.

[6] William Reno, *Warlord Politics and African States*, Boulder, Colo.: Lynne Rienner Publishers, 1999, p. 123. For more details on the role of the Liberian civil war in the onset of the Sierra Leone conflict, see Paul Richards, *Fighting for the Rain Forest: War, Youth and Resources in Sierra Leone*, Oxford, UK: International African Institute in association with James Currey, 1996, pp. 2–4; Hirsch, 2001, p. 32; Paul Williams, "Fighting for Freetown: British Military Intervention in Sierra Leone," *Contemporary Security Policy*, Vol. 22, No. 3, 2001, pp. 140–168, p. 145; and Moore, Squire, and MacBailey, 2003, p. 9.

[7] Hirsch, 2001, p. 25.

the conflict.[8] During the war, the RUF was not the only group to use diamonds. Many elements of the army engaged in illicit mining, as did progovernment militias.[9]

Cultural and Social

The rural region of Sierra Leone bordering Liberia was vulnerable to the RUF incursion because of the human, as well as physical, terrain.[10] The Sierra Leonean population is divided among several ethnic and social groups, limiting the sense of national identity. The lack of national identity made it easier for the RUF to find recruits.

The first dividing line runs between the capital and the rest of the country. During the colonial period, the British established a colony in Freetown and concentrated their presence in the capital. In the rest of the country (the "Protectorate"), they largely delegated political authority to traditional local chiefs.[11] This divide between the "Westernized" capital and the countryside holds to this day. A second important dividing line runs between ethnic groups. Tribes and ethnicities usually lived together rather peacefully during the pre-independence era, but this changed as politicians started to rely on their own tribes to garner political support and as the population grew.[12] Although the role of ethnic tensions as a cause of the war should not be overstated,[13]

---

[8]   On this issue, see, for instance, Ola Olsson, "Conflict Diamonds," *Journal of Development Economics*, Vol. 82, No. 2, March 2007, pp. 267–286, p. 268.

[9]   Reno, 1999, p. 127; V. A. B. Davies, "Sierra Leone: Ironic Tragedy," *Journal of African Economies*, Vol. 9, No. 3, 2000, pp. 349–369, p. 360.

[10]   On tensions between the border area and Freetown that pre-date the war, see Richards, 1996, pp. 22, 42–48.

[11]   Thomson, 2007, p. 2.

[12]   Hirsch, 2001, p. 24.

[13]   John Bellows and Edward Miguel, "War and Institutions: New Evidence from Sierra Leone," *American Economic Review*, Vol. 96, No. 2, 2006, pp. 394–399, p. 395, claim that "neither ethnic nor religious divisions played a central role in driving the conflict," and Alfred B. Zack-Williams, "Sierra Leone: The Political Economy of Civil War, 1991–98," *Third World Quarterly*, Vol. 20, No. 1, February 1999, pp. 143–162, p. 148, states that the war in Sierra Leone "did not assume the ethnic and/or religious dimensions of other crises, such as those in Liberia or Sudan." It is also worth noting that RUF membership transcended

the resentment generated by successive leaders favoring one ethnicity or one region over the others played an important role in destroying the legitimacy of the state and the loyalty of the population toward anything larger than their group, region, or party. When the RUF entered Sierra Leone in 1991, leaders easily found supporters in the southeastern region who felt aggrieved by the policies of President Joseph Momoh from the northern-backed All People's Congress (APC) party.[14]

Another important factor that facilitated and sustained the conflict was the emergence of a disaffected youth population.[15] Before and shortly after independence, Sierra Leone's system of higher education had an excellent reputation; Fourah Bay College, in particular, attracted students from all over the region, earning it the nickname "the Athens of West Africa."[16] During the rule of President Siaka Stevens from 1968 to 1985, this situation dramatically changed. Public spending on education was nearly halved between the mid-1970s and the late 1980s.[17] The overwhelming majority of youth grew up without education and struggled to find employment.[18] In 1985, Sierra Leone had the lowest adult literacy rate out of the 160 countries listed in the UNDP's 1991 Human Development Report—13.3 percent.[19] During the war, the lack of educational and economic opportunities played an important role in making recruits available for the different fighting

---

ethnic groups (phone discussion with Col. [Ret.] Thomas Dempsey, former U.S. military attaché for Liberia and Sierra Leone [1998–1999], February 12, 2010).

[14] Davies, 2000, p. 358.

[15] Paul Collier and Anke Hoeffler found that high rates of secondary-school enrollment reduce the risk of conflict. See Collier and Hoeffler, 2004b, p. 574.

[16] Hirsch, 2001, p. 23; Davies, 2000, p. 349.

[17] Ibrahim Abdullah, "Bush Path to Destruction: The Origin and Character of the Revolutionary United Front/Sierra Leone," *Journal of Modern African Studies*, Vol. 36, No. 2, June 1998, pp. 203–235, p. 211.

[18] Hirsch, 2001, p. 30.

[19] UNDP, *Human Development Report 1991: Financing Human Development*, New York: Oxford University Press, 1991, p. 121.

factions. The RUF promised them food and money but also, in some cases, scholarships to study abroad.[20]

Overall, the war only compounded the difficulties of a population that was already struggling to make a living before the conflict. The RUF's systematic mutilation of civilians had dramatic social and economic consequences for a rural population largely made of farmers. A large number of combatants were women and children, many of whom were subjected to abuse and exposed to sexually transmitted diseases, such as HIV/AIDS.[21] Sierra Leone's youth issue was made more acute by the conflict. Almost 7,000 of the combatants demobilized by the UN Mission in Sierra Leone (UNAMSIL) were child soldiers.[22]

Economic

In spite of its many natural resources, Sierra Leone's economy steadily declined during the postindependence years. By 1991, the country was at the bottom of the UNDP HDI,[23] and the value of agricultural production had plummeted to $10 million.[24] In the mid-1980s, Sierra Leone's foreign debt was already equivalent to nearly 300 percent of its export revenue.[25]

---

[20] Macartan Humphreys and Jeremy Weinstein, *What the Fighters Say: A Survey of Ex-Combatants in Sierra Leone, June–August 2003*, New York: Columbia University, Stanford University, and Post-Conflict Reintegration Initiative for Development and Empowerment, July 2004, p. 26.

[21] Zack-Williams, 1999, p. 154.

[22] "Sierra Leone: Disarmament and Rehabilation [sic] Completed After Five Years," Integrated Regional Information Networks, February 4, 2004. This number includes only child soldiers who took part in the disarmament, demobilization, and reintegration (DDR) program. The overall number of child soldiers is much larger. Girls, in particular, are believed to have represented about 30 percent of child soldiers but only 8 percent of those child soldiers who took part in the DDR program (Coalition to Stop the Use of Child Soldiers, *Child Soldiers: Global Report 2008*, London, 2008).

[23] Sierra Leone ranked 160th out of 160 countries in UNDP's 1991 HDI (UNDP, 1991, p. 121).

[24] Zack-Williams, 1999, p. 149.

[25] David Fashole Luke and Stephen P. Riley, "The Politics of Economic Decline in Sierra Leone," *Journal of Modern African Studies*, Vol. 27, No. 1, March 1989, pp. 133–141, p. 138.

Rural areas, which are home to 80 percent of Sierra Leone's population, were affected even more acutely than the capital was.[26] In 1990, only 22 percent of the population in rural areas had access to clean water, as opposed to 83 percent in the cities.[27] President Stevens' disinterest in the development of rural areas can be explained by the fact that his political clients were mostly located in Freetown, making it politically unnecessary for him to provide services to the rest of the country. The south of the country, which does not traditionally support the APC (President Stevens' party), received the least government funding for development, fueling lasting resentment among the population.[28]

The mismanagement of the diamond industry played a large part in the fall in revenues experienced by Sierra Leone from 1970 to 1990.[29] In the 1960s, diamonds provided Sierra Leone with revenue amounting to one-fifth of the country's GDP and 70 percent of its foreign exchange earnings.[30] Stevens garnered support for his party before the 1967 elections by promising illicit miners that he would not interfere with their activities if they helped him get elected. As a result, by 1988, most of the diamond mining had shifted to the illicit sphere: The value of licitly exported diamonds had plummeted to $22,000.[31] When President Momoh attempted to reassert the state's authority over the mining industry, he did so through two military operations that resulted in an estimated 25,000 miners losing their livelihoods without

---

[26] Davies, 2000, p. 354.

[27] Davies, 2000, p. 355.

[28] Zack-Williams, 1999, p. 145. On how this neglect of the countryside facilitated the onset of war in several ways, see Davies, 2000, p. 355.

[29] For a detailed history of diamond mining in Sierra Leone, see Ian Smillie, Lansana Gberie, and Ralph Hazleton, *The Heart of the Matter: Sierra Leone, Diamonds and Human Security—Completed Report*, Ottawa: Partnership Africa Canada, 2000.

[30] Reno, 1999, p. 116; International Crisis Group, *Sierra Leone: The Election Opportunity*, Africa Report 129, July 12, 2007c, pp. 9–10.

[31] Reno, 1999, p. 120. On the collapse of Sierra Leone's national mining industry, see, for instance, Davies, 2000, p. 354.

any sustainable alternative.[32] Many joined the ranks of the RUF when the war broke out.[33]

The overall economic situation was only made worse by the war, which destroyed half of the country's infrastructure.[34] Although state revenue remained minimal, by early 1995, the military absorbed an estimated 75 percent of public spending.[35] The state lost what little control it had over its resources; the RUF looted the countryside, plundering natural and mining resources (a practice called "Operation Pay Yourself").

Political

Sierra Leone's patronage system facilitated the war in several ways. First, such systems are particularly vulnerable to external shocks, such as economic crises, because they are based on a leader or ruling coalition providing privileges to its supporters rather than on the creation of a political and moral community. When there are no more resources to distribute to political clients, the system collapses.[36] Second, large segments of the population did not benefit from the patronage networks and resented the government for not providing them with the most-basic public services.[37] This segment of the population was the first one to take up arms with the RUF when the war broke out in 1991. Third, the patronage system created a highly fragmented state, with patronage networks competing against each other.[38] Finally, because the system stifled dissent from those who do not benefit from it, violence became an option for the disgruntled population.[39]

---

[32] Reno, 1999, p. 121.

[33] Reno, 1995, p. 124.

[34] Moore, Squire, and MacBailey, 2003, p. 1.

[35] Reno, 1999, p. 126.

[36] Williams, 2001, p. 143.

[37] Zack-Williams, 1999, p. 159.

[38] Reno, 1995, pp. 127–128.

[39] Williams, 2001, p. 143.

Institutional

Prior to the conflict, the lack of effective state institutions enabled rampant corruption and the shrinking of the formal economy, especially in the extractive industries,[40] and allowed President Stevens to put into place an elaborate patronage system funded by large-scale looting of state revenue.[41] Stevens' replacement in 1985 by Momoh did nothing to improve the situation. At that point, the state was nearing bankruptcy. Unpaid civil servants looted government property and offices, while the capital experienced shortages of fuel, electricity, and water.[42] Many emigrated.[43]

The lack of capacity of Sierra Leone's army cannot directly be counted among the root causes of war, but it contributed to prolonging the war. President Stevens purposefully sidelined the country's armed forces during his rule, relying instead on a paramilitary unit (the Internal Security Unit) whose focus was regime security.[44] The number of troops was never higher than 2,000–3,000.[45] During the war, appalling fighting conditions for the military resulted in large numbers of soldiers colluding with the RUF, looting property, and engaging in illicit mining.[46] The Sierra Leone Police (SLP) was another dysfunctional institution, with unskilled and underpaid personnel who lacked

---

[40] Davies, 2000, p. 354.

[41] Reno, 1995, pp. 79–103; Zack-Williams, 1999, p. 144. It is estimated that, by the end of his life, Stevens had accumulated close to $500 million in personal wealth (Reno, 1999, p. 116).

[42] Davies, 2000, p. 354; Hirsch, 2001, p. 30.

[43] Hirsch, 2001, p. 30.

[44] Reno, 1999, p. 116; Hirsch, 2001, p. 36; International Crisis Group, *Sierra Leone: Time for a New Military and Political Strategy*, Africa Report 28, April 11, 2001, p. 5.

[45] Reno, 1999, p. 116; International Crisis Group, 2001, p. 5.

[46] International Crisis Group, 2001, p. 6; Hirsch, 2001, p. 36; Krijn Peters and Paul Richards, "'Why We Fight': Voices of Youth Combatants in Sierra Leone," *Africa: Journal of the International African Institute*, Vol. 68, No. 2, 1998, pp. 183–210, pp. 184–185.

equipment and vehicles and earned a reputation for inefficiency and corruption.[47]

Nation-Building Efforts

Nation-building in Sierra Leone started before the conflict officially ended in January 2002. As early as 1998, the United Kingdom started to elaborate plans for a reform of the security sector with the Sierra Leonean government.[48] In 1999, the United Nations deployed a peace-keeping force, UNAMSIL, which succeeded the Nigeria-led Economic Community of West African States Monitoring Group that had been deployed in 1997. The international community addressed governance and economic issues with a particular focus on offering more opportunities to the young, who had been the prime recruits of the RUF. Improving governance included efforts aimed at increasing accountability of public officials, countering rampant corruption, decentralizing government, and reforming the army and police. On the economic front, measures included restructuring and monitoring the diamond industry and more generally restoring the state's ability to generate revenue. As their programs met or failed to meet expectations, donors readjusted their focus and strategies—addressing issues that they had initially ignored, involving new actors, and sometimes revising their programs to tackle the most-challenging local factors with which they were confronted.

Geographical and Geopolitical

After the war, Sierra Leone remained vulnerable to its neighbors' instability, especially until Liberia's conflict ended in 2003. Although the continuation of the war in Liberia did not directly undermine the

---

[47] Horn and Olonisakin, 2006, p. 111; Sarah Meek, "Policing Sierra Leone," in Mark Malan, Sarah Meek, Thokozani Thusi, Jeremy Ginifer, and Patrick Coker, eds., *Sierra Leone: Building the Road to Recovery*, Pretoria: Institute for Security Studies, Monograph 80, March 1, 2003, pp. 105–116, p. 105.

[48] Thomson, 2007, pp. 5–8.

peace process in Sierra Leone, it resulted in continued insecurity in the border area with at least one case of an incursion by Liberian rebels in January 2003.[49] UNAMSIL helped monitor the border jointly with the UN Mission in Liberia (UNMIL), a multidimensional peacekeeping operation established in 1993 under Chapter VII of the UN Charter.[50] The most important security measure, however, was provided by the United Kingdom's "over-the-horizon guarantee" to intervene militarily if the government were to fall under grave threat again.[51]

With UN support, in 2004, Sierra Leone reactivated a dormant regional mechanism, the Mano River Union, which had been created in 1973 to increase trade among its member states.[52] An unresolved territorial dispute between Sierra Leone and Guinea, in which both claimed ownership of the border town of Yenga, made cooperation within the union difficult, leading the United Kingdom and France to provide technical experts to both countries in order to examine the issue and hold consultations in the disputed area.[53]

Cultural and Social

In an attempt to heal the traumas of the war, the government, with the support of international donors, set up two transitional justice mechanisms: the Special Court for Sierra Leone, which was tasked with bringing to trial those most responsible for war crimes and crimes against humanity, and the Truth and Reconciliation Commission, whose aim

---

[49] International Crisis Group, *Tackling Liberia: The Eye of the Regional Storm*, Africa Report 662, April 30, 2003b, p. 13.

[50] UN Security Council, *Twenty-Seventh Report of the Secretary-General on the United Nations Mission in Sierra Leone*, S/2005/777, December 12, 2005, ¶ 16. Regarding UNMIL and the predecessor, more-limited, UN missions and offices in Liberia, see UNMIL, "UNMIL Background," undated.

[51] International Crisis Group, *Liberia and Sierra Leone: Rebuilding Failed States*, Africa Report 87, December 8, 2004, pp. 2, 21.

[52] Sierra Leone and Liberia were the founding members of the Mano River Union. Guinea joined in 1980 (Peter Robson, "The Mano River Union," *Journal of Modern African Studies*, Vol. 20, No. 4, December 1982, pp. 613–628, pp. 613–614; UN Security Council, 2005, ¶ 16).

[53] UN Security Council, 2005, ¶ 17.

was to establish a consensual narrative of the conflict based on testimonies of those who were affected by the war.[54]

In order to weaken the effect of ethnic and regional divisions and promote a stronger civil society, the United Kingdom and other donors provided support to several civil associations.[55] The UK DFID launched the Enhancing the Interaction and Interface Between Civil Society and the State to Improve Poor People's Lives program, which was renewed in 2008 in spite of mixed reviews. An independent evaluation had found it to be, ultimately, "a much-needed platform for engagement between the civil society and various arms of the government."[56] Understanding that the violence during the war was partly due to the lack of other means of public expression, efforts were also made to promote free media.[57]

Reintegrating Sierra Leone's former combatants was another priority. More than 70,000 combatants benefited from the United Nations–managed DDR program completed in 2004.[58] The reintegration program was criticized on several counts. It taught former combatants skills (as carpenters, plumbers, blacksmiths, and auto mechanics) that are in low demand in a country as poor as Sierra Leone.[59] Some beneficiaries simply resold the tool kit they had been given once they realized that they would not find work.[60] The DDR program also largely overlooked the needs of female ex-combatants; they represented less than 7 percent of the total number of combatants formally demo-

---

[54] International Crisis Group, *Sierra Leone's Truth and Reconciliation Commission: A Fresh Start?* Africa Briefing 12, December 20, 2002, pp. 1–2.

[55] Williams, 2001, p. 163.

[56] Quoted in Nick Chapman and Charlotte Vaillant, *Synthesis of Country Programme Evaluations Conducted in Fragile States*, London: UK Department for International Development, 2010, p. 29.

[57] On this issue, see, for instance, Thomson, 2007, p. 27.

[58] "Sierra Leone: Disarmament," 2004.

[59] International Crisis Group, 2004, p. 15.

[60] Joseph Hanlon, "Is the International Community Helping to Recreate the Preconditions for War in Sierra Leone?" *Round Table*, Vol. 94, No. 381, September 2005, pp. 459–472, p. 466.

bilized, while their estimated participation in the war was 10 to 50 percent, varying among the warring factions.[61]

International donors also focused on the education system. Between 2003 and 2007, 153 primary and secondary schools were built or repaired.[62] In 2001, the government had begun an effort to provide free and mandatory primary education for boys and girls,[63] and, as a result, literacy rates rose sharply, reaching 41 percent of adults and 58 percent of youth in 2009—two indicators that nonetheless remain below the regional average.[64]

Economic

Economic assistance started before the conflict ended in 2002. In November 1999, the IMF unveiled an Emergency Post-Conflict Assistance program, followed by further aid from the United Kingdom, the European Union, and the World Bank.[65] An important effort was also made to help the state gain more revenue not only through tax collection but also by countering the plundering of its resources. For example, the U.S. Coast Guard donated three patrol boats to Sierra Leone for use in countering illegal fishing, which was estimated to cost the country $10 million per year.[66] Another important step in giving Sierra

---

[61] Andreu Solà-Martín, "Is Peacebuilding Sustainable in Sierra Leone?" *Global Change, Peace and Security*, Vol. 21, No. 3, October 2009, pp. 291–307, p. 299; Megan MacKenzie, "Securitization and Desecuritization: Female Soldiers and the Reconstruction of Women in Post-Conflict Sierra Leone," *Security Studies*, Vol. 18, No. 2, 2009, pp. 241–261, p. 245.

[62] International Crisis Group, 2007c, p. 8.

[63] Catherine Bolten, "The Agricultural Impasse: Creating 'Normal' Post-War Development in Northern Sierra Leone," *Journal of Political Ecology*, Vol. 16, 2009, pp. 70–86, p. 72.

[64] UN Educational, Scientific and Cultural Organization (UNESCO) Institute for Statistics (UIS), "Education (all levels) Profile: Sierra Leone," *UIS Statistics in Brief*, undated, referenced November 16, 2011. *Adult* is defined as 15 years of age and above; youth are between ages 15 and 24. Regional literacy rates are 62 percent for adults and 71 percent for youth.

[65] Thomson, 2007, p. 7.

[66] International Crisis Group, 2004, p. 16, n. 86.

Leone's government more control over its budget was the cancellation, in 2006, of the country's $1.6 billion external debt.[67]

Even before the war ended, a large international movement worked to prevent the funding of rebel groups through the plundering of diamond resources (so-called "conflict diamonds"). The Kimberley Process, an international system for certifying the origin of diamonds, was established based on an international agreement reached in Kimberley, South Africa. The government of Sierra Leone, supported by international donors and particularly the United Kingdom, attempted to regulate and improve the management of its diamond-mining industry. In 2001, it established the Diamond Area Community Development Fund (DACDF) to return to local communities part of the benefits generated by mining activities.[68] The following year, the World Bank, DFID, and USAID supported the Ministry of Mineral Resources in setting up a program through which district mining committees would issue diamond-mining licenses. Illegal mining remained extensive, prompting UNAMSIL to take further steps toward enforcement by recording the Global Positioning System (GPS) coordinates of licensed artisanal mining plots with the help of military observers.[69]

Subsequently, another initiative to "clean" the diamond industry, the Kono Peace Diamond Alliance (Kono PDA), was launched in August 2003 with the support of USAID and DFID.[70] This alliance gathered miners, local chiefs, diamond traders, government officials, members of civil society, and international donors and provided diverse forms of technical support, including courses in diamond evaluation through the Integrated Diamond Management Program (IDMP).[71]

---

[67] International Crisis Group, 2007c, p. 8; Solà-Martín, 2009, p. 300.

[68] Partnership Africa Canada, *Diamonds and Human Security: Annual Review 2009*, 2009, p. 16; International Crisis Group, *Sierra Leone: The State of Security and Governance*, Africa Report 67, September 2, 2003c, p. 28.

[69] Solà-Martín, 2009, p. 302.

[70] International Crisis Group, 2003c, p. 25.

[71] Dobbins, Jones, Crane, Rathmell, et al., 2005, p. 146.

The program had limited success.[72] A 2007 USAID evaluation noted that the Kono PDA, although an effective coalition, was not capable of managing donor funding. IDMP was more generally pointed to as a program in which donors failed to adapt because, "[a]lthough most of the other partners and donors were going down different tracks by 2004 the program continued unchanged even when it became clear that some of its strategic choices and underlying assumptions were not accurate."[73]

Political

Improving governance was perceived as one of the top priorities to stabilize Sierra Leone in the postwar period. The two main parties that ruled Sierra Leone's political life prior to the war—the APC of Ernest Bai Koroma and the Sierra Leone People's Party (SLPP) of Ahmad Tejan Kabbah—remained the key political players after the war. The SLPP won the 2002 presidential and parliamentary elections, which observers described as "reasonably fair."[74] During the 2004 district council elections, however, the International Crisis Group denounced pressures on voters in favor of SLPP candidates, as well as the use of coercive methods to prevent independent candidates from participating or to deny them a fair chance of victory.[75]

The following presidential and parliamentary elections in 2007, won this time by the APC, were considered a success because of their large turnout and were described again as "free and fair," thanks to the work of the National Electoral Commission.[76] They were marred by

---

[72] Jean Pierre Tutusaus, Sue Nelson, and Arthur Abadje, *USAID/Sierra Leone Diamond Sector Program Evaluation*, Washington, D.C.: U.S. Agency for International Development, July 20, 2007, p. 14.

[73] Tutusaus, Nelson, and Abadje, 2007, p. ix.

[74] "Internal Affairs (Sierra Leone): Internal Affairs," *Jane's Sentinel Security Assessment: West Africa*, July 28, 2010.

[75] International Crisis Group, 2004, p. 18.

[76] UN Security Council, *First Report of the Secretary-General on the United Nations Integrated Peacebuilding Office in Sierra Leone*, S/2009/59, January 30, 2009a, ¶ 68; Freedom House, "Sierra Leone: Freedom in the World 2008," c. 2008.

some incidents of violence between ALP and SLPP supporters, voter intimidation, and accusations of ballot stuffing.[77] Nevertheless, the general fairness of elections led to a small improvement in 2008 of Sierra Leone's Freedom House score for political rights.[78] Some issues remain, however, including occasional harassment of journalists.[79] The patronage networks that ruled political life in Sierra Leone prior to the war are still prevalent, and change in political practices has been slow.[80]

Institutional

Sierra Leone's parliament created the Anti-Corruption Commission (ACC) in 2000 to investigate alleged corruption cases, assist the public administration in changing its practices, and more broadly change mentalities among the population about corruption.[81] The United Kingdom, through DFID, provided funds and personnel to facilitate the work of the commission, but a 2007 review of the program noted "little real progress" since the previous review in 2005 and even some reversals.[82] The report recommended that the UK government end its support to the commission—which it did.[83] Noting that,

> [w]ithout the functioning support institutions (in particular an incorrupt Judiciary, functioning Attorney General's Office, functioning and effective Auditor General's Office empowered to publish its reports regardless of Parliamentary debate, incorrupt

---

[77] Maya M. Christensen and Mats Utas, "Mercenaries of Democracy: The 'Politricks' of Remobilized Combatants in the 2007 General Elections, Sierra Leone," *African Affairs*, Vol. 107, No. 429, 2008, pp. 515–539, pp. 518–519, 532–534.

[78] Freedom House, 2008.

[79] "Internal Affairs (Sierra Leone)," 2010.

[80] Taylor Brown, Richard Fanthorpe, Janet Gardener, Lansana Gberie, and M. Gibril Sesay, *Sierra Leone: Drivers of Change*, Bristol, UK: IDL Group, March 2005.

[81] International Crisis Group, *Sierra Leone: A New Era of Reform?* Africa Report 143, July 31, 2008, p. 17.

[82] Joel Cutting and Gladwell Otieno, *Annual Review of DFID Support to the Anti-Corruption Commission Phase 2 in Sierra Leone*, London: UK Department for International Development, January 25, 2007, p. 21.

[83] Cutting and Otieno, 2007, pp. 29–30.

police force, and strong independent media) the ACC cannot operate effectively,

this evaluation also suggested that much-broader justice-sector reform is needed before investing in anticorruption can prove useful.[84]

Excessive centralization of authority was one of the root causes of war in Sierra Leone. UNAMSIL, the World Bank, and UNDP all funded and supported programs for decentralization.[85] DFID launched an ambitious Paramount Chiefs Restoration Program (PCRP), whose aim was to reestablish traditional chiefs in their position, elect new chiefs if needed, give them houses, and provide them with a code of practice.[86] The United Kingdom spent more than $3 million on this project, which received the support of UNAMSIL.[87]

The program prompted some criticism. One issue was that the chiefs' control of customary law was felt by part of the population to be iniquitous.[88] Another was the lack of transparency of the decision process leading to the nomination of chiefs.[89] Numerous chiefs were also

---

[84] Cutting and Otieno, 2007, pp. 29–30.

[85] UN Security Council, *First Report of the Secretary-General on the United Nations Integrated Office in Sierra Leone*, S/2006/269, April 28, 2006, ¶ 28; Dobbins, Jones, Crane, Rathmell, et al., 2005, pp. 143–145; Paul Jackson, "Chiefs, Money and Politicians: Rebuilding Local Government in Post-War Sierra Leone," *Public Administration and Development*, Vol. 25, 2005, pp. 49–58, p. 51. On this issue, see also Paul Jackson, "Reshuffling an Old Deck of Cards? The Politics of Local Government in Sierra Leone," *Journal of African Economies*, Vol. 106, No. 422, January 2007, pp. 95–111, p. 102; and Edward Sawyer, "Remove or Reform? A Case for (Restructuring) Chiefdom Governance in Post-Conflict Sierra Leone," *African Affairs*, Vol. 107, No. 428, 2008, pp. 387–403, p. 402.

[86] International Crisis Group, 2004, p. 24; Richard Fanthorpe, "On the Limits of Liberal Peace: Chiefs and Democratic Decentralization in Post-War Sierra Leone," *African Affairs*, Vol. 105, No. 418, January 2006, pp. 27–49, p. 31.

[87] Richard Fanthorpe, *Post-War Reconstruction in Rural Sierra Leone: What Political Structures May Prove Viable? Final Report*, London: UK Department for International Development, 2004, ¶ 1.2.

[88] Fanthorpe, 2006, p. 32; Hanlon, 2005, p. 462. These accusations were voiced in particular during the consultations that the PCRP carried out between 1999 and 2001 in 75 chiefdoms in the south of the country in order to identify the population's main grievances (Fanthorpe, 2006, pp. 39–40).

[89] International Crisis Group, 2003c, p. 17; Fanthorpe, 2006, pp. 40–42.

accused of serving their patrons in Freetown rather than local communities.[90] Last, chiefs often constituted the upper level of a patronage network through which they distributed resources or jobs to their supporters, to the exclusion of the rest of the community.[91] Several studies, as well as DFID's own local consultations, have nevertheless shown that, in spite of these shortcomings, the population sees the PCRP as fulfilling a critical role (especially in the justice system) and generally supports this institution—but also welcomes its reform.[92] The PCRP was completed in June 2002 under its new name, the Chiefdom Governance Reform Program.[93] A 2009 World Bank report noted that the reform part of the program "never took off" because of the "lack of political commitment and poor leadership" of the governmental institutions involved.[94]

Meanwhile, DFID, along with the European Union, the World Bank, UNDP, and the United States, worked on a parallel decentralization track—the reestablishment of the elected district councils that President Stevens had dissolved in 1972.[95] The Local Government Act of 2004 devolved some state prerogatives to these councils.[96] One persistent issue, however, has been the modalities of power sharing between the two local authorities—the PCRP and the district councils. Theoretically, councilors focus on reconstruction and development, while members of the PCRP are in charge of customary law and community policing, but both play a role in collecting local taxes.[97] Local councilors generally struggled to establish their authority against

---

[90] Fanthorpe, 2006, pp. 40–42; International Crisis Group, 2007c, p. 11.

[91] International Crisis Group, 2003c, p. 17.

[92] Fanthorpe, 2006, p. 44; see also P. Jackson, 2005, p. 57; and Sawyer, 2008, pp. 393–397.

[93] Yongmei Zhou, ed., *Decentralization, Democracy, and Development: Recent Experience from Sierra Leone*, Washington, D.C.: World Bank, 2009, p. xix; Fanthorpe, 2004, ¶ 1.3.

[94] Zhou, 2009, p. xx.

[95] International Crisis Group, 2003c, pp. 17–18; Fanthorpe, 2006, p. 35; 2003 DFID concept note cited in Fanthorpe, 2006, p. 34, n. 22.

[96] Fanthorpe, 2004, ¶ 1.5.

[97] Fanthorpe, 2006, p. 35; Hanlon, 2005, p. 462.

the PCRP; they also found it difficult, after 30 years without local councils, to know exactly what their position entailed.[98] Consequently, USAID undertook to fund programs to help newly elected councilors understand better their role and responsibilities and to educate the chiefs about their relationships to the councils.[99]

Sierra Leone's security sector underwent substantial reforms. In 1999, the United Kingdom launched its ambitious Sierra Leone Security Sector Reform Programme, sending an International Military Advisory and Assistance Team to train and restructure the Sierra Leonean army and reform the Ministry of Defense.[100] The army was downsized by almost half and received equipment from a wide range of donors.[101] The SLP was another institution in need of assistance. Nine hundred police officers were killed during the war.[102] UNAMSIL's CIVPOL element and the UK Commonwealth Police (through its Commonwealth Community Safety and Security Project) took the lead in this reform.[103] Among their priorities were deploying the police in the countryside and promoting "visible policing" as a way to build confidence between the SLP and the population.[104]

---

[98] Hanlon, 2005, p. 463; International Crisis Group, 2007c, p. 11; P. Jackson, 2007, pp. 104–105.

[99] Phone discussion with Thomas Hull, former U.S. Ambassador to Sierra Leone (2004–2007), April 16, 2010.

[100] International Crisis Group, 2004, p. 2; Hanlon, 2005, p. 469; Horn and Olonisakin, 2006, p. 119; Jeremy Ginifer, "The Challenge of the Security Sector and Security Reform Processes in Democratic Transitions: The Case of Sierra Leone," *Democratization*, Vol. 13, No. 5, 2006, pp. 791–810, p. 799.

[101] UN Security Council, 2005, ¶ 28; UN Security Council, 2006, ¶ 25; UN Secretary-General, *United Nations Integrated Office in Sierra Leone (third report)*, S/2006/922, November 18, 2006, ¶ 23; Economist Intelligence Unit, "Country Report: Sierra Leone," December 2009, p. 13; UN Security Council, *Sixth Report of the Secretary-General on the United Nations Integrated Office in Sierra Leone*, S/2008/281, April 29, 2008a, ¶ 14.

[102] Meek, 2003, pp. 105–106.

[103] International Crisis Group, 2003c, p. 9, n. 76.

[104] Phone discussion with Kieran Mitton, researcher, Conflict Security and Development Group, King's College London, February 12, 2010; Peter Albrecht and Paul Jackson, *Security System Transformation in Sierra Leone, 1997–2007*, Birmingham, UK: Global Facilitation Network for Security Sector Reform, University of Birmingham, 2009, p. 35.

As for the justice system, DFID funded the reconstruction of courts that were destroyed during the war, but the entire system is short of staff and plagued by corruption.[105] The Justice Sector Development Programme launched in 2005 remained effectively confined to Freetown.[106] It was succeeded in 2010 by the Improved Access to Security and Justice Programme, which attempted to better reach out to provinces and take into account traditional justice and security providers.[107]

Outcomes

The international community has had at least limited success in mitigating all the factors that led to and sustained the conflict in Sierra Leone. Peace was eventually established in neighboring Liberia, which removed a critically important source of destabilizing outside influence. Governance and respect for human rights have improved, democratic reforms were instituted, authority was decentralized, and the economy strengthened.

Local Attitudes

In 2005, the UN Peacekeeping Best Practices Section requested an independent survey of the population's perception of UNAMSIL. This survey shows that, at that time, a majority still lacked confidence in the country's ability to ensure its own security. More than 70 percent of respondents stated that they would rather see UNAMSIL stay longer than leave the country.[108] There was, in particular, a fear that the 2007 elections could result in an outbreak of violence—a fear that fortunately did not materialize.[109]

---

[105] Thomson, 2007, p. 26.

[106] Peter Albrecht, *Betwixt and Between: Chiefs and Reform of Sierra Leone's Justice Sector*, Copenhagen: Danish Institute for International Studies, Working Paper 2010:33, 2010, p. 6.

[107] Albrecht, 2010, pp. 6, 17.

[108] Jean Krasno, *Public Opinion Survey of UNAMSIL's Work in Sierra Leone*, United Nations Peacekeeping Best Practices Unit, July 2005, p. 10.

[109] Krasno, 2005, p. 24.

Geographical and Geopolitical

The end of the war in Liberia and the reform of that government helped consolidate peace in Sierra Leone, and vice versa. The Mano River Union has proved useful in promoting cooperation among Sierra Leone, Liberia, Guinea, and, since 2008, Côte d'Ivoire.[110] The resolution of the political crisis in Guinea increases the likelihood of a resolution of the Yenga dispute.[111] Instability in Côte d'Ivoire and the continuation of major drug trafficking in the region make the strengthening of regional consultation and coordination mechanisms more important than ever.

Cultural and Social

According to the United Nations, the reparation program of the Truth and Reconciliation Commission has made "significant progress," and 28,000 war victims have been identified.[112] As of 2011, the commission's recommendations had not been fully implemented, however, and the reparation program still needed additional donor funding to provide benefits to all identified war victims.[113]

The Special Court for Sierra Leone had raised expectations: It was supposed to be more cost-effective, faster, and closer to the people affected by the war than previous international tribunals for Rwanda and for the former Yugoslavia.[114] On this latter point, the court developed an ambitious outreach program toward victims, with mixed results.[115] It was, however, successful in indicting and arresting quickly some high-profile protagonists in the war. In May 2012, it sentenced

---

[110] "West Africa: Cote d'Ivore [sic] Joins MRU Today," *News* (Monrovia), May 15, 2008.

[111] Economist Intelligence Unit, "Country Report: Sierra Leone," September 2011, p. 9.

[112] UN Security Council, *Third Report of the Secretary-General on the United Nations Integrated Peacebuilding Office in Sierra Leone*, S/2009/438, September 1, 2009c, ¶ 36.

[113] UN Security Council, *Sixth Report of the Secretary-General on the United Nations Integrated Peacebuilding Office in Sierra Leone*, S/2011/119, March 9, 2011, ¶¶ 38, 39.

[114] Rachel Kerr and Jessica Lincoln, *The Special Court for Sierra Leone: Outreach, Legacy and Impact—Final Report*, London: King's College London, War Crimes Research Group, Department of War Studies, February 2008, p. 3.

[115] Kerr and Lincoln, 2008, pp. 24–25.

former Liberian president Charles Taylor to 50 years in prison for crimes committed during the war in Sierra Leone.[116]

Ethnic and regional divisions remain an important feature of Sierra Leone's social fabric, but less so than before the war. The conflict contributed to weakening old patronage networks, which are being replaced with other types of social affiliations, such as church groups, associations, Islamic fraternities, and initiation societies.[117] This phenomenon is much more visible in the cities than in the countryside, but, because the urban population became much larger during and after the war, this social change is significant.[118] The situation of youth—more than one-third of the population—remains difficult.[119] A 2009 World Bank report found that young people were less likely to find employment (especially in the public sector) and to be paid for their work than adults.[120]

Economic

Sierra Leone's economic progress has been mixed. As of 2011, real GDP growth was on the increase, but so were inflation and the country's current-account deficit,[121] and the country was ranked 180th out of 187 countries on the HDI. Sierra Leone's diamond exports have surged from $1 million in value in 1999 to $100 million to $150 million in 2009, but declines in world market prices for diamonds have cut this value by about one-fourth in subsequent years.[122] Estimates of the size

---

[116]Marlise Simons and J. David Goodman, "Ex–Liberian Leader Gets 50 Years for War Crimes," *New York Times*, May 30, 2012.

[117]International Crisis Group, 2008, p. 6.

[118]International Crisis Group, 2008, pp. 6, 23.

[119]The World Bank defines "young people" as people between the ages of 15 and 35.

[120]Pia Peeters, Wendy Cunningham, Gayatri Acharya, and Arvil Van Adams, *Youth Employment in Sierra Leone: Sustainable Livelihood Opportunities in a Post-Conflict Setting*, Washington, D.C.: World Bank, 2009, p. 7.

[121]Economist Intelligence Unit, 2011, p. 3.

[122]International Crisis Group, 2007c, p. 10; Partnership Africa Canada, 2009, p. 2.

and commercial attractiveness of Sierra Leone's iron ore deposits and nascent offshore oil production have been revised upward.[123]

In Sierra Leone, the mining sector remains anything but transparent. In 2009, a report found that the main issues confronting the mining sector were largely the same as before the war.[124] Most of the mechanisms that were put into place to regulate the industry have proven insufficient: The results of the presidential task force to review the mining sector were disappointing;[125] illegal mining remains extensive;[126] the Ministry of Mineral Resources is inefficient and poorly managed;[127] the 120 newly appointed mine-monitoring officers in charge of monitoring the extraction activities in the mines receive little training and meager pay, making them easy to corrupt;[128] and the DACDF funds that were supposed to return some mining benefits to local communities are distributed along lines described as "arbitrary" and "opaque."[129] Some diamonds are processed properly thanks to the Kimberley Process, but others are still smuggled out of the country, depriving the state of revenue.[130] It remains to be seen whether the establishment of the National Minerals Agency announced in July 2011 and the planned review of all existing mining agreements against the standards of the Extractive Industry Transparency Initiative will result in an improvement of this situation.[131]

---

[123]UN Security Council, 2011, ¶ 19.

[124]Mark Curtis, *Sierra Leone at the Crossroads: Seizing the Chance to Benefit from Mining*, Freetown: National Advocacy Coalition on Extractives, March 2009, pp. 6–9.

[125]Partnership Africa Canada, 2009, p. 15.

[126]International Crisis Group, 2007c, p. 10.

[127]International Crisis Group, 2007c, p. 10.

[128]Partnership Africa Canada, 2009, p. 16.

[129]Partnership Africa Canada, 2009, pp. 16–17; P. Jackson, 2007, p. 100.

[130]Phone discussion with Thomas Hull, former U.S. Ambassador to Sierra Leone (2004–2007), April 16, 2010.

[131]Economist Intelligence Unit, 2011, p. 3.

Political

Although elections since 2002 have generally been considered "free and fair," efforts to eliminate the political use of violence so common during the prewar era have been slow and incomplete.[132] Several violent incidents took place around the 2008 local council elections and again in 2011, ahead of the 2012 presidential and parliamentary elections.[133] Since 2008, a project to revise the 1991 constitution has been ongoing, but it still had not come to fruition as of 2012, in spite of encouragement from UN Secretary-General Ban Ki-Moon to advance this reform.[134] Freedom House ratings for civil liberties and political rights remained stagnant between 2008 and 2012,[135] suggesting that earlier advances in this regard have stalled.

Institutional

The government adopted the new Anti-Corruption Act and an official anticorruption strategy in 2008 and 2009, respectively, but they have done little to reduce corruption levels. In 2009, Sierra Leone's Corruption Perceptions Index ranking was the same as in 2003.[136] A 2008 report by the UN Office on Drugs and Crime (UNODC) concluded that the control of corruption had deteriorated over the previous decade.[137] The most recent chairman of the ACC aims to add compliance and justice capacity-building to its mandate, but the commission itself is losing credibility after failing on several occasions to impose strong penalties on officials under its scrutiny.[138]

---

[132] Christensen and Utas, 2008, p. 538.

[133] Freedom House, "Sierra Leone: Freedom in the World 2011," c. 2011; Freedom House, "Sierra Leone: Freedom in the World 2012," c. 2012b.

[134] "Internal Affairs (Sierra Leone)," 2010; "Sierra Leone: Fighting for Women's Right to Land," Integrated Regional Information Networks, June 22, 2012.

[135] Freedom House, 2012b.

[136] Sierra Leone's rank in 2003 was 113th out of 133 countries surveyed (Transparency International, *Corruption Perceptions Index 2003*, 2003).

[137] Based on figures from the Worldwide Governance Indicators (WGI) (UNODC, *Drug Trafficking as a Security Threat in West Africa*, October 28, 2008, p. 39).

[138] Economist Intelligence Unit, 2011, p. 8.

A key step in decentralization, the July 2008 local council elections were deemed "successful" by the United Nations, which also underlined the need to increase the capacity and authority of local councils.[139] Serious issues remain, however. The division of power between paramount chiefs and local councilors is still unclear.[140] The fact, in particular, that local councils now establish what share of the local tax paramount chiefs are allowed to collect may be a source of conflict in some chiefdoms. Another problem concerns the reform of salaries of the chiefdom staffs, which used to be paid by the central government but are now to be covered by the local taxes raised by the chiefs. This new system, less reliable for chiefdom staff, has reportedly resulted in increased corruption.[141] Local capacity is still an unsolved issue: Almost all civil servants seconded by the central government to local councils chose to return to Freetown, citing "rural hardship, lack of job security and upward mobility, and uncompetitive compensation policy"[142] to justify their decisions.

The overall performance of the army has reached a point at which the reform can be deemed a success, even though soldiers' accommodations and logistical support are still lacking.[143] This result contrasts with those achieved by the SLP.[144] In 2006, a UN report highlighted rampant corrupt police practices largely due to irregular and low pay, as well as lack of experience and skills.[145] As of 2010, police brutality was on the decline, but corruption remains high, although the Police Complaints, Discipline, and Internal Investigations Department seems to

---

[139] UN Security Council, 2009a, ¶ 39.

[140] UN Security Council, 2008a, ¶ 38.

[141] P. Jackson, 2007, pp. 99–100.

[142] Zhou, 2009, p. xxix.

[143] UN Security Council, 2009a, ¶ 38; Ginifer, 2006, p. 799.

[144] Economist Intelligence Unit, 2009, p. 13.

[145] UN Security Council, 2006, ¶ 22.

be gaining momentum and increasingly taking in complaints against police officers.[146]

Conclusions

What Local Factors Posed the Greatest Challenges?

The local factors within each category that were most important in shaping the environment in which nation-builders sought to promote an enduring peace included the following.

Geographical and Geopolitical

Spillover conflict from neighboring Liberia triggered the war in Sierra Leone, and diamond resources in the country fueled it. After the war and until war ended in Liberia, Sierra Leone's vulnerability to such spillover was mitigated by activities of the UN peacekeeping mission and the United Kingdom's security guarantee. The end of Liberia's conflict and improved regional cooperation have helped consolidate peace in Sierra Leone.

Cultural and Social

Two key factors that contributed to the conflict in Sierra Leone were the country's geographic and ethnic divisions, which inhibited a sense of national identity, and the lack of educational or economic opportunities for youth, which created a large pool of recruits for rebel forces. Geographic and ethnic divisions continue to be a feature of the societal fabric, but their salience as a risk factor for conflict has lessened somewhat. Educational opportunities have improved, but unemployment remains high for youth, who comprise one-third of the population.

Economic

One important economic factor that fueled resentment of the government and thus facilitated rebel recruitment was the inequitable distribution of development resources and provision of public services based

---

[146]U.S. Department of State, *2010 Human Rights Report: Sierra Leone*, Washington, D.C., April 8, 2011a.

on clientelism. Another was the government's mishandling of the diamond industry. After the conflict, licit diamond production soared, but structural problems in the management and regulation of the industry persisted.

Political

Sierra Leone's patronage system was an important source of grievances and social fragmentation giving rise to the conflict. Patronage networks are still prevalent in the country, although, at the same time, democratic processes are taking hold.

Institutional

Institutional weaknesses contributed to the conflict by enabling rampant corruption and looting of the state's resources to fund patronage, and thus generating grievances against the government. Weak military capabilities contributed to prolonging the conflict. Since the conflict, the military has improved considerably through efforts spearheaded by the United Kingdom, but, in other areas, including the police, institutional development remains very much a work in progress, and corruption continues to plague institutional performance.

Were Local Factors Modified or Circumvented to Promote Enduring Peace?

In the ten years since the end of its civil war, Sierra Leone remained at peace and democratization made significant advances, but government effectiveness improved only slightly. Per capita GDP increased by 72.7 percent, but socioeconomic development remained very low. Table 7.1 shows these outcomes, alongside key resources applied by nation-building interveners.

Nation-building in Sierra Leone has required reconstructing a failed state rather than simply stabilizing a postconflict country. This has required a very broadly conceived program of social and institutional reforms. As of 2012, the overall situation in Sierra Leone was peaceful but fragile. The country's socioeconomic performance is still extremely weak, earning it the 180th rank out of 187 countries

Table 7.1
Postintervention Performance and Nation-Building Inputs in Sierra Leone

Performance Indicator	Year of Intervention (2000)	5 Years Later	10 Years Later
At peace?	—	Yes	Yes
Government effectiveness (10-point scale)	2.87	3.07	3.36
Freedom Index (10-point scale)	4.75	6.25	7.00
HDI (10-point scale)	2.50	3.10	3.30
Growth in per capita GDP (in 1st 5 years and in 10 years after intervention) (%)	—	51.1	72.7
Nation-Building Input			
Peak military presence per capita, number of troops per 1,000 inhabitants	4.5		
Peak international civilian police presence per capita, number of police per 1,000 inhabitants	0.02		
Average annual per capita assistance in the first 5 years (constant 2010 US$)	93.10		

SOURCES: World Bank, undated (d); Freedom House, various years; UNDP, undated; IMF, undated; Dobbins, Jones, Crane, Chivvis, et al., 2008, Figures 9.2, 9.4, 9.9; UN Peace Operations, various years; World Bank, undated (c).

in UNDP's 2011 HDI.[147] Corruption still constrains state revenue and weakens the confidence of the population in public institutions; the army and more so the police lack skills and equipment; the new decentralized governance system is still seeking a balance between traditional chiefs and local councilors; and young men remain disproportionately unemployed compared with other categories of the population. Although many of the factors that gave rise to the conflict have not been successfully addressed to any great extent, the external factor that triggered the conflict has been resolved. Sierra Leone should thus be considered vulnerable to conflict should some new trigger emerge.

---

[147] UNDP, 2011.

Democratic Republic of the Congo

With the end of the Cold War, Zairian dictator Mobutu Sese Seko began to lose his grip on power. Laurent Kabila overthrew him in 1997, and then war broke out in the Congo, centered in the east, as Kabila fought with his Rwandan and Ugandan backers, who sought to oust

Figure 8.1
Map of the Democratic Republic of the Congo

SOURCE: CIA, "Congo, Democratic Republic of the,"
The World Factbook, 2012c.
RAND RR167-8.1

him. When Angola, Zimbabwe, and Namibia intervened on Kabila's behalf, the newly renamed Democratic Republic of the Congo (DRC) descended into the bloodiest and most complex war in recent African history. By most estimates, several million people died. Neighboring militaries withdrew following the 2002 Sun City peace accords, and a political process to stabilize the country was begun. Violence persisted at varying levels in the eastern DRC, however, and surged once more in 2012 with the emergence of a new rebel group, the M23, apparently back by Rwanda.[1] This chapter addresses the nation-building efforts pursued prior to the resurgence of civil war in late 2012.

Nation-building in the DRC could be expected to be challenging. The DRC has many significant risk factors for continued conflict, including low per capita income, a long war, a large population, and years of long-standing ethnic and tribal conflicts that cross national boundaries. The DRC covers a large, heavily forested land area, and it possesses large quantities of easily extractable gems and ores.

Local Factors Before the Peace

Geographical and Geopolitical
Located in the Congo River Basin, the DRC is a huge country: 2,344,858 square kilometers in size, the 12th-largest country in the world (see Figure 8.1). The DRC only has a 37-kilometer strip of coast between Angola to the south and the Republic of Congo (commonly called Congo-Brazzaville) to the north, but the Congo River provides access to shipping.

In 2012, the population was 68 million, which gave an overall population density of 29 inhabitants per square kilometer.[2] The population is concentrated in the far west in Kinshasa and in a few popula-

---

[1]   Jeffrey Gettleman, "Congo Slips into Chaos Again as Rebels Gain," *New York Times*, November 25, 2012, p. A1. See also International Crisis Group, *Eastern Congo: Why Stabilisation Failed*, Africa Briefing 91, October 4, 2012.

[2]   UN Department of Economic and Social Affairs, *World Population Prospects, the 2010 Revision*, updated October 20, 2011.

tion centers in the eastern provinces.[3] The population density of the eastern provinces has created substantial pressure on the land and thus potential for conflict.[4]

The DRC is home to a large portion of the second-largest forested area in the world, the forests of the Congo River Basin. The country thus has large swaths of rugged terrain that are near impassible. There are almost no roads linking Kinshasa, the capital, with the provinces; transportation is almost exclusively by air or boat along the Congo River system.

Geopolitically, the DRC is situated in an unstable part of the world. To the south lies Angola, for decades the site of one of the main proxy wars of the Cold War. To the north, the DRC borders the Central African Republic and Sudan, only slightly more stable. To the east lie the Great Lakes, Uganda, Burundi, and Rwanda, the epicenter of Africa's worst genocide in living memory.

Cultural and Social

The DRC is home to several ethnic groups and tribes. The enduring social importance of traditional leaders and power structures is indicated by the fact that land in much of the country was, under Mobutu, under communal ownership rather than private or state control.[5] Local government was largely the purview of these traditional power structures.

In the eastern DRC, where most of the fighting has taken place, ethnic tensions mixed with tribal tensions. In the Kivus, for example, tensions existed between Hutu and Tutsi ethnic groups from Rwanda (known as Banyarwanda) whom the Belgians had moved into the Congo and the indigenous (known as Kanyarwanda) Hunde, Nande, and Nyanga tribes. Pastoral Hema and agriculturalist Lendu tribes indigenous to the eastern Ituri district have had longstanding disputes

---

[3] Herbst, 2000, pp. 146–147.

[4] Lemarchand, 2009, p. 222.

[5] Herbst, 2000, p. 188.

over land.[6] Another group, the Banyamulegne Tutsis, who migrated to the Kivus prior to Belgian rule, were considered suspect by indigenous tribes.

The war hardened existing ethnic and tribal divisions, which increasingly became fault lines for conflict. Conflict also tended to erode the authority of traditional power structures to the benefit of warlords and militias. Warlords began to supplant elders and tribal leaders at the local level.[7]

Social development was at a level commensurate with the country's low level of economic development. In 1998, life expectancy was 45 years; by 2011, it was still only 48 years.[8] Health care and other services were minimal before the war; the war only made things worse. Eighty percent of the population was living below the World Bank's poverty line in 2001, and 71 percent in 2005; it has made little progress since. In addition, the DRC has suffered greatly from the HIV/AIDS pandemic that has hit Africa. The war left a large number of injured victims, as well as refugees, orphans, and street children, in its wake.[9]

A brighter spot in an otherwise-bleak scene was the apparent strength of civil society, which has played an important role during the war and peace process. In many instances, churches and NGOs stepped into the role once played by the state, providing various basic services on a local basis.[10]

Economic

The DRC was already one of the world's poorest countries under Belgian rule, yet the situation declined further under Mobutu. The instability of the 1990s led to further erosion of economic conditions, with

---

[6]   Lemarchand, 2009, pp. 13–15, 235–236.

[7]   Koen Vlassenroot and Timothy Raeymaekers, eds., *Conflict and Social Transformation in Eastern DR Congo*, Gent: Academia Press Scientific Publishers, 2004, p. 22–23.

[8]   World Bank, "World DataBank," undated (b), referenced August 2012.

[9]   IMF, *Democratic Republic of the Congo: Poverty Reduction Strategy Paper*, Country Report 07/330, September 2007b.

[10]   International Crisis Group, *Escaping the Conflict Trap: Promoting Good Governance in the Congo*, Africa Report 114, July 20, 2006.

overall per capita GDP falling from $380 (in constant dollars) in 1960 to $141 in 1997, in part because of the global decline in world copper prices, which reduced mining exports.[11] Mobutu's regime also ended in hyperinflation, which ran 10,000 percent in 1994.[12] Mobutu elevated "corruption to the level of an institution," as one leading expert put it.[13]

This economic decline occurred despite substantial endowments of natural resources, many of which are mined in the eastern provinces of Nord-Kivu and Sud-Kivu, as well as in Katanga, Kasai-Oriental, and the Ituri district of Orientale province bordering Uganda in the northeast. Exports of coltan, cobalt, cassiterite, copper, diamonds, and gold helped sustain Mobutu's regime.

The war took a further toll on this already-poor country. The few roads that existed fell into disrepair, and large areas lost access to electricity and clean water. Investment stopped, and public debt ballooned. Exports came to halt. Even subsistence farming was negatively affected by the constant looting and destruction of buildings, livestock, and other property. The economy that emerged from the war was largely based on subsistence agriculture; agriculture's share of the economy increased from 30 percent in 1980 to 54 percent in 2001.[14]

The war began as a primarily political conflict, but, over time, economic agendas increasingly motivated the violence.[15] The state lost control of the mines in the east and thus an important source of revenue. Rebel groups began looting mineral resources and thereby gained both financing and an incentive to keep fighting. Because these resources

---

[11] World Bank, *Transitional Support Strategy for the Democratic Republic of the Congo*, Report 27751, January 26, 2004.

[12] Philippe Beaugrand, *Zaïre's Hyperinflation, 1990–96*, Washington, D.C.: International Monetary Fund, Working Paper WP/97/50, April 1997.

[13] Gérard Prunier, *Africa's World War: Congo, the Rwandan Genocide, and the Making of a Continental Catastrophe*, Oxford, UK: Oxford University Press, 2009, p. 318.

[14] World Bank, 2004.

[15] Stephen Jackson, "Making a Killing: Criminality and Coping in the Kivu War Economy," *Review of African Political Economy*, Vol. 29, No. 93–94, September–December 2002, pp. 516–536; Theodore Trefon, Van Hoyweghen Saskia, and Stefaan Smis, "Editorial: State Failure in the Congo—Perceptions and Realities," *Review of African Political Economy*, Vol. 29, No. 93–94, September–December 2002, pp. 379–388.

were widely dispersed around the vast country, the security and political situation became highly fragmented.[16] Access to and plunder of the DRC's natural resources played a driving role in the conflict.

The interventions of Uganda and especially Rwanda have even been characterized as "African imperialism," whereby the military costs of fighting in the DRC were more than compensated by the material gains from access to Congolese minerals. Zimbabwe and Angola both gained access to mining concessions through their support for Kabila during the war. In many cases, extraction of Congolese resources exacerbated previously existing social and ethnic tensions, most notably when it came to Congolese views of the Banyarwanda and, by extension, Banyamulenge peoples.[17]

After the war, the situation around the mines in the Kivus and Ituri was chaotic, with various rebel groups controlling mines. Fighting for control over the mines was not uncommon. Legal and illegal networks, meanwhile, supported an estimated 2 million so-called "artisanal" miners nationwide; these included ex-combatants from all sides.[18]

Political

The DRC has never been a stable democracy. From its colonization by Belgium in the late 19th century until independence in 1960, Congolese enjoyed few liberties and little political representation. Putative efforts to establish democracy upon independence failed when the military revolted, the province of Katanga seceded, and civil war broke out. UN troops intervened to put down the rebelling military and quell smaller secessionist efforts. Mobutu assumed power in the aftermath of the crisis, and he consolidated power in 1965. For three decades, he held the state together through patronage rather than the

---

[16] William Reno, *Warlord Politics and African States*, Boulder, Colo.: Lynne Rienner Publishers, 1998, pp. 149–151.

[17] Lemarchand, 2009, p. 254.

[18] UN Security Council, *Report of the Secretary-General Pursuant to Paragraph 8 of Resolution 1698 (2006) Concerning the Democratic Republic of the Congo*, S/2007/68, February 8, 2007.

provision of public services. As is typical of many dictators, he purposefully kept his government factionalized to avoid challenges to his authority.[19] He maintained power through elaborate payoff networks, rather than investing in the institutions of the state, which remained chronically weak.[20]

Mobutu could sustain this system as long as the United States and other powers with which he aligned were willing to provide material support. The end of the Cold War, however, ended this foreign largesse while increasing pressure for political liberalization. Mobutu responded by printing money so he could try to bribe his political opposition, but this only created hyperinflation and further weakened his grip on power.[21] Security forces, the legal system, and social services had all broken down by the time Zaire collapsed into civil war in 1997. Internationally supported peace negotiations were ongoing throughout the conflict. A peace accord reached at Lusaka in 1999 failed, but a second attempt at Pretoria in 2002 proved more successful—in part because rebel leader Laurent Kabila had been assassinated and his son and successor Joseph was more interested in peace.

Separate agreements stipulated the withdrawal of foreign forces and the establishment of a power-sharing arrangement. Joseph Kabila remained president but with four vice presidents: one from each of the two main rebel groups, one from Kabila's own party, and one from the unarmed political opposition. Ministerial positions and parliamentary seats were also divided among the various parties to the conflict.[22] A provisional constitution was agreed, and an 18-month transitional period was established, during which military forces would be demobilized and reintegrated into the Congolese national army, a new consti-

---

[19] International Crisis Group, 2006.

[20] Lemarchand, 2009, pp. 218–219.

[21] Lemarchand, 2009, pp. 218–219.

[22] Rachel L. Swarns, "Congo and Its Rebels Sign Accord to End War," *New York Times*, December 18, 2002; Prunier, 2009, p. 277.

tution would be ratified by referendum, and certain key laws would be promulgated. After the transitional period, elections would be held.[23]

Institutional

Before the war, state institutions were the private domain of Mobutu and were highly corrupt. They largely ceased to function during the war and remained extremely weak afterward. The DRC lacked the financial and human capital necessary to develop government institutions. Corruption only made things worse: An estimated 80 percent of customs revenue was embezzled during the transition, and one-quarter of the national budget was unaccounted for.[24] Security forces were in disarray, with large segments of the national army formally at war with one another and only nominally loyal to the central government. The justice system and most national ministries barely functioned. Administrative capacity was extremely limited.

Nation-Building Efforts

Limited resources relative to the size of the country were applied to international efforts to grapple with the enormous challenges in the DRC. As postconflict reconstruction got under way in the DRC, the attention of the United States and other Western powers was focused on interventions in Afghanistan and Iraq. However, it is doubtful that substantially more resources would have been made available to the DRC absent those other operations because the Congo was simply too big and too distant from most of the developed world. The complexity of nation-building in such a poor, large, and institutionally weak country and the fact that violence was continuing in the east meant that the only politically feasible approach was a slow, gradual process aimed at restoring a modicum of stability over time.

---

[23] Richard Cornwell, "The Democratic Republic of the Congo: From Fiction to Fact?" *African Security Review*, Vol. 14, No. 4, 2005, pp. 41–42.

[24] International Crisis Group, *Congo: Staying Engaged After the Elections*, Africa Briefing 44, January 9, 2007a.

The international effort was led by the United Nations and supported by the European Union, World Bank, IMF, United States, and several European countries. The UN mission initially was established in 1999 on the heels of the Lusaka Ceasefire Agreement and gradually saw its role expanded through a series of UN Security Council resolutions. The mission's mandate ultimately authorized 19,815 military personnel, which made it the largest UN operation in history.[25] The cost of the UN operation reached nearly $1.4 billion annually.[26] There were also two EU military operations of limited duration to bolster the peace—one in 2003 to shore up a deteriorating situation in the east that threatened to derail the peace accords and another in 2005 during the elections. Nonmilitary dimensions of the overall international effort included humanitarian relief, development aid, DDR, democratization, and regional diplomacy.

Geographical and Geopolitical
By mid-2003, most of the neighboring powers involved in the war had withdrawn, largely of their own accord.[27] Uganda and Rwanda, however, continued to intervene in the eastern DRC, both directly and indirectly through rebel proxies.

During the peace negotiations, Uganda had withdrawn some 10,000 of its 13,000 troops in the northeast and was to pull out the remainder as set forth in the Luanda Agreement of September 2002. By spring 2003, however, it had still not done so when conflict broke out again in the town of Bunia, threatening to undermine the peace accords altogether.[28] The European Union deployed a bridging force to inhibit further deterioration in the security situation while the United

---

[25] The hybrid UN/African Union peacekeeping mission in Darfur, established in 2008, had nearly as many authorized military personnel and more police, making the total number of personnel authorized there slightly higher.

[26] This figure is the budget for 2011–2012. See United Nations Organization Stabilization Mission in the Democratic Republic of the Congo (MONUSCO), "MONUSCO Facts and Figures," undated, referenced July 4, 2012.

[27] Prunier, 2009, pp. 285–290.

[28] Prunier, 2009, pp. 292–293.

Nations could be reinforced. Meanwhile, the United States threatened to suspend its assistance programs to Uganda unless Ugandan troops exited the DRC once and for all. This pressure helped to bring Ugandan involvement to an end.[29]

Rwanda was a different story. Rwandan-linked forces and proxies continued to intervene in the east. In the first half of 2004, intrigue between Kigali and Kinshasa, combined with the private interests of some Congolese military leaders in the region, resulted in a major crisis in the town of Bukavu. Because it implicated members of the transitional government, the crisis threatened to derail political progress in Kinshasa. U.S. officials were dispatched to the region to attempt to negotiate a settlement, but with little effect. The European Union increased its rhetorical and financial support for the UN peacekeeping mission, whose presence in the area was at risk of being overrun by rebel groups. South African envoys sent to Kinshasa and Kigali were able to defuse the crisis.[30]

In the following years, international actors continued to work to convince these governments to cut off support for their proxy groups operating in the east. Eventually, rapprochement between the DRC and Rwanda resulted in direct cooperation to address instability in the eastern DRC. In 2008, Uganda and the Congolese Army joined with UN forces in an effort to oust the Ugandan rebel group the Lord's Resistance Army, which had been operating intermittently in the northeastern DRC. In 2009, Rwandan forces entered the DRC at Kinshasa's invitation to chase out rebel groups once supported by the Rwandan government.

Following a lull in violence around the elections, the situation in the Kivus deteriorated again in late 2006 largely because of actions of the Democratic Forces for the Liberation of Rwanda (Forces démocratiques de libération du Rwanda, or FDLR), a group once linked to Rwanda, and the National Congress for the Defence of the People (Congrès national pour la défense du peuple, CNDP), a group once linked to the government of the DRC but now operating indepen-

---

[29] Prunier, 2009, pp. 293.

[30] Prunier, 2009, pp. 297–300.

dently under the warlord Laurent Nkunda. These two groups fought against each other and the Congolese army for control of regional mining operations.

Recognizing the role of natural resources in the fighting, UN and Congolese forces began targeting the FDLR's grip on the mines in the Kivus. This effort was complicated, however, by the willingness of some Congolese troops to cooperate with the FDLR in illegal exploitation of the mines.[31] In an effort to trace the source of mineral exports, in 2009, UN mission personnel began conducting random checks at Bukavu and Goma airports in conjunction with Congolese authorities.[32]

Under pressure from the United States and other international actors, the DRC, Rwanda, Burundi, and Uganda agreed to engage in Tripartite Plus talks. These talks helped to improve regional cooperation, for example, through the creation of the Joint Verification Mechanism to address cross-border issues.

In the summer and fall of 2008, Nkunda's forces came close to capturing the provincial capital of Goma, on the border with Rwanda and the site of the UN regional headquarters. This provoked a new round of international engagement. On October 29, 2008, the UN Secretary-General appointed former Nigerian president Olusegun Obasanjo as special envoy for the Great Lakes region, with the express mission of facilitating negotiations between Kigali and Kinshasa. A subsequent UN report explicitly identified the link between Nkunda and Rwanda, and pressure on Rwanda mounted to rein in Nkunda. Sweden and the Netherlands withheld aid to Rwanda, which also came under pressure from the United States and the United Kingdom. An

---

[31] UN Security Council, *Report of the Secretary-General on the Deployment of the African Union–United Nations Hybrid Operation in Darfur*, S/2008/443, July 7, 2008b, ¶ 28; UN Security Council, *Fourth Special Report of the Secretary-General on the United Nations Organization Mission in the Democratic Republic of the Congo*, S/2008/728, November 21, 2008c, ¶ 23.

[32] UN Security Council, *Thirtieth Report of the Secretary-General on the United Nations Organization Mission in the Democratic Republic of the Congo*, S/2009/623, December 4, 2009d, ¶ 38; UN Security Council, *Twenty-Eighth Report of the Secretary-General on the United Nations Organization Mission in the Democratic Republic of the Congo*, S/2009/335, June 30, 2009b, ¶ 47.

agreement was reached whereby the DRC and Rwanda would normal-ize diplomatic relations, enhance economic cooperation, and seek to work together to eliminate the FDLR and bring Nkunda to heel.

Rwandan forces again entered the DRC in 2009 under the terms of this agreement. Somewhat miraculously, at nearly the same moment, Nkunda was overthrown by his own chief of staff (who proved more amenable to negotiation) and was subsequently arrested in Rwanda. Reintegration of Nkunda's forces into the national army proceeded apace. Meanwhile, Rwandan–Congolese cooperation reduced the FDLR's numbers and pushed them back from major population cen-ters and resources. They were far from eliminated, however, by the time the joint operations came to an end a few months later.

Cultural and Social

The international nation-building strategy in the DRC did not focus on Congolese culture and society. Resources were dedicated to imme-diately pressing needs, such as security, economic stabilization, and elections. Ethnic, tribal, and land tensions in the east of the coun-try were not addressed at Sun City; they hardened with the constant interference of Congolese and foreign armed groups in this region.[33] The plight of returning refugees and internally displaced people—who were often radicalized during the war and wanted their land back— and of former combatants, whose reintegration benefits had been mini-mal, only added pressure to these unresolved issues.[34]

The activities of armed groups in eastern Congo led to ever-increasing numbers of displaced persons and human rights violations, including the use of rape as a weapon of war. Such crimes are, however, rarely addressed by the Congolese justice system, which lacks capac-ity and is not trusted by victims.[35] In April 2009, the UN Organiza-

---

[33] International Crisis Group, *The Kivus: The Forgotten Crucible of the Congo Conflict*, Africa Report 56, January 24, 2003a, p. 28; International Crisis Group, *The Congo's Transition Is Failing: Crisis in the Kivus*, Africa Report 91, March 30, 2005a, pp. 9–10.

[34] International Crisis Group, *Congo: Five Priorities for a Peacebuilding Strategy*, Africa Report 150, May 11, 2009a, pp. 16–17.

[35] International Crisis Group, 2009a, p. 17.

tion Mission in the Democratic Republic of the Congo (MONUC) launched an overall strategy in the fight against sexual violence in the DRC to better address, among other issues, this problem of impunity by bringing together the efforts of different UN agencies, as well as local and international NGOs.[36]

Economic

The economy began to improve almost immediately, although not dramatically, in the aftermath of the 2002 peace accords. Foreign donors, especially the Bretton Woods institutions and the European Union, played a major role, with some 20 foreign agencies involved in economic reconstruction and development. Total foreign assistance, excluding expenses for peacekeeping operations, elections, and humanitarian assistance, rose from $200 million in 2001 to some $800 million in 2004 and 2005. This latter figure remains low by historical postconflict standards; it represents only $15 per capita annually.[37] According to the World Bank, this amount equals roughly the cost of election support (for 2006) and humanitarian assistance combined.[38]

The focus from 2001 to 2005 was on macroeconomic stabilization. An agreement in September 2001 had reduced the DRC's foreign debt service bill to $160 million annually. In 2002, the Club of Paris canceled $4.6 billion of the DRC's $10.3 billion in foreign debt.[39] These efforts, combined with others, helped to bring inflation under control.[40] Because of the lack of a tax base, public finances relied heavily on aid, with more than 40 percent of the budget coming from inter-

---

[36] Eoin Young, "Launch of Overall Strategy in the Fight Against Sexual Violence in the DRC," United Nations Organization Mission in the Democratic Republic of the Congo, April 2, 2009.

[37] World Bank, *International Development Association Country Assistance Strategy for the Democratic Republic of the Congo for the Period FY08–FY11*, Vol. I, Report 41474-ZR, November 16, 2007, pp. 1, 11.

[38] World Bank, 2007, p. 11.

[39] Prunier, 2009, pp. 316–317.

[40] For further discussion, see Dobbins, Jones, Crane, Chivvis, et al., 2008, pp. 130–131.

national donors.[41] There was also a parallel effort to effect structural reform of government finances.

Other initiatives focused largely on immediate needs. From 2003 to 2005, total donor funds went to emergency nonhumanitarian aid (25 percent), health and other social services (14 percent), budget support (12 percent), community development (11 percent), demobilization and reintegration (9 percent), democracy-building (8 percent), and capacity-building (7 percent). Infrastructure received only 5 percent of total donor funding.[42]

In February 2008, the DRC became a candidate country in the Extractive Industries Transparency Initiative, which was designed to reduce corruption and increase investment in the mining industry. Some progress was made toward greater transparency in granting and renegotiating mining contracts, although those processes remained generally murky, complicating and discouraging foreign investment.[43]

Reducing illegal exploitation of the DRC's mining resources was difficult for several reasons. There were a large number of small and medium-sized organizations involved in illegal mining, and the United Nations judged direct action against known perpetrators likely to be ineffective because, although financial or other sanctions might eliminate a few criminals, others would most probably take their place. Of equal concern was that any successful actions would have a major negative impact on the livelihood of the artisanal miners, whose income from mining was estimated to support between one-fifth and one-quarter of the DRC's population.[44] Rather than risk violence for little benefit, the UN mission chose to work with the government to try to reduce corruption and strengthen state control over territory.

---

[41] Prunier, 2009, p. 318.

[42] This breakdown does not include the costs of the peacekeeping mission, support to the political process, or humanitarian aid (World Bank, 2007, p. 10).

[43] Anthony W. Gambino, *Congo: Securing Peace, Sustaining Progress*, New York: Council on Foreign Relations, 2008, p. 22, 41.

[44] UN Security Council, 2007. See also S. Jackson, 2002, pp. 516–536.

Political

The primary focus of the international postconflict effort on the political front was elections, the first of which was originally slated for 2004. The date for the first elections was repeatedly pushed back, but, by 2006, further delays were judged unwise due to growing popular discontent. Substantial resources were invested in peacekeeping during the balloting, with enhanced monitoring, special funding packages, and the eventual deployment of an EU military force to bolster security. Elections resulted in a government led by Joseph Kabila, the DRC's wartime president. After losing in a runoff, his main adversary, Jean-Pierre Bemba, did not contest the results. Although the international community deserves some credit for the success of the elections, many also criticized the outcome as lopsided in favor of one side and therefore tending to alienate others and destabilize the fragile peace.[45]

In 2011, the DRC held elections again, and Joseph Kabila retained the presidency, defeating his opponent, Étienne Tshisekedi. Despite significant participation (close to 19 million registered voters participated) and a general lack of election-related violence, the outcome was widely judged by international observers to be flawed because of technical and logistical issues, isolated incidents of voter intimidation, and a lack of transparency of the tabulation process.[46]

Institutional

International actors also focused on reforming and strengthening the DRC's security forces. Several countries sent bilateral security force assistance missions. The World Bank ran an extensive DDR, repatriation, and resettlement program. Efforts to unify the various factions of the Congolese army and to build its capacity were still ongoing as of 2012.

---

[45] Lemarchand, 2009, p. 260; Séverine Autesserre, "The Trouble with Congo: How Local Disputes Fuel Regional Conflict," *Foreign Affairs*, Vol. 87, No. 3, May–June 2008, pp. 94–110.

[46] U.S. Department of State, "Congo, Democratic Republic of the (04/30/12)," April 30, 2012.

Other institutions received less attention. The World Bank worked to improve the management of state finances, reform the mining sector, and improve the civil service. Some bilateral assistance efforts were made to strengthen institutions, including two small EU advisory missions.

Across the board, corruption remained a major obstacle to institutional development. Some actors, including USAID, sought to avoid working with the government and preferred to channel funds to society through NGOs.[47] Some observers criticized the UN mission for not putting more pressure on the government to root out corruption.[48]

Outcomes

During the ten years following the 2002 accords, violence abated and regional cooperation improved, but then Rwandan interference resumed, and conflict resurged in the eastern DRC in late 2012. In the interim, the DRC had twice held elections and the economy had grown, but the country was still extremely poor. Kinshasa struggled to assert control over vast territory. In 2010, the Polity IV Project rated the DRC as extremely fragile, with only Somalia and Sudan receiving lower scores in the global rankings.[49]

Local Attitudes

Given the DRC's size, it is unsurprising that local attitudes toward nation-building operations—to the limited extent they have been gauged—varied significantly from place to place. The most notable variation was between the east and west. An external study commissioned in late 2005 by the UN Peacekeeping Best Practices Section found that the UN mission was unpopular in the west but that resi-

---

[47] Gambino, 2008, p. 39.

[48] International Crisis Group, 2006.

[49] Monty Marshall and Benjamin R. Cole, *Global Report 2011: Conflict, Governance, and State Fragility*, Vienna, Va.: Center for Systemic Peace, December 1, 2011, p. 30. For details on how this State Fragility Index was calculated, see Marshall and Cole, 2011, p. 36.

dents of the east held much more-favorable views of UN work. In other words, where the UN presence was smaller, attitudes were more hostile, and, where stability and security were fragile, the UN mission was viewed more favorably. In Nord-Kivu (in the east), for example, 50 percent of respondents reported that the presence of the UN mission made them feel safer, whereas only 24 percent of the population reported the same in the western province of Bandundu. The significance of these figures is unclear, however, given that, nationally, 60 percent polled believed that it was time for the UN mission to leave, while half those polled also believed that, if the UN left, the war was likely to restart. In general, respondents to the poll appeared to have a favorable view of an African Union role.[50]

Geographical and Geopolitical

During the decade prior to 2012, the regional situation improved, especially with regard to relations between the DRC and Rwanda. The cooperation of the Rwandan government in stabilizing the DRC was inconsistent and did not result in an end to violence, though its conduct, including its willingness to arrest Nkunda, indicated that Kigali could have a positive effect on the situation in the eastern DRC when it wished to do so. Renewed tensions began to threaten the DRC–Rwanda rapprochement in April 2012. The DRC accused Rwanda of sponsoring a mutiny among Congolese troops in Nord-Kivu—an assertion denied by Rwanda but supported by a UN Group of Experts.[51] By the end of 2012, conflict in the east had surged once again.

Relations have improved with Uganda, which was held liable by the International Court of Justice in 2005 to pay reparations for infringement on the DRC's sovereignty. In June 2008, both countries, along with Sudan, agreed to cooperate to root out the Ugandan rebel group the Lord's Resistance Army from its strongholds in the DRC

---

[50] BERCI International, *Peacekeeping Operations in the Democratic Republic of the Congo: The Perception of the Population*, Peacekeeping Best Practices Section, United Nations Department of Peacekeeping Operations, November 2005.

[51] "Border Dynamics: Mutineers Threaten Security in Eastern DRC," *Jane's Intelligence Review*, July 19, 2012.

and Sudan and launched joint operations against the group. Natural resources, however, may be a source of tension in the future because oil reserves were recently discovered near the DRC–Uganda border.[52]

Cultural and Social

Congolese culture and society changed little as a result of international efforts, which, as noted earlier, were not focused on these domains. Ethnic tensions remain and, in the east, may even have been exacerbated by the fighting between Nkunda's pro-Rwandan forces and "real Congolese." Tribal structures have endured, except where they have been supplanted by power structures that emerged from the war. The level of social development remains extremely low.

Economic

Beginning in 2002, inflation was tamed and the economy began to grow again (see Figures 8.2 and 8.3). Growth decelerated sharply during the 2009 global economic downturn but recovered quickly and exceeded 2008 rates in 2010 and 2011 (see Figure 8.2). Foreign investment was significant; between 2003 and 2007, the government reported $2.7 billion in foreign investment.[53] As in many other postconflict situations, however, growth, in part, reflected the extremely low postwar starting point. Given the small size of the DRC economy in general, growth of 5 to 10 percent per year still generates low per capita GDP.

The DRC remains very poor. Per capita gross national income was $130 in 2006 (compared with an average of $842 in sub-Saharan Africa) and still only $190 per person in 2011. The country is very far from meeting UN Millennium Development Goals.[54] Corruption is widespread, inhibiting public service delivery and complicating relations with donors. The country was ranked 160th of 176 countries on Transparency International's 2012 Corruption Perceptions Index.[55]

---

[52] "External Affairs (Democratic Republic of Congo)," *Jane's Sentinel Security Assessment: Central Africa*, December 16, 2011.

[53] World Bank, 2007, p. 6.

[54] World Bank, 2007, pp. 44, 46.

[55] Transparency International, *Corruption Perceptions Index 2012*, 2012.

Figure 8.2
Annual Growth in Gross Domestic Product in the Democratic Republic of the Congo

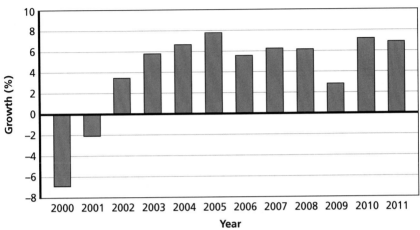

SOURCE: World Bank, undated (c).
RAND *RR167-8.2*

Figure 8.3
Annual Inflation Rate in the Democratic Republic of the Congo as Measured by the Gross Domestic Product Deflator

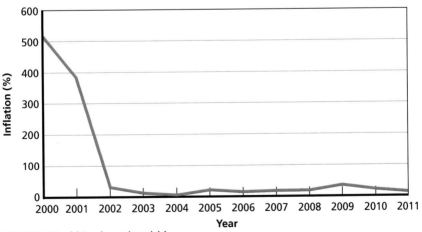

SOURCE: World Bank, undated (c).
RAND *RR167-8.3*

Infrastructure remains so poor that private-sector economic growth is severely constrained. By 2007, there were only 600 kilometers of paved roads.[56] Of the ten provincial capitals, only one can be accessed by land from the capital. Electrification rates are the lowest in Africa.[57] Meanwhile, scant progress has been made in reforming the mining sector, public enterprises, the civil service, the social sectors, customs administration, and the central bank.[58]

Political

Violence during the 2006 elections was successfully avoided. Some analysts thought that election outcomes contributed to the renewal of postelection violence in the east, but a more likely explanation is that the elections simply postponed violence that was bound to occur anyway.[59] Joseph Kabila was reelected in 2011, in polling marred by violence and logistical delays. The elections were judged flawed by independent observers, such as the Carter Center, as well as by official missions, including from the European Union. Nevertheless, these elections appear to have been accepted by the population, and there has been no return to widespread violence. The regime, in spite of the elections, remains largely autocratic. Kabila's presidency has been marked by widespread corruption, control of the justice system by the executive, and bribing and intimidation of the opposition.[60]

The governance indicators of "voice and accountability" and "government effectiveness" have slightly improved since 1998, but this progress has been irregular, and both scores have stagnated since

---

[56] World Bank, 2007, p. 8.

[57] World Bank, 2007, p. 8.

[58] IMF, *Democratic Republic of the Congo: 2007 Article IV Consultation—Staff Report; Staff Supplement; Staff Statement; Public Information Notice on the Executive Board Discussion; and Statement by the Executive Director for the Democratic Republic of the Congo*, Country Report 07/327, September 2007a, p. 5.

[59] Autesserre, 2008.

[60] Séverine Autesserre, *The Trouble with the Congo: Local Violence and the Failure of International Peacebuilding*, Cambridge, UK: Cambridge University Press, 2010, p. 234.

2008.[61] Development of democracy remains stunted: Freedom House characterized the DRC as "not free" and has given it scores of 6 on a 1–7 scale (7 being the worst) for protection of both civil liberties and political rights.[62]

Institutional

The state remains weak and lacking in legitimacy. Institutions are highly corrupt. Political motivations remain mostly predatory in nature; control of the government and bureaucracy are used as opportunities for graft.

Conclusions

What Local Factors Posed the Greatest Challenges?

The local factors within each category that were most important in shaping the environment in which nation-builders sought to promote an enduring peace included the following.

Geographical and Geopolitical

Interference by the DRC's neighbors, either directly or through proxies, has been a persistent source of conflict in the country. Regional cooperation improved in the years after the peace agreement, though not without backsliding. Cooperation with Rwanda threatened to unravel in 2012. Given the multiple sources of instability in the region and the DRC's fragility, new triggers for conflict between the DRC and other neighbors could emerge as well.

Cultural and Social

Tensions, including over land, between the DRC's multiple ethnic and tribal groups have contributed to conflict, especially in the east. The

---

[61] World Bank, undated (d). The DRC had a "voice and accountability" score of −1.9 in 1998 and −1.4 in 2010 (−2.5 being the lowest possible score and +2.5 the highest). Its "government and effectiveness" score was −2.0 in 1998 and −1.7 in 2010.

[62] Freedom House, *Freedom in the World 2012: The Arab Uprisings and Their Global Repercussions*, c. 2012a.

war, in turn, exacerbated these tensions, as well as eroding traditional power structures. Issues in this domain remain unresolved.

Economic

The lootability of the DRC's mineral resources helped to perpetuate the conflict, both by enabling financing of Congolese rebel groups and by motivating intervention on the part of neighboring countries. Severe poverty, minimal infrastructure, and rampant corruption posed major constraints on efforts to reinforce the peace agreement with socioeconomic improvements.

Political

The DRC has a long history of authoritarianism. Elections were a primary focus of the international postconflict nation-building effort. Though the results have been accepted, successive elections have been flawed and the government remains autocratic.

Institutional

Institutions in the DRC have long been—and remain—corrupt, poorly resourced, and lacking in capabilities to provide public services. This general institutional weakness has contributed to the country's vulnerability to conflict. The government has been largely incapable of exerting authority throughout the DRC's vast territory.

Were Local Factors Modified or Circumvented to Promote Enduring Peace?

During the years following the 2002 peace agreement and before the resurgence of violence in 2012, the DRC enjoyed a fragile relative peace, democratization barely advanced, and government effectiveness regressed slightly. Per capita income increased by only 8.2 percent, and the DRC ended the decade dead last in HDI rankings of 187 countries. Poor performance across these dimensions at least partly reflects the fact that the country remained in conflict in certain areas throughout much of the preceding decade. Table 8.1 shows these outcomes, alongside key resources applied by nation-building interveners.

In light of these adverse conditions, the progress that had been made in reducing violence was creditable, even though the situation

Table 8.1
Postintervention Performance and Nation-Building Inputs in the Democratic Republic of the Congo

Performance Indicator	Year of Intervention (1999)	5 Years Later	10 Years Later
At peace?	—	Yes	Yes[a]
Government effectiveness (10-point scale)	3.36	3.27	3.11
Freedom Index (10-point scale)	1.75	2.50	2.50
HDI (10-point scale)	2.20	2.60	2.80
Cumulative growth in per capita GDP (in 1st 5 years and in 10 years after intervention) (%)	—	–5.7	8.2
Nation-Building Input			
Peak military presence per capita, number of troops per 1,000 inhabitants	0.3		
Peak international civilian police presence per capita, number of police per 1,000 inhabitants	0.02		
Average annual per capita assistance in the first 5 years (constant 2010 US$)	36.46		

SOURCES: World Bank, undated (d); Freedom House, various years; UNDP, undated; IMF, undated; Dobbins, Jones, Crane, Chivvis, et al., 2008, Figures 9.2, 9.4, 9.9; UN Peace Operations, various years; World Bank, undated (c).

[a] Civil war in the eastern DRC resumed in 2012.

remained fragile and violence resurged in 2012. One area in which the international effort had comparative success was addressing the geopolitical problems that the DRC faced. This was in part because regional states were responsive to the tools that more-distant intervening actors possessed for resolving these problems. That responsiveness was limited by neighboring states' perception of their own interests, however, as shown by Rwanda's off-again, on-again support for Congolese rebel groups.

The DRC's sheer size, abysmal level of development, bad neighborhood, lootable natural resources, and tribal and ethnic differences made nation-building extremely difficult. Because the international community viewed the DRC as having limited geostrategic significance, the resources devoted to nation-building were limited relative to the scale of the challenges. At as much as $1.4 billion annually, the cost of the UN mission is large in absolute terms, but it is small when viewed on a per capita basis in comparison with the cost of peacekeeping missions in Kosovo or East Timor, for instance.[63] The work of the United Nations, European Union, and others produced some positive results—particularly in reducing the destabilizing interference of the DRC's neighbors—and the situation would surely have been worse absent international efforts. Nevertheless, more than a decade after the UN mission's creation, the DRC remains unstable, corrupt, and poor.

Over time, international actors have come to recognize the extent to which natural resources in the east were contributing to the region's insecurity and the extent to which the problem called for concerted regional action. Lacking physical control of the territory, however, there was little that could be done to stem the outflow of minerals. International trusteeship and other proposals for reasserting control over these resources may work, provided they can be set up, but this seems unlikely.

In general, the international approach to building peace in the DRC has been top down and has been criticized for neglecting the local roots of conflicts and for spending abundantly on national election resources that might otherwise have been used for local institution-building and conflict resolution.[64] Although a more explicitly local

---

[63] Budget estimates are based on UN General Assembly, "Financing of the Support Account for Peacekeeping Operations and the United Nations Logistics Base at Brindisi, Italy: Note by the Secretary-General," A/C.5/66/17, June 12, 2012.

[64] Autesserre, 2008; Séverine Autesserre, "Hobbes and the Congo: Frames, Local Violence, and International Intervention," *International Organization*, Vol. 63, Spring 2009, pp. 249–280; Seth Kaplan, "The Wrong Prescription for the Congo," *Orbis*, Vol. 51, No. 2, 2007, pp. 299–311.

approach might have paid dividends, it would very likely have been more expensive, especially given the security situation in the neediest areas. And the politics of the capital and the broader region also required attention in order to improve security.

The requirements for progress in the DRC may be somewhat clearer now than they were more than a decade ago, but the scale of the challenges remains immense, and the resources that can be put toward the problems will continue to be a crucial limitation on achieving self-sustaining peace. Such a goal remains elusive; critically, it will depend on strong governance improvements in the DRC. But, without the international effort, regional cooperation might not have advanced to the degree that it did, the humanitarian situation would be even worse than it is, and prospects for improvement would be even dimmer.

CHAPTER NINE

Estimating the Challenges and Comparing with Outcomes

In this chapter, we turn to a larger set of the 20 main post–Cold War nation-building operations organized by the United Nations, NATO, or a coalition of willing nations, including the six looked at in more detail in preceding chapters. In each of these 20 cases, we assess the overall degree of difficulty of achieving nation-building objectives imposed by local factors, such as geography, ethnicity, and levels of development. We then compare our estimates of difficulty with the degree of progress achieved in each case in promoting peace, democracy, government effectiveness, economic growth, and human development over five- and ten-year periods following the arrival of international forces. Such a comparison will enable us to assess whether there appears to be any pattern of association of progress with degree of difficulty due to local conditions.

We find that each of the six societies examined in the preceding chapters registered at least some progress in the areas of security, democratization, and economic and social well-being in the decade following the arrival of international forces. All but the DRC also registered some slight progress in government effectiveness. Similarly, in the larger set of 20 cases, there has been, on average, at least some, often significant, progress in each area. Overall, we did not find degree of difficulty to be an obstacle to progress, although it clearly limited absolute results—that is to say, for instance, that poor states did not end up rich, just less poor.

To estimate the relative degree of difficulty faced by interveners engaged in nation-building, we employ a statistical model for analyzing the risk of civil war onset developed by Fearon and Laitin.[1] Among the variables included in the Fearon and Laitin model are levels of ethnic and religious fractionalization, per capita GDP, level of democracy, size of population, proportion of mountainous terrain, political instability, prior conflict, and whether or not the state in question is new or established. Because the primary goal of nation-building is preventing the recurrence of civil war, the greater the risk of civil war onset, the more difficult it should be to achieve that goal. To be clear, our purpose is not to test the Fearon and Laitin model on a small set of cases. Rather, we use the model to estimate the probability of civil war onset for each of the 20 countries in our set as a way of approximating the overall level of difficulty of each case and ordering them on this basis. The countries with the highest probabilities of conflict onset should be, at least roughly, the most-challenging cases for nation-building, and the ones with the lowest probabilities should be the easier cases.[2]

To assess the degree of progress achieved in each of the 20 nation-building interventions, we use statistical indicators to evaluate each country's postconflict performance along several dimensions. Because establishing enduring peace is the principal goal of nation-building, the most important indicator we consider is whether a country is at peace after five years and as of the year of this writing, 2012. We use a widely accepted measure of peace that is based on the number of battle deaths per year, more than 1,000 being the threshold.[3]

---

[1]   Fearon and Laitin, 2003.

[2]   When we used the Fearon and Laitin model to estimate probabilities of civil war onset for the 20 countries discussed in this chapter, we set the "prior war" control variable at zero because we are calculating these probabilities for countries where a civil war has ended and are interested in the risk of renewed conflict in contexts in which war has terminated. See Fearon and Laitin, 2003, pp. 82–83. Because of the way in which the Fearon and Laitin model is constructed, setting the "prior war" control variable at one (meaning that there was a civil war ongoing in the prior year) reduces the probabilities for all 20 countries. In other words, under this model, being engaged in an ongoing civil war (as indicated by the "prior war" variable) reduces the probability of onset of a new civil war.

[3]   We use the definition of *civil war* developed by the Correlates of War Project: sustained combat, involving organized armed forces, resulting in a minimum of 1,000 battle-related fatalities within a 12-month period. See Meredith Reid Sarkees, *The COW Typology of War: Defining and Categorizing Wars (version 4 of the data)*, undated. On the distinction between

We use the Freedom Index, a score developed by Freedom House, to measure progress toward democratization.[4] A country's Freedom Index score is the average of its separate political rights and civil liberties scores. We have converted the seven-point Freedom Index scale to a ten-point scale, with a score of 1 being the worst and 10 the best (we also inverted the Freedom Index scores so that they can be compared more easily with the government effectiveness and human development scores).

We employ the World Bank's Worldwide Governance Indicators (WGI) scores for government effectiveness (one of several dimensions of governance on which the WGI reports) to measure progress in that area.[5] This index is based on surveys of users of government services and captures perceptions of the quality of public services (such as education, transportation, and basic health), the quality of the civil service and the degree of its independence from political pressures, the quality of policy formulation and implementation, and the credibility of the government's commitment to such policies.[6] The government effectiveness score is an index that ranges from –2.5 to 2.5 and has a normal distribution with a mean of zero. An average country, in other words, will have a score of zero (and the world average each year will be zero), the best performer will have a score of 2.5, and the worst performer will have a score of –2.5. As with the Freedom House scores, we have converted this index to a ten-point scale, with a score of 1 indicating the least government effectiveness and 10 the most.

To determine progress achieved in socioeconomic development, we use two measures. First, we look at improvement in terms of national income—specifically, the cumulative growth in per capita GDP in percentages during the first five years and during the first ten

---

the widely used definitions of *civil* and of *armed conflict* (25 or more battle-related deaths per year), see Lotta Themnér and Peter Wallensteen, "Armed Conflict, 1946–2010," *Journal of Peace Research*, Vol. 48, No. 4, July 2011, pp. 525–536.

[4]   Freedom House, 2012a.

[5]   The government effectiveness indicator is one of several governance indicators published by the World Bank, undated (d). The World Bank ranks a total of 212 countries.

[6]   World Bank, undated (d).

years following the intervention.[7] Second, we look at changes in the 20 countries' HDI scores, which are calculated by UNDP. The HDI is a composite measure of achievement in human development across three basic dimensions: health, education, and living standards. It combines indicators of life expectancy, educational attainment, and income and is, in this sense, a broader measure of progress in socioeconomic development than growth in per capita GDP. HDI scores fall between 0 and 1, which, for purposes of comparison, we have converted to a ten-point scale, as we did for measures of democracy and governance.

Sustaining Peace

Table 9.1 ranks the 20 interventions in order of difficulty employing the Fearon and Laitin methodology for estimating risk of civil war onset. We assess the degree of difficulty using the date of intervention as the estimation point. Calculating difficulty on the basis of conditions at the time the intervention was launched reflects the risk of renewed conflict before nation-building efforts—which would be aimed at reducing that risk—were under way. The probabilities of civil war onset for each country are shown in the third column. Bosnia's top ranking among the probabilities may seem surprising as compared with, say, the DRC or Côte d'Ivoire. The reason Bosnia stands out is that the Fearon and Laitin model estimates the odds of civil war onset as 5.25 times greater in the first two years of a state's independent existence than in other years.[8]

The fourth and fifth columns indicate whether the societies in question were at peace (i.e., whether there were fewer than 1,000 battle deaths per annum due to either civil war or international conflict) five years after the intervention and, because we are concerned with *endurance* of peace, in the most recent year, 2012. Table 9.1 also pres-

---

[7] We calculated growth in per capita income using statistics on population and growth in GDP from IMF, "International Financial Statistics (IFS) Query Builder," undated, referenced 2012.

[8] Fearon and Laitin, 2003, p. 85.

Table 9.1
Peace Endurance

Difficulty Rankings: Countries Ordered from Highest to Lowest Probability of Renewed Civil War Within 5 Years	Year of Intervention	Probability of Civil War Onset Within 5 Years from Start of Intervention (%)	At Peace 5 Years After Intervention	At Peace in 2012	Peak International Presence per Capita, Number per 1,000 Inhabitants	
					Military Troops	Civilian Police
1. Bosnia	1995	39.80	Yes	Yes	17.5	0.59
2. Sudan	2005	17.50	Yes[a]	Yes[a]	0.29	0.02
3. Kosovo	1999	15.10	Yes	Yes	19.3	2.38
4. Sierra Leone	2000	12.70	Yes	Yes	4.5	0.02
5. East Timor	1999	11.40	Yes	Yes	9.8	1.56
6. Afghanistan	2001	10.30	No	No	1.6	0
7. DRC	1999	8.80	Yes[a]	No	0.3	0.02
8. Somalia	1992	6.90	No	No	5.7	0.01
9. Iraq	2003	6.70	No	No	6.5	0
10. Mozambique	1992	6.20	Yes	Yes	0.4	0.07
11. Haiti	2004	5.40	Yes	Yes	0.78	0.19
12. Liberia	2003	5.30	Yes	Yes	4.72	0.36

Table 9.1—Continued

Difficulty Rankings: Countries Ordered from Highest to Lowest Probability of Renewed Civil War Within 5 Years	Year of Intervention	Probability of Civil War Onset Within 5 Years from Start of Intervention (%)	At Peace 5 Years After Intervention	At Peace in 2012	Peak International Presence per Capita, Number per 1,000 Inhabitants	
					Military Troops	Civilian Police
13. El Salvador	1992	5.30	Yes	Yes	0.1	0.06
14. Namibia	1988	5.00	Yes	Yes	3.4	1.07
15. Cambodia	1991	4.30	Yes	Yes	1.5	0.3
16. Eastern Slavonia[b]	1995	3.60	Yes	Yes	35.3	4.35
17. Albania	1997	2.70	Yes	Yes	2.3	0.08
18. Macedonia	2001	2.60	Yes	Yes	2.4	0.2
19. Côte d'Ivoire	2002	2.30	Yes	Yes	0.45	0.07
20. Solomon Islands	2003	0.60	Yes	Yes	3.96	0.66

SOURCES: Dobbins, Jones, Crane, Chivvis, et al., 2008, Figures 9.2 and 9.4; UN Peacekeeping Operations, 2004, 2005, 2006, 2008.

[a] For Sudan and the DRC, see the discussion of ongoing violence in the text that follows.

[b] For Eastern Slavonia, a region of Croatia, we use data for Croatia throughout this report.

NOTE: See text for explanation of difficulty rankings.

ents indicators of the magnitude of resources international interveners applied that were directly related to establishing peace. The sixth and seventh columns show the peak per capita density of international troops and police within the ten-year period after intervention.

Table 9.1 reveals that, for these 20 cases, there was no correlation between the probability of civil war onset absent an intervention and success in preventing a renewal of civil war where there was, in fact, an intervention.[9] The four countries where peace has not been achieved are within the top half of the list in terms of anticipatable difficulty but not among the most-difficult cases. In other words, looking only at the set of cases in which there have been major international interventions (a much smaller number of cases than the number on which the Fearon and Laitin model is based), the model's estimates of the relative likelihood of renewed civil war do not appear to hold up. This suggests that the influence of structural conditions in these countries on whether civil war recurred was outweighed by the influence of a factor not considered in the model—that is, international peacekeeping intervention. Put differently, these interventions reduced the risk of renewed conflict, even in several of the most-difficult cases.

Looking beneath the surface of these data, we see that the *type* of intervention matters considerably in whether the intervention succeeds in producing enduring peace. All but one (the DRC) of the 17 peacekeeping missions produced peace, and none of the three peace-enforcement missions did so.[10] That is to say, all but one of the interventions that were initiated on the basis of a peace agreement or with the consent of the warring parties succeeded in establishing peace, whereas the three that lacked such consent—Somalia, Afghanistan, and Iraq—did not.

---

[9] In Table 9.1, there is no statistically significant correlation between probability of war and peace status five years after intervention or peace status in 2012. The p-value is 0.91, meaning that there is a 91-percent likelihood that the correlation between probability of war and peace status in 2012 (0.0269) would be observed purely by chance.

[10] Our use of the terms *peacekeeping* and *peace enforcement* to describe different missions in this volume is not meant to distinguish between missions undertaken under the authority of Chapter VI versus Chapter VII of the UN Charter. Some of the missions that we characterize as having been launched with local consent were authorized under Chapter VII.

Bosnia and Kosovo are sometimes regarded as peace-enforcement missions because the peace agreements in both cases were coerced, but, in both cases, peace agreements were in place when NATO ground troops arrived, and the entry thus had the consent, however grudging, of all the parties. Some of the UN peacekeeping missions among the 17 interventions noted were conducted under Chapter VII of the UN Charter, which authorizes the use of force, and these are also sometimes referred to as peace-enforcement missions, but, again, the entry of troops was not opposed but rather had the agreement of the warring parties, even if some level of eventual resistance was anticipated.

In some of the 17 peacekeeping cases, peace has not been uniformly sustained from the time of intervention until 2012. Côte d'Ivoire, for example, experienced a high level of violence related to contested presidential election results in 2011.[11] As of 2012, however, the violence had abated following the arrest of former president Laurent Gbagbo and his replacement by Alassane Ouattara, but the security situation remained fragile. In East Timor, international forces had to be reinserted in 2003 when fighting broke out on their initial departure.

Neither is peace firmly established in all these cases. Peace is especially fragile in Sudan, where civilian populations are particularly vulnerable to tribal violence that has involved rival communities in lethal raids whose death toll is often difficult to determine. Local officials cited 2,000–3,000 killed in a single raid in the town of Pibor in January 2012.[12] In March–April 2012, clashes also took place between Sudanese and South Sudanese armies along the border between Sudan and its newly independent neighbor to the south, albeit with limited

---

[11] As of April 2011, these clashes had already caused at least 400 deaths in the capital city, Abidjan (Louis Charbonneau, "Death Toll in Ivory Coast's Abidjan to Rise Sharply: U.N.," Reuters, April 11, 2011). In the western town of Duékoué, election-related intercommunal violence resulted in large-scale massacres in March 2011, with an estimated 330 killed according to the United Nations and 1,000 according to aid organizations (Adam Nossiter, "Hundreds Killed in Ivory Coast Town as Conflict Intensifies," *New York Times*, April 2, 2011). More than 100 more people were killed in ethnic violence in the same region during that period (Andrew Harding, "Ivory Coast: More Than 100 Bodies Found, Says UN," BBC News, April 8, 2011).

[12] "South Sudan Horror at Deadly Cattle Vendetta," BBC News, January 16, 2012.

casualties.[13] Violence also continues in the Darfur region of Sudan, although, again, the numbers of deaths are difficult to determine.[14]

In the DRC, during much of 2012, violence persisted but with the number of deaths directly attributable to ongoing conflict being uncertain. The United Nations estimated that at least 264 civilians were killed in ethnic violence between May and September 2012 solely in the region of Nord-Kivu, with potentially many more uncounted victims.[15] The advocacy group Genocide Watch estimated that ethnic violence killed 700 people in Nord-Kivu and Sud-Kivu between April and October 2012.[16] As of November 2012, however, civil war had resumed in the eastern DRC, with a new rebel group, the M23, having made significant gains against a dysfunctional DRC army and taken control of the important city of Goma.[17]

Large population size is considered a risk factor in the Fearon and Laitin model, and Sudan and the DRC are the two largest of the 20 societies. In these cases, the challenges of weak governance, insecurity, and large territories and populations are compounded by the difficulty of securing adequate international assets to help them establish enduring peace.

Table 9.1 shows some correlation between level of anticipatable difficulty and level of international effort; that is to say, those societies with a higher propensity to renewed conflict, with the exception of Sudan at the high end of difficulty and Eastern Slavonia at the low end, tended to attract higher per capita levels of international troop deploy-

---

[13] See, for instance, "Sudan and South Sudan in Fierce Oil Border Clashes," BBC News, March 27, 2012.

[14] For example, Khartoum announced in September 2012 that its forces had killed 45 insurgents in Darfur, but this number could not be verified ("'Dozens Killed' as Sudan's Army and Rebels Clash," BBC News, September 7, 2012).

[15] UN Joint Human Rights Office, *Report of the United Nations Joint Human Rights Office on Human Rights Violations Perpetrated by Armed Groups During Attacks on Villages in Ufamandu I and II, Nyamaboko I and II and Kibabi Groupements, Masisi Territory, North Kivu Province, Between April and September 2012*, November 2012, ¶ 20.

[16] "Genocide and Mass Atrocity Warning: Democratic Republic of the Congo—The Kivus," *Genocide Watch*, October 3, 2012.

[17] Gettleman, 2012, p. A1.

ments (but not higher per capita levels of police deployments).[18] It is also true, however, that the smaller societies, regardless of anticipatable difficulties, had higher international troop and police densities. The sizes of international troop and police deployments are driven by both demand (level of anticipated difficulty) and supply.

That the table indicates that peacekeeping is more successful than peace enforcement is hardly surprising. It is notable, however, that Table 9.1 suggests that, aside from consent of the parties and perhaps size, there are no other local conditions that systematically preclude at least some degree of success in achieving peace, the prime objective of any peacekeeping mission. Peace was achieved in most of these 20 cases regardless of variation in level of difficulty calculated on the basis of varied local conditions.

Promoting Democracy

Table 9.2 shows levels of anticipatable difficulty alongside progress in democratization. The fourth, fifth, and sixth columns show each society's Freedom Index at intervention, after five years, and after ten years, or, if ten years have not passed, in 2011, the last year for which figures were available.[19] The seventh column shows the net change in Freedom Index scores over ten years. (As noted earlier, we have inverted and converted Freedom House's seven-point Freedom Index to a ten-point index, with 10 being the best possible score.)

With the exceptions of Sudan and Côte d'Ivoire, every one of these 20 societies, even those that remained in conflict, registered advances in democratization over ten years and, in some cases, quite significantly so. On a scale of 1 to 10, these 10 societies experienced an average (mean) improvement of 2.15 points, or 21.5 percentage points.

---

[18] If we remove Sudan and Eastern Slavonia from the sample, there is a positive significant correlation between the probability of war and peak international military presence per capita at the 1-percent level (the correlation is 0.74, with a p-value of 0.0005); the correlation is also positive but not significant for peak international civilian police presence.

[19] Freedom House's latest report (Freedom House, 2012a) presents data for 2011.

Table 9.2
Democratization

Difficulty Rankings: Countries Ordered from Highest to Lowest Probability of Renewed Civil War Within 5 Years	Year of Intervention	Probability of Civil War Onset Within 5 Years from Start of Intervention (%)	Freedom Index at Intervention	Freedom Index 5 Years Later	Freedom Index 10 Years Later, or in 2011	Net Change in Freedom Index in 10 Years
1. Bosnia	1995	39.80	2.5	4.75	6.25	+3.75
2. Sudan	2005	17.50	1	1	1	0
3. Kosovo	1999	15.10	1[a]	NA	4.75	+3.75[a]
4. Sierra Leone	2000	12.70	4.75	6.25	7	+2.25
5. East Timor	1999	11.40	1[a]	7	6.25	+6.25[a]
6. Afghanistan	2001	10.30	1	4	2.5	+1.5
7. DRC	1999	8.80	1.75	2.5	2.5	+0.75
8. Somalia	1992	0.30	1	1	1.75	+0.75
9. Iraq	2003	6.70	1	2.5	3.25	+2.25
10. Mozambique	1992	6.20	4	6.25	6.25	+2.25
11. Haiti	2004	5.40	2.5	4.75	4.75	+2.25
12. Liberia	2003	5.30	2.5	6.25	6.25	+3.75
13. El Salvador	1992	5.30	7	7.75	7.75	+0.75

Table 9.2—Continued

Difficulty Rankings: Countries Ordered from Highest to Lowest Probability of Renewed Civil War Within 5 Years	Year of Intervention	Probability of Civil War Onset Within 5 Years from Start of Intervention (%)	Freedom Index at Intervention	Freedom Index 5 Years Later	Freedom Index 10 Years Later, or in 2011	Net Change in Freedom Index in 10 Years
14. Namibia	1988	5.00	6.25	7.75	7.75	+1.5
15. Cambodia	1991	4.30	2.5	2.5	3.25	+0.75
16. Eastern Slavonia	1995	3.60	5.5	7.75	8.5	+3
17. Albania	1997	2.70	5.5	7	7	+1.5
18. Macedonia	2001	2.60	5.5	7	7	+1.5
19. Côte d'Ivoire	2002	2.30	2.5	1.75	2.50	0
20. Solomon Islands	2003	0.60	1.75	6.25	6.25	+4.5
Mean						+2.15
Median						+1.875

SOURCES: Freedom House, *Freedom in the World* reports, various years.

[a] Freedom House has no separate rating for Kosovo or East Timor in the pre-intervention context. Given that both societies had suffered massive repression in the period immediately prior to the arrival of international forces, we have suggested a rating of 1 (the lowest) for the condition at the time of intervention. If Kosovo and East Timor were not included in our calculations of the average change in Freedom Index scores over ten years, the mean would be +1.83 and the median would be +1.5, somewhat lower than the average improvement when they are included. NA = not available.

This effect generally remains stable or increases over time. Between five and ten years after intervention, seven countries saw their scores increase, while only two (East Timor and Afghanistan) experienced a decrease. All other countries remained stable.[20] Few of these territories (El Salvador, Namibia, and Eastern Slavonia) became fully consolidated democracies, however, as measured by falling within Freedom House's category of "free" societies—that is, those whose scores are within the upper third of the scale.[21]

These figures indicate no correlation between the degree of anticipatable difficulty and the degree of progress toward democratization.[22] Indeed, Bosnia, the hardest case, registered the second-greatest gain. The highest gain, in contrast, was in the easiest case, Solomon Islands. There was even some improvement in the four societies in which peace was not established: the DRC, Somalia, Afghanistan, and Iraq.

Improving Governance

Table 9.3 compares difficulty in preventing renewed conflict to changes in government effectiveness. The fourth, fifth, and sixth columns show each society's government effectiveness index at intervention, after five years and after ten, or, if ten years have not passed, in 2010, the last year for which these data were available. The seventh column shows the net change in government effectiveness over ten years.

---

[20] This excludes Kosovo, for which a comparison between five and ten years after intervention was not possible because Kosovo was internationally administered at the five-year mark.

[21] Using Freedom Index scores, Freedom House categorizes countries as "free," "partly free," and "not free." See Freedom House, 2012a, for the designations for each country. Based on our conversion of the Freedom Index to a ten-point scale with 10 as the best possible score, the three categories correspond to scores of 1 to 3.75 for "not free," 4 to 7 for "partly free," and 7.25 to 10 for "free."

[22] There is no statistically significant correlation between probability of civil war and net change in Freedom Index over ten years (the correlation is only 0.25, with a p-value of 0.28). Table 9.2 indicates a slight inverse relationship between Freedom Index scores at five and ten years and relative degree of anticipatable difficulty in preventing renewed conflict, but the relationship is not statistically significant.

Table 9.3
Government Effectiveness

Difficulty Rankings: Countries Ordered from Highest to Lowest Probability of Renewed Civil War Within 5 Years	Year of Intervention	Probability of Civil War Onset Within 5 Years from Start of Intervention (%)	Government Effectiveness at Intervention	Government Effectiveness 5 Years Later	Government Effectiveness 10 Years Later or in 2010	Net Change in Government Effectiveness in 10 Years
1. Bosnia	1995	39.80	3.24	4.6	5.19	+1.95
2. Sudan	2005	17.50	2.96	3.03	3.03	+0.07
3. Kosovo	1999	15.10	NA	NA	4.78	NA
4. Sierra Leone	2000	12.70	2.87	3.07	3.36	+0.49
5. East Timor	1999	11.40	NA	3.43	3.43	NA
6. Afghanistan	2001	10.30	1.32	2.82	2.85	+1.53
7. DRC	1999	8.80	3.36	3.27	3.11	−0.25
8. Somalia	1992	6.90	1.73	1.61	2.62	+0.89
9. Iraq	2003	6.70	2.44	3.25	3.29	+0.85
10. Mozambique	1992	6.20	5.24	4.8	4.71	−0.53
11. Haiti	2004	5.40	2.54	2.81	2.60	+0.06
12. Liberia	2003	5.30	2.81	3.07	3.36	+0.55
13. El Salvador	1992	5.30	4.28	4.58	4.64	+0.36

Table 9.3—Continued

Difficulty Rankings: Countries Ordered from Highest to Lowest Probability of Renewed Civil War Within 5 Years	Year of Intervention	Probability of Civil War Onset Within 5 Years from Start of Intervention (%)	Government Effectiveness at Intervention	Government Effectiveness 5 Years Later	Government Effectiveness 10 Years Later or in 2010	Net Change in Government Effectiveness in 10 Years
14. Namibia	1988	5.00	NA	6.42	5.88	NA
15. Cambodia	1991	4.30	3.92	3.92	3.99	+0.07
16. Eastern Slavonia	1995	3.60	5.62	6.06	6.45	+0.83
17. Albania	1997	2.70	4.06	4.47	4.83	+0.77
18. Macedonia	2001	2.60	4.09	5.37	5.18	+1.09
19. Côte d'Ivoire	2002	2.30	3.81	3.25	3.11	–0.7
20. Solomon Islands	2003	0.60	1.41	3.72	3.79	+2.38
Mean						+0.61
Median						+0.55

SOURCE: World Bank, undated (d). NA = not available.

It will be noted that, in this area, the level of improvement is limited. Indeed, three societies showed regression in their scores. Those changes in government effectiveness that occurred have proven relatively consistent over the years. Countries that experienced improved government effectiveness after five years of intervention generally saw this effectiveness improve further after ten years (Bosnia, Sierra Leone, Afghanistan, Iraq, Liberia, El Salvador, Eastern Slavonia, Albania, and Solomon Islands). Countries whose government effectiveness had declined after five years of intervention generally saw it decline further after ten years (the DRC, Mozambique, and Côte d'Ivoire). Only Somalia, Haiti, and Macedonia have experienced variations in their government effectiveness scores between five and ten years after intervention. Again, there is no correlation between levels of anticipatable difficulty in preventing renewed conflict and improvements or declines in government effectiveness.[23]

These 20 societies achieved an average of 0.61 improvement on a scale of 10 (or 6.1 percentage points) in the first decade after intervention.[24] While this degree of improvement is not dramatic, it is significant in that any rise in government effectiveness scores represents an advance relative to the world average. As explained earlier, the WGI government effectiveness scale is an index for which the world average each year is always the midpoint (with our conversion to a ten-point scale, the world average is always five). Individual countries' scores are thus relative to each other, and an improved score does not necessarily

---

[23] The correlation between probability of war and net change in government effectiveness over ten years is only 0.28, with a p-value of 0.27.

[24] This calculation does not include Kosovo or East Timor because, in both cases, there were no governments in place when international forces arrived, and government effectiveness ratings are not available for the years of intervention or, in Kosovo's case, for five years later. East Timor had never had an indigenous government in a formal sense, and Kosovo's indigenous provincial government had been disbanded a decade earlier. In both cases, international administrators governed the territories for several years after the interventions, while indigenous governments were created from scratch. It therefore seems reasonable to assume a very low level of government effectiveness at the onset of these two interventions. With this assumption, the increases over ten years to government effectiveness ratings of 4.78 for Kosovo and 3.43 for East Timor were well above the averages that we calculated without including those two countries.

indicate an absolute advancement, but it does demonstrate improvement compared with the rest of the world. In other words, though these 20 postintervention societies mostly continued to have below-average government effectiveness, they did generally improve in this respect relative to the rest of the world.

Achieving Economic Growth

Table 9.4 shows cumulative growth in per capita GDP over the five- and ten-year periods following each intervention, as well as average annual per capita foreign assistance provided to each country over the first five years following the interventions.

Table 9.4 shows a definite correlation between degree of anticipatable difficulty and degree of economic improvement, but not in the direction that might have been expected: Several of the most-difficult cases achieved the greatest economic growth.[25] In at least some of these cases, such as Bosnia and Kosovo, this can be at least partly explained by the abundant international assistance these societies received.

Overall, this is a group of poor and very poor countries (leaving aside oil wealth in Iraq and more–recently discovered hydrocarbon resources in East Timor), as shown in Table 9.5. Fewer than one-third—the Balkan countries, El Salvador, and East Timor—have per capita GNIs of more than $4,000 (roughly the cutoff for the upper-middle income level) after ten years, and fewer do after five years.[26] None of the poor societies in the group was raised out of poverty, but nearly all achieved significant economic growth, and all 15 for which

---

[25] There is a positive significant correlation both between the probability of war and growth in per capita GDP over the first five years and the probability of war and growth in per capita GDP over the first ten years after intervention (at the 1 percent level). For five years the correlation is 0.77 with a p-value of only 0.0001, and for ten years the correlation is 0.80 with the same p-value.

[26] East Timor has seen its national income rise in recent years due to hydrocarbon exploitation, but it still has a low level of socioeconomic development, well below the average for the east Asia and Pacific region. As of 2011, East Timor's HDI rank was 147 of 187 countries.

Table 9.4
Growth in per Capita Gross Domestic Product

Difficulty Rankings: Countries Ordered from Highest to Lowest Probability of Renewed Civil War Within 5 Years	Year of Intervention	Probability of Civil War Onset Within 5 Years from Start of Intervention (%)	Growth in per Capita GDP in 1st 5 years After Intervention (%)	Growth in per Capita GDP in 1st 10 Years After Intervention (%)	Average Annual per Capita Assistance in the First 5 Years (constant 2010 US$)
1. Bosnia	1995	39.80	155.2	213.7	384.00
2. Sudan	2005	17.50	28.8	NA	69.69
3. Kosovo	1999	15.10	20.1	83.2	273.93
4. Sierra Leone	2000	12.70	51.1	72.7	93.10
5. East Timor	1999	11.40	17.8	42.7	361.00
6. Afghanistan	2001	10.30	68.4	130.9	62.72
7. DRC	1999	8.80	-5.7	8.2	36.46
8. Somalia	1992	6.90	NA	NA	89.85
9. Iraq	2003	6.70	78.5	84.4[a]	369.32
10. Mozambique	1992	6.20	27.6	68.8	104.98
11. Haiti	2004	5.40	-5.3	-5.3[a]	74.15
12. Liberia	2003	5.30	12.9	16.4[b]	138.59
13. El Salvador	1992	5.30	8.6	20.6	79.57

Table 9.4—Continued

Difficulty Rankings: Countries Ordered from Highest to Lowest Probability of Renewed Civil War Within 5 Years	Year of Intervention	Probability of Civil War Onset Within 5 Years from Start of Intervention (%)	Growth in per Capita GDP in 1st 5 years After Intervention (%)	Growth in per Capita GDP in 1st 10 Years After Intervention (%)	Average Annual per Capita Assistance in the First 5 Years (constant 2010 US$)
14. Namibia	1988	5.00	4.0	14.2	118.10
15. Cambodia	1991	4.30	17.2	53.6	38.36
16. Eastern Slavonia	1995	3.60	20.6	54.5	19.77
17. Albania	1997	2.70	35.8	75.3	148.84
18. Macedonia	2001	2.60	17.7	35.9	161.66
19. Côte d'Ivoire	2002	2.30	–7.4	–7.4[c]	26.40
20. Solomon Islands	2003	0.60	23.2	20.8[a]	488.58
Mean			29.9	54.6	156.95
Median			20.1	48.1	99.04

SOURCES: IMF, undated; Dobbins, Jones, Crane, Chivvis, et al., 2008, Figure 9.9; World Bank, undated (c).

[a] Based on the most-recent data available (2009).

[b] Based on the most-recent data available (2010).

[c] Based on the most-recent data available (2008).

NOTE: NA = not available.

Table 9.5
Per Capita Gross National Income

Difficulty Rankings: Countries Ordered from Highest to Lowest Probability of Renewed Civil War Within 5 Years	Year of Intervention	PPP per Capita GNI at Intervention ($)	PPP per Capita GNI 5 Years Later ($)	PPP per Capita GNI 10 Years Later ($)
1. Bosnia	1995	1,180	5,010	6,610
2. Sudan	2005	1,530	2,020	NA
3. Kosovo	1999	NA	NA	NA
4. Sierra Leone	2000	360	610	820
5. East Timor	1999	900	1,320	4,410
6. Afghanistan	2001	490	890	910
7. DRC	1999	230	240	310
8. Somalia	1992	NA	NA	NA
9. Iraq	2003	2,330	3,370	3,770
10. Mozambique	1992	260	360	510
11. Haiti	2004	1,010	1,170	1,190
12. Liberia	2003	210	370	520
13. El Salvador	1992	2,980	3,990	4,810

Table 9.5—Continued

Difficulty Rankings: Countries Ordered from Highest to Lowest Probability of Renewed Civil War Within 5 Years	Year of Intervention	PPP per Capita GNI at Intervention ($)	PPP per Capita GNI 5 Years Later ($)	PPP per Capita GNI 10 Years Later ($)
14. Namibia	1988	2,440	3,270	3,870
15. Cambodia	1991	650	670	960
16. Eastern Slavonia	1995	7,990	10,720	14,930
17. Albania	1997	3,090	4,980	7,390
18. Macedonia	2001	5,790	8,730	11,490
19. Côte d'Ivoire	2002	1,490	1,670	1,730
20. Solomon Islands	2003	1,860	2,250	2,360

SOURCE: GNI per capita PPP (current international $) data are drawn from World Bank, undated (a).

NOTE: This table shows GNI per capita based on PPP. PPP GNI is GNI converted to international dollars using PPP rates. We show per capita income, in terms of PPP, for the date of intervention and five and ten years later so that the relative levels of economic development among the 20 countries at these three points in time can be considered. However, it is important to note that changes in PPP per capita income are not the same as changes in per capita GDP as measured using economic growth rates and population because data for the two different measures are collected using different methodologies. Changes in PPP per capita income for a particular country over time do not indicate economic improvement or the lack of it; growth figures are the correct indicator of economic improvement or deterioration. NA = not available.

there are sufficient data achieved improvements in socioeconomic development as measured by HDI scores, as discussed below.

To put these 20 countries' economic growth performance in perspective, Appendix B compares each country's performance with economic growth over the same period among its global income group and within its geographical region. More than half of these countries outperformed either their income group or region or, in the cases of eight countries, both. Seven countries underperformed by comparison with both their income groups and regions. (For two countries, we lack sufficient data.) Several of the underperformers experienced renewed violence during the ten-year period after interventions (particularly the DRC, East Timor, and Haiti, which also experienced hurricanes and a devastating earthquake), probably hampering economic activity, though continuing conflict did not bar overperformance by Afghanistan and Iraq. Levels of economic assistance do not appear to explain the distinctions; four of the seven underperformers were among the top ten recipients of aid among the 20 countries. In sum, the majority of these postintervention societies performed economically as well as or better than their more-tranquil peers.

Advancing Human Development

Table 9.6 charts changes in each society's HDI score. This index adds indicators of health and education to indicators of economic performance (i.e., changes in per capita national income) and thus provides a more comprehensive measurement of improvements and declines in overall living standards.

Again, there is no correlation between levels of anticipatable difficulty and gains in human development. Indeed, several of the most-difficult cases achieved the greatest improvements in their HDI scores. This is most notable for Afghanistan, which, although not at peace, recorded the greatest HDI score improvement, nearly double that of the next-most-sizable advance (by East Timor). Because Afghanistan started from such a low base, it nevertheless has not risen out of the low human development category, illustrating that where a society begins

Table 9.6
Human Development Index Scores

Difficulty Rankings: Countries Ordered from Highest to Lowest Probability of Renewed Civil War Within 5 Years	Year of Intervention	Probability of Civil War Onset Within 5 Years from Start of Intervention (%)	HDI at Intervention	HDI 5 Years Later	HDI 10 Years Later or in 2010	Net Change in HDI in 10 Years
1. Bosnia	1995	39.80	NA	NA	7.2	NA
2. Sudan	2005	17.50	3.8	4.1	4.1	+0.3
3. Kosovo	1999	15.10	NA	NA	NA	NA
4. Sierra Leone	2000	12.70	2.5	3.1	3.3	+0.8
5. East Timor	1999	11.40	4.0[a]	4.5[b]	4.9	+0.9
6. Afghanistan	2001	10.30	2.3[a]	3.4[b]	4.0	+1.7
7. DRC	1999	8.80	2.2[a]	2.6[b]	2.8	+0.6
8. Somalia	1992	6.90	NA	NA	NA	NA
9. Iraq	2003	6.70	5.5[b]	5.6	5.7	+0.2
10. Mozambique	1992	6.20	2.1[c]	2.5[a]	2.6[b]	+0.5
11. Haiti	2004	5.40	4.3[b]	4.5	4.5	+0.2
12. Liberia	2003	5.30	3.0[b]	3.3	3.3	+0.3
13. El Salvador	1992	5.30	5.8[c]	6.2[a]	6.5[b]	+0.7

Table 9.6—Continued

Difficulty Rankings: Countries Ordered from Highest to Lowest Probability of Renewed Civil War Within 5 Years	Year of Intervention	Probability of Civil War Onset Within 5 Years from Start of Intervention (%)	HDI at Intervention	HDI 5 Years Later	HDI 10 Years Later or in 2010	Net Change in HDI in 10 Years
14. Namibia	1988	5.00	5.6[d]	5.9[c]	6.1	+0.5
15. Cambodia	1991	4.30	NA	4.2[c]	4.4[a]	NA
16. Eastern Slavonia	1995	3.60	7.1	7.8	7.9	+0.8
17. Albania	1997	2.70	6.9[a]	7.2[b]	7.3	+0.4
18. Macedonia	2001	2.60	NA	7.0[b]	7.3	NA
19. Côte d'Ivoire	2002	2.30	3.8[b]	3.8	4.0	+0.2
20. Solomon Islands	2003	0.60	5.0[b]	5.1	5.1	+0.1
Mean						+0.6
Median						+0.5

SOURCE: UNDP, "International Human Development Indicators: Do-It-Yourself Data Tables," undated.

[a] 2000.

[b] 2005.

[c] 1995.

[d] 1990.

NOTE: Prior to 2005, the HDI was produced in five-year increments. As previously noted, we have converted the 0–1 HDI scores to a ten-point scale. NA = not available.

on any of these indices will affect where it ends at any given point in time but will not necessarily affect the rate of progress it can achieve.[27]

Summing Up

When we consider all the tables in this chapter, these data show that even the poorest countries are not excluded from achieving peace, recording gains in socioeconomic development, or advancing democracy. But, with the exception of lower-middle-income Namibia, the more economically developed countries as indicated by level of per capita national income—Eastern Slavonia (Croatia), Bosnia, Macedonia, and Albania—all had the highest government effectiveness scores after five and after ten years. Two of these four, Eastern Slavonia and Macedonia, already had upper-middle income levels when the interventions there commenced. On the other hand, Afghanistan and Solomon Islands had the first- and third-greatest improvements in effectiveness, Bosnia being the second.

Table 9.7 summarizes the net changes for each of the 20 countries in the performance indicators discussed in this chapter.

In sum, the great majority of these 20 societies saw improvements in security while achieving among them, on average, progress in every area of performance that we measured. This progress includes a mean increase of 55 percent in per capita income, mean improvements of 21.5 percentage points (2.15 points on a ten-point scale) in democratization, and 6 percentage points each (0.6 points out of ten) in human development and government effectiveness. In the next chapter, we explore explanations for these outcomes.

---

[27] The cutoff point between the low and medium human development categories for 2011 was around 0.5. Afghanistan ranked 172nd of 187 countries in HDI rankings for 2011 (unchanged from 2010). HDI rankings place countries in four categories of human development: low, medium, high, and very high. Of the territories in Table 9.5 for which there are data, only those in the Balkans are in the high or (for Eastern Slavonia, that is, Croatia) very high category (UNDP, undated).

Table 9.7
Summary of Net Changes in Performance Indicators Following 20 Major Post–Cold War Nation-Building Interventions

Difficulty Rankings: Countries Ordered from Highest to Lowest Probability of Renewed Civil War Within 5 Years	Probability of Civil War Onset Within 5 Years from Start of Intervention (%)	At Peace in 2012	In First 10 Years After Intervention			
			Net Change in Freedom Index (10-point scale)	Net Change in Government Effectiveness (10-point scale)	Net Change in HDI Score (10-point scale)	Cumulative Growth in per Capita GDP (%)
1. Bosnia	39.80	Yes	+3.75	+1.95	NA	213.7
2. Sudan	17.50	Yes	0	+0.07	+0.3	NA
3. Kosovo	15.10	Yes	+3.75[a]	NA	NA	83.2
4. Sierra Leone	12.70	Yes	+2.25	+0.49	+0.8	72.7
5. East Timor	11.40	Yes	+6.25[a]	NA	+0.9	42.7
6. Afghanistan	10.30	No	+1.5	+1.53	+1.7	130.9
7. DRC	8.80	No	+0.75	−0.25	+0.6	8.2
8. Somalia	0.30	No	+0.75	+0.89	NA	NA
9. Iraq	6.70	No	+2.25	+0.85	+0.2	84.4[b]
10. Mozambique	6.20	Yes	+2.25	−0.53	+0.5	68.8
11. Haiti	5.40	Yes	+2.25	+0.06	+0.2	−5.3[b]
12. Liberia	5.30	Yes	+3.75	+0.55	+0.3	16.4[c]
13. El Salvador	5.30	Yes	+0.75	+0.36	+0.7	20.6

Table 9.7—Continued

Difficulty Rankings: Countries Ordered from Highest to Lowest Probability of Renewed Civil War Within 5 Years	Probability of Civil War Onset Within 5 Years from Start of Intervention (%)	At Peace in 2012	Net Change in Freedom Index (10-point scale)	In First 10 Years After Intervention		
				Net Change in Government Effectiveness (10-point scale)	Net Change in HDI Score (10-point scale)	Cumulative Growth in per Capita GDP (%)
14. Namibia	5.00	Yes	+1.5	NA	+0.5	14.2
15. Cambodia	4.30	Yes	+0.75	+0.07	NA	53.6
16. Eastern Slavonia	3.60	Yes	+3	+0.83	+0.8	54.5
17. Albania	2.70	Yes	+1.5	+0.77	+0.4	75.3
18. Macedonia	2.60	Yes	+1.5	+1.09	NA	35.9
19. Côte d'Ivoire	2.30	Yes	0	-0.7	+0.2	-7.4[d]
20. Solomon Islands	0.60	Yes	+4.5	+2.38	+0.1	20.8[b]
Mean			+2.15	+0.61	+0.6	54.6
Median			+1.875	+0.55	+0.5	48.1

Table 9.7—Continued

Difficulty Rankings: Countries Ordered from Highest to Lowest Probability of Renewed Civil War Within 5 Years	Probability of Civil War Onset Within 5 Years from Start of Intervention (%)	At Peace in 2012	In First 10 Years After Intervention			
			Net Change in Freedom Index (10-point scale)	Net Change in Government Effectiveness (10-point scale)	Net Change in HDI Score (10-point scale)	Cumulative Growth in per Capita GDP (%)

SOURCES: Freedom House, various years; World Bank, undated (d); UNDP, undated; IMF, undated

[a] For Kosovo and East Timor, we assume a Freedom Index rating of 1 (the lowest) for the condition at the time of intervention because those societies had suffered massive repression in the period immediately prior to the arrival of international forces.

[b] Based on the most-recent data available (2009).

[c] Based on the most-recent data available (2010).

[d] Based on the most-recent data available (2008).

NOTE: NA = not available.

CHAPTER TEN

Conclusions

The case studies explored in this volume aim to answer two principal questions: First, what local factors were important in each case in giving rise to conflict and threatening to perpetuate it? And second, were external actors able to modify or work around those factors to promote enduring peace, and, if so, how? The answers to the first question illuminate which local circumstances pose the greatest challenges to nation-building, as well as the best opportunities for nation-building success. The answers to the second offer insights into how nation-building interveners may most effectively target their efforts in inevitable future operations to end conflicts and stabilize countries in their aftermath. The concluding sections of each case study offer specific answers for that particular society; in this chapter, we synthesize those answers and draw from our statistical analysis in Chapter Nine to provide broader conclusions.

We chose the six societies covered in Chapters Three through Eight among the larger field of significant post–Cold War nation-building operations with a view to securing maximum variety of size, location, level of development, ethnic and religious fractionalization, terrain, and other local conditions that the relevant literature suggests should have the most influence on prospects for securing peace. Yet, despite the very different societies chosen for this study, the factors that had the most influence on both conflict and peace proved rather similar.[1]

---

[1] We did not include Afghanistan or Iraq among our six case studies because we (and many others) have already examined the factors at play in these two operations at some length.

The Transformational Limits of Nation-Building

Our case studies show that the transformational effects that nation-building has on local conditions are limited but that nonetheless in five of the six countries we examined in detail—with the DRC, having seen a resumption of civil war, being an exception—nation-building operations were followed by improved security, greater enjoyment of political rights and civil liberties, higher levels of national income, and, to lesser extents, improved human development and government effectiveness. Similar gains were experienced in most of the 20 countries discussed in Chapter Nine.

In the six cases, many local factors that contributed to one degree or another to conflict defied modification or elimination. For example, in El Salvador, landlessness remained a problem; in Cambodia, nationalism and xenophobia endured; the inequitable distribution of resources persisted in Sierra Leone; ethnic divisions hardened in Bosnia; regional and political identity differences continued to produce civil unrest in East Timor; and institutions continued to be extremely weak in the DRC. Though, as our statistical performance indicators show, improvements were achieved to varying degrees in these countries, governments largely remained ineffective deliverers of public services, poor societies remained poor, lootable resources continued to be looted, security organ capabilities were still weak, and in none of the cases was corruption seriously diminished. The countries that were better off to begin with institutionally and economically were better off at the conclusion of nation-building interventions, as compared with those that started out with greater limitations. Yet they were almost all measurably better off than when these operations began.

In some respects, the nation-building interveners, as well as local leaders, did not make concerted efforts to alter or eliminate particular factors that had contributed to conflict in the past. In Cambodia, for instance, minimal efforts were made to confront the social and cultural

---

Neither did we include Somalia, where the U.S. and UN peace-enforcement activities were abandoned early on. Thus, most of our six cases represent some degree of success and are, in this sense, not fully representative. We did include Afghanistan, Iraq, and Somalia among the 20 cases considered in our statistical analyses in Chapter Nine, however.

conditions that facilitated the rise of the Khmer Rouge. In Bosnia, only belated and half-hearted attempts were made to bridge ethnic divides in society by, for example, trying to weed ethnic divisiveness out of the education system. Ethnic, tribal, and land-related tensions in the eastern DRC received little attention. In other respects, concerted efforts were met with stiff resistance. For example, management and regulation of the diamond industry in Sierra Leone was a focus of attention, but reform efforts proved insufficient to overcome the incentives for illegal extraction and corrupt profit-taking.

The case studies also show that some types of local conditions can be more readily modified than others. Institutional weakness, for instance, was not generally amenable to transformation within the time frame of nation-building operations, though there were some important examples otherwise, such as improvement of the military in Sierra Leone. Lack of skilled human resources was a significant constraint in this regard and one that could not be quickly ameliorated even where financial resources were in good supply, as the experience in East Timor shows. The challenge of institutional development is reflected in the limited improvement in the countries' government effectiveness scores. Effective delivery of public services requires a functioning bureaucracy.

On the other hand, economic recovery from wartime devastation generally was achieved. In addition, most of the six countries, freed from conflict and, in some instances, from authoritarian preconflict regimes, made progress in adopting formal democratic practices, as well as in democratization more substantively. Only El Salvador, however, has a fully consolidated democracy; Bosnia, East Timor, and Sierra Leone are rated by Freedom House as "partly free," while Cambodia and the DRC remain "not free."[2]

In the six cases, a relatively narrow set of factors made the crucial difference between war and peace; these are discussed in the next section. Where nation-building has succeeded in achieving its primary purpose of establishing enduring peace, interveners were able to modify or sufficiently mitigate these crucial factors. It is likely, but dif-

---

[2]   Freedom House, 2012a.

ficult to prove, that even modest achievements with respect to other, harder-to-change factors reinforced these successes.

To say that nation-building has not transformed many problematic local factors is not to say that these countries are not better off. As shown in Chapter Nine, many improvements have been achieved. In some instances, those improvements may simply be attributable to the end of conflict (often accomplished with the help of external actors), which opens up economic and social opportunities. But, in others, nation-building activities can be credited, as shown in the case studies. Moreover, it is apparent that, even where some local factors that contributed to conflict have not been modified and where politics have continued to be unstable or security fragile, the lengthy presence of external actors has staved off conflict. In East Timor, foreign security forces are still present because they are needed to quell occasional civil unrest; a large UN peacekeeping operation continues to work at reducing violence in the DRC;[3] and, in Bosnia, the lifespan of the OHR has exceeded all expectations because of domestic leaders' continued inability to exercise effective self-government.

Factors Crucial to Establishing Enduring Peace

Two factors emerged in the case studies as crucial to producing conflict and crucial for nation-builders to resolve or mitigate if they are to successfully promote enduring peace. The first is geopolitical circumstances—that is to say, the behavior of external state actors—and the second is the political and economic influence of domestic patronage networks. These factors also help explain the patterns of statistical indicators of nation-building outcomes discussed in Chapter Nine.

---

[3] The mission, now named MONUSCO, had more than 23,000 personnel as of the end of September 2012 (MONUSCO, undated).

Geopolitics

The most influential factor promoting war and peace was the behavior of external actors. In a sense, this connection is axiomatic because the very act of intervening for the purpose of nation-building is an activity undertaken by outside actors. But the effect of geopolitics went well beyond the dispatch of a peacekeeping force. In each of these six cases, the regional and global situation had a profound effect in fomenting or sustaining the conflict and then in its enduring termination.

Civil war in Cambodia, an ethnically homogenous society historically characterized by deference to authority, was triggered by U.S. and North and South Vietnamese incursions and then sustained by Vietnamese, Chinese, Soviet, and U.S. support for contending factions. Peace came largely as a result of détente, not so much between the United States and the Soviet Union as between China and the Soviet Union. With the removal of malign external influences, Cambodia gradually returned to its earlier state—poor and poorly governed but peaceful. It also became somewhat more prosperous.

The civil war in El Salvador grew out of extreme economic disparities but became embroiled in the wider regional competition between the United States and the Soviet Union and their local proxies. Once the superpower competition ended, the war in El Salvador was also quickly brought to an end with support from both Washington and Moscow.

The war in Bosnia was fought along ethnic lines but instigated and driven by the aspirations of national leaders in neighboring Serbia and Croatia. The forces they supported and the Bosnian Muslim forces, which lacked an external patron, fought themselves essentially to a standstill, at which point international pressures became sufficient to persuade Serbia and Croatia to bridle their local clients and to lead all the conflict parties to make peace.

Tiny East Timor was entirely at the mercy of its neighbors. It was misgoverned and brutalized for decades by Indonesia, liberated by Australia, and then governed for several years by the United Nations. It was international political and economic pressures on the government of Indonesia that caused that government to both abandon its claims to

East Timor and then rein in its local agents who had been terrorizing the newly freed society.

The civil war in Sierra Leone was sparked by an invasion of dissident elements located in neighboring Liberia supported by a faction in that country's own civil conflict. The UN peacekeeping operation gained traction only once the former colonial power, the United Kingdom, stepped in to sharply suppress insurgent elements. Peace in Sierra Leone was consolidated only once the civil war in Liberia also ended.

Conflict in the DRC stemmed originally from the disintegration of the Mobutu regime but was perpetuated by repeated military incursions by several neighboring states and their support of local clients. Although international troops and economic assistance were certainly important in restoring some degree of peace after the 1999 UN intervention, the decisive factor was the eventual withdrawal by neighboring states of their troops and of their support for contending factions within the DRC—under international economic and political pressure but also because of their own motivations. The reduction in violence persisted so long as the DRC's neighbors cooperated with Kinshasa in suppressing transnational armed groups still active on its territory. But this fragile relative peace broke down in 2012 when apparent Rwandan backing once again enabled rebel gains and a consequent surge in violence in the eastern DRC.

Patronage Networks

A second major factor influencing the course of nation-building efforts was the persistence of strong patronage networks controlling much of political and economic life in these societies. Regional experts have tended to view and explain these patronage networks as more or less unique cultural or historical phenomena, and certainly such networks were extended through a variety of channels—ethnic, religious, tribal, clan, linguistic, or geographic—but their actions and effects were remarkably similar.

Whereas the international community has had considerable success in altering the geopolitical sources of conflict in each of the six cases, it had much less success in weakening the hold of patronage networks that were competing for wealth and power. These patronage networks could be and often were co-opted into power-sharing arrangements that produced peace and even some modicum of democracy, but they could almost never be persuaded to support institutional and policy reforms that would curb their own rent-seeking capacity.

In Bosnia, these networks, some formed in the former Yugoslavia, were strengthened and criminalized and took on ethnic coloration during the civil war, and they have continued to dominate the political and economic life of the country ever since. In Sierra Leone and the DRC, patronage was organized around tribes and ethnic groups; in El Salvador, around social class; and, in East Timor, along linguistic and geographic lines. In Cambodia, the utter lack of government institutions at the end of the conflict led to the reemergence of a patronage system as a means of distributing what few resources existed. Although competing patrons sometimes collaborated to divide the political and economic pies, they all resisted strengthening of any state institutions they could not capture and exploit.

The ability of a more or less united international community to alter geopolitical realities and co-opt local patronage networks thus largely explains the achievement registered in these six cases of peace, some democratization, and varying levels of socioeconomic improvement. The resistance of these networks to strengthening the state and curbing their own ability to tap its resources helps explain the lack of improvement in government effectiveness.

The Impact of Geopolitics and Patronage Networks in 20 Cases

These same factors also help explain the patterns of performance indicators in the larger set of 20 societies that experienced nation-building interventions discussed in Chapter Nine. All of the other factors usually cited as sources of conflict—such as poverty, geography, size, prior democratic experience, and ethnic or religious fractionalization—certainly affected the pace of change in these societies, yet none of these factors, except perhaps size, either explains most of the disparities in results or has prevented some degree of success.

Geopolitics and the strength of patronage networks also best explain the four failures among these 20 cases, specifically Afghanistan, Iraq, Somalia, and the DRC. The first two countries were invaded by the United States, so neither was there a peace agreement in place when international forces arrived nor did their presence enjoy the consent of the parties to the preceding conflicts. In both cases, the United States chose not to co-opt the dominant patronage network, the Pashtun Islamists in Afghanistan and the Sunni secularists in Iraq. Denied their accustomed access to wealth and power, these networks chose to resist. Equally and perhaps even more importantly, they received substantial external support in order to do so.

The United States enjoyed some degree of regional support for its invasion of Afghanistan. Pakistan very reluctantly acquiesced, but all the other regional states supported the intervention. Iran was soon antagonized by being included in President George W. Bush's "axis of evil," while Pakistan soon resumed support for Afghan Pashtun militant Islamists.

The United States had almost no regional support for its invasion of Iraq. Among that country's six neighbors, only Kuwait supported the U.S. intervention. Once the George W. Bush administration began touting its intention to turn Iraq into a democratic model that would ultimately inspire similar changes among all of its neighbors, regional hostility to the project hardened further. Iran and Syria began supporting the operations of Shi'a and Sunni extremists, respectively; Turkey staged several small military incursions into the Kurdish north and threatened larger such actions; and Saudi Arabia and the other Sunni states withheld relations with the new Shi'a-dominated government in Baghdad while individuals within those states financed terrorist attacks.

In both cases, therefore, the United States sought to exclude the hitherto-most-powerful patronage networks in the country from even the slightest share of power, influence, and wealth and, at the same time, it failed to secure the support of neighboring states. In some cases, indeed, the United States went out of its way to antagonize neighbors directly, by threatening Iran with a preemptive strike on its nuclear program, or indirectly in case of the Sunni autocracies, by challenging their legitimacy.

It is nevertheless striking that, despite the failure to bring peace to Afghanistan, in the past decade, that society has registered the greatest improvement in human development and the second-greatest improvement in per capita GDP and government effectiveness of these 20 countries. These results, which contrast sharply with the popular image of present-day Afghanistan, cannot be entirely explained by external aid flows because Afghanistan was not among the largest foreign aid recipients on a per capita basis. Neither is it simply that Afghanistan started from a lower base because Liberia, Mozambique, Sierra Leone, and the DRC were all poorer to begin with and grew less rapidly. Dramatic advances in Afghanistan's school enrollment and life expectancy, declines in infant mortality, and rapid economic growth even in some of the most-conflicted areas of the country do reflect the emphasis of the Afghan government's counterinsurgency and development strategies in pushing resources and public services out into the hinterland.

Somalia also suffered from neighbors' interference, but the main cause of resistance to the U.S. and international military presence in 1993 was a United Nations–led grassroots democratization campaign that was bound to antagonize every warlord in the country. In the DRC, such interference was a crucial factor causing the conflict that precipitated the 1999 UN intervention, as well as the resurgence of conflict in 2012 even while that intervention continued. In some of the years in between, a fragile relative peace prevailed while neighbors' interference was in abeyance.

Dissimilar Societies, Similar Instruments

None of the foregoing analysis is meant to suggest that the unique geography, culture, and level of development of each of the six societies examined in Chapters Three through Eight, and the 20 societies surveyed in Chapter Nine, made no difference to the nation-building outcomes. Rather, to the extent that these factors presented impediments to peace, they were, to some considerable degree, overcome. Nation-builders became reasonably adept at understanding local power dynamics and co-opting feuding patronage networks into more-peaceful, to some degree more-democratic, and almost always more economically productive forms of competition.

They did so using the same limited set of tools. Although every society is, in many respects, unique, the instruments with which the intervening powers seek to promote peace are few and largely similar from one instance to the next, consisting essentially of compulsion (military force), persuasion (diplomacy), and various forms of assistance with economic and political development. The quantity and quality of such tools made available do make a difference to the outcomes, as we have emphasized in prior publications, but so do the skill with which they are employed and their responsiveness to the local context, as we have tried to illustrate in our six case studies here.

Among these tools, diplomacy turns out to be the most decisive, when enabled by economic and sometimes military leverage. Thus, just as geopolitics proved to be the most important factor in both sustaining and ending conflict in each of the six case studies, so diplomacy proved decisive, not just in mediating peace agreements but, perhaps more importantly, in altering the geopolitical—that is to say, the external—circumstances that gave rise to or enabled these conflicts.

It should not be surprising that it has proven easier to alter the behavior of governments than to reengineer societies. Neither should it be surprising that an altered geopolitical environment can greatly improve the prospects for peace and development. It is also important to recognize, however, that even the most-skillful diplomacy and the most-favorable regional environments would likely not have sufficed to bring enduring peace to most of these war-torn societies had the international community not also been willing to commit military manpower and economic assistance to the effort to disengage adversaries, demobilize combatants, reintegrate former fighters into civilian life, and create new political and economic avenues through which formerly warring factions, contending patronage networks, and influential political leaders (the three tend to be synonymous) could continue to compete for power and wealth through peaceful rather than violent means. Other RAND studies—in particular, *The Beginner's Guide to Nation-Building*—provide detail on the instruments and policies whereby these changes have been effectuated.[4] Where such efforts have

---

[4]   Dobbins, Jones, Crane, and DeGrasse, 2007.

been inadequately resourced or unwisely executed, the result has been subpar outcomes, even in favorable geopolitical circumstances. Inadequate attention to reintegration of former combatants, for instance, left a legacy of heightened criminal violence in El Salvador. UN forces in Sierra Leone were outmatched by local insurgents until rescued by UK troops. Foreign forces left East Timor prematurely and had to be returned once civil unrest ignited. International resources for the DRC were never enough to fully overcome the challenges of size, distance, and difficult terrain.

Changing the behavior of malign external actors and co-opting local patronage networks may be the two most-important keys to success in nation-building, but the quantity and quality of inputs, in the form of both manpower and money, also influence outcomes.

Establishing Realistic Expectations

The prominence of a few spectacular (and massively expensive) nation-building failures and the relative obscurity of most of the successes has created an impression among the general Western public, and even among more-expert audiences, that this activity seldom succeeds and that it is, in any case, inordinately expensive. One result has been that both Democratic and Republican U.S. administrations have insisted that they will not conduct nation-building, even as they repeatedly engage in it.

Contrary to this negative stereotype, however, the great majority of international interventions in the past two decades have been followed by improved security, some measurable degree of democratization, significant economic growth, and a corresponding improvement in human development. Most of these missions have not been expensive when compared with the benefits accrued, even if those benefits are calculated in purely economic terms.[5]

---

[5] Paul Collier and Anke Hoeffler, *The Challenge of Reducing the Global Incidence of Civil War*, Oxford, UK: Centre for the Study of African Economies, Department of Economics, Oxford University, March 26, 2004a.

How then to explain that even much of the expert and academic literature on relatively successful operations tends to be so critical? These generally downbeat assessments would seem to result from exaggerated expectations and resultant frustration on the part of both field operatives and expert observers at the slow pace and limited nature of the desired societal change. Five or ten years on, poor populations remain poor and bad governments remain bad. That these populations are no longer killing each other in large numbers tends to be discounted as the conflict recedes into the past. That these societies are mostly more democratic and more prosperous, with healthier and better-educated populations, also tends to be discounted because these changes are so gradual and the absolute situations still so unsatisfactory.

This monograph suggests benchmarks by which to measure progress in current and future nation-building–type operations. Any mission that results, after ten years, in better than a 21.5-percentage-point rise in a country's Freedom Index, more than 55-percent growth in its per capita income, or better than a 6-percentage-point improvement in either its HDI or government effectiveness scores will be doing better than the post–Cold War averages to date.

Other measures may also become available. Transparency International's Corruption Perceptions Index does not extend far enough back to cover the older cases we examined but should be available to benchmark future operations. Better statistics are gradually being developed to measure the intensity of violent conflict, and these, too, should ultimately allow more-precise measurement of progress in promoting security than the binary judgment we have employed in this study.

As the statistical analysis in Chapter Nine shows, the great majority of postconflict missions in the past two decades have resulted in improved security, progress in democratization, significant economic growth, and improvements in human development, and most have done so with a modest commitment of international military and civilian manpower and economic assistance. Our case studies demonstrate that transformation of many of the specific conditions that gave rise to or fueled a conflict may not be feasible in the time frame of nation-building operations, but they also show that such broad transformation has not proven essential to achieving the primary goal of nation-building—establishing peace—or its subsidiary goals of political and economic reform.

Operations that have enjoyed local consent and regional support almost always have achieved peace, even when a degree of coercion was employed to secure both. Nearly all these operations have also helped produce freer, more-democratic, and more-prosperous societies. Clearly, local conditions limited absolute outcomes, and, clearly, some of these indigenous obstacles have not been subject to rapid alteration, but neither have most of the oft-cited barriers to nation-building operations blocked significant progress.

Performance Indicators and Nation-Building Inputs for 20 Major Post–Cold War Nation-Building Interventions

This appendix shows performance indicators and nation-building inputs for the 20 major post–Cold War nation-building interventions discussed in Chapter Nine (including the six interventions discussed in Chapters Six through Eight), ordered from highest to lowest probability of renewed conflict within five years after intervention. This appendix brings together all of the indicator and input data presented in the preceding chapters, with the addition of average annual growth rates.

In all tables in this appendix, for the average annual rate of growth in per capita GDP, the data in the "5 Years Later" column are the average for the *first five* years after intervention, and the data in the "10 Years Later" column are the average for the *second five* years after intervention. Cumulative growth in per capita GDP is shown over the *five years* after intervention and over the *ten years* after intervention. For government effectiveness and HDI, the data in the "10 Years Later" column represent the respective scores ten years after intervention or in 2010. Similarly, for the Freedom Index, the data in the "10 Years Later" column represent the score ten years after intervention or in 2011, the latest year for which data are available.

Government effectiveness, Freedom Index, and HDI scores are all shown here converted to a ten-point scale, with 1 as the worst score and 10 as the best.

Table A.1
Performance Indicators and Nation-Building Inputs for Bosnia

Performance Indicator	Year of Intervention (1995)	5 Years Later	10 Years Later
At peace?	—	Yes	Yes
Government effectiveness	3.24	4.60	5.19
Freedom Index	2.50	4.75	6.25
PPP per capita income ($)	1,180	5,010	6,610
Average annual rate of growth in per capita GDP (%)	—	20.6	4.21
Cumulative growth in per capita GDP (%)	—	155.20	213.70
HDI	NA	NA	7.20
Nation-Building Input			
Peak military presence per capita, number of troops per 1,000 inhabitants	17.5		
Peak international civilian police presence per capita, number of police per 1,000 inhabitants	0.59		
Average annual per capita assistance in the first five years (constant 2010 US$)	384		

SOURCES: World Bank, undated (d); Freedom House, various years; World Bank, undated (a); IMF, undated; UNDP, undated; Dobbins, Jones, Crane, Chivvis, et al., 2008, Figures 9.2, 9.4, 9.9; UN Peace Operations, various years; World Bank, undated (c).

NOTE: NA = not available.

Table A.2
Performance Indicators and Nation-Building Inputs for Sudan

Performance Indicator	Year of Intervention (2005)	5 Years Later	10 Years Later
At peace?	—	Yes	Yes (2012)
Government effectiveness	2.96	3.03	3.03
Freedom Index	1.00	1.00	1.00
PPP per capita income ($)	1,530	2,020	NA
Average annual rate of growth in per capita GDP (%)	—	5.33	NA
Cumulative growth in per capita GDP (%)	—	28.8	NA
HDI	3.80	4.10	4.10
Nation-Building Input			
Peak military presence per capita, number of troops per 1,000 inhabitants	0.29		
Peak international civilian police presence per capita, number of police per 1,000 inhabitants	0.02		
Average annual per capita assistance in the first five years (constant 2010 US$)	69.69		

SOURCES: World Bank, undated (d); Freedom House, various years; World Bank, undated (a); IMF, undated; UNDP, undated; Dobbins, Jones, Crane, Chivvis, et al., 2008, Figures 9.2, 9.4, 9.9; UN Peace Operations, various years; World Bank, undated (c).

NOTE: NA = not available.

Table A.3
Performance Indicators and Nation-Building Inputs for Kosovo

Performance Indicator	Year of Intervention (1999)	5 Years Later	10 Years Later
At peace?	—	Yes	Yes
Government effectiveness	NA	NA	4.78
Freedom Index	1.00[a]	NA	4.75
PPP per capita income ($)	NA	NA	NA
Average annual rate of growth in per capita GDP (%)	—	3.73	3.80
Cumulative growth in per capita GDP (%)	—	20.1	83.2
HDI	NA	NA	NA
Nation-Building Input			
Peak military presence per capita, number of troops per 1,000 inhabitants	19.3		
Peak international civilian police presence per capita, number of police per 1,000 inhabitants	2.38		
Average annual per capita assistance in the first five years (constant 2010 US$)	273.93		

SOURCES: World Bank, undated (d); Freedom House, various years; World Bank, undated (a); IMF, undated; UNDP, undated; Dobbins, Jones, Crane, Chivvis, et al., 2008, Figures 9.2, 9.4, 9.9; UN Peace Operations, various years; World Bank, undated (c).

[a] Freedom House has no separate index for Kosovo or East Timor in the pre-intervention context. Given that both societies had suffered massive repression in the period immediately prior to the arrival of international forces, we have suggested a rating of 1 (the lowest), for the condition at the time of intervention.

NOTE: NA = not available.

Table A.4
Performance Indicators and Nation-Building Inputs for Sierra Leone

Performance Indicator	Year of Intervention (2000)	5 Years Later	10 Years Later
At peace?	—	Yes	Yes
Government effectiveness	2.87	3.07	3.36
Freedom Index	4.75	6.25	7.00
PPP per capita income ($)	360	610	820
Average annual rate of growth in per capita GDP (%)	—	8.61	NA
Cumulative growth in per capita GDP (%)	—	51.1	72.7
HDI	2.50	3.10	3.30
Nation-Building Input			
Peak military presence per capita, number of troops per 1,000 inhabitants	4.50		
Peak international civilian police presence per capita, number of police per 1,000 inhabitants	0.02		
Average annual per capita assistance in the first five years (constant 2010 US$)	93.10		

SOURCES: World Bank, undated (d); Freedom House, various years; World Bank, undated (a); IMF, undated; UNDP, undated; Dobbins, Jones, Crane, Chivvis, et al., 2008, Figures 9.2, 9.4, 9.9; UN Peace Operations, various years; World Bank, undated (c).

NOTE: NA = not available.

Table A.5
Performance Indicators and Nation-Building Inputs for East Timor

Performance Indicator	Year of Intervention (1999)	5 Years Later	10 Years Later
At peace?	—	Yes	Yes
Government effectiveness	NA	3.43	3.43
Freedom Index	1.00[a]	7.00	6.25
PPP per capita income ($)	900	1,320	4,410
Average annual rate of growth in per capita GDP (%)	—	3.32	3.91
Cumulative growth in per capita GDP (%)	—	17.8	42.7
HDI	4.00[b]	4.50[c]	4.90
Nation-Building Input			
Peak military presence per capita, number of troops per 1,000 inhabitants	9.80		
Peak international civilian police presence per capita, number of police per 1,000 inhabitants	1.56		
Average annual per capita assistance in the first five years (constant 2010 US$)	361		

SOURCES: World Bank, undated (d); Freedom House, various years; World Bank, undated (a); IMF, undated; UNDP, undated; Dobbins, Jones, Crane, Chivvis, et al., 2008, Figures 9.2, 9.4, 9.9; UN Peace Operations, various years; World Bank, undated (c).

[a] Freedom House has no separate index for Kosovo or East Timor in the pre-intervention context. Given that both societies had suffered massive repression in the period immediately prior to the arrival of international forces, we have suggested a rating of 1 (the lowest), for the condition at the time of intervention.

[b] Data are for 2000.

[c] Data are for 2005.

NOTE: NA = not available.

Table A.6
Performance Indicators and Nation-Building Inputs for Afghanistan

Performance Indicator	Year of Intervention (2001)	5 Years Later	10 Years Later
At peace?	—	No	No
Government effectiveness	1.32	2.82	2.85
Freedom Index	1.00	4.00	2.50
PPP per capita income ($)	490	890	910
Average annual rate of growth in per capita GDP (%)	—	10.98	6.52
Cumulative growth in per capita GDP (%)	—	68.4	130.9
HDI	2.30[a]	3.40[b]	4.00
Nation-Building Input			
Peak military presence per capita, number of troops per 1,000 inhabitants	1.60		
Peak international civilian police presence per capita, number of police per 1,000 inhabitants	0.00		
Average annual per capita assistance in the first five years (constant 2010 US$)	62.72		

SOURCES: World Bank, undated (d); Freedom House, various years; World Bank, undated (a); IMF, undated; UNDP, undated; Dobbins, Jones, Crane, Chivvis, et al., 2008, Figures 9.2, 9.4, 9.9; UN Peace Operations, various years; World Bank, undated (c).

[a] Data are for 2000.

[b] Data are for 2005.

NOTE: NA = not available.

Table A.7
Performance Indicators and Nation-Building Inputs for the Democratic Republic of the Congo

Performance Indicator	Year of Intervention (1999)	5 Years Later	10 Years Later
At peace?	—	Yes	Yes[a]
Government effectiveness	3.36	3.27	3.11
Freedom Index	1.75	2.50	2.50
PPP per capita income ($)	230	240	310
Average annual rate of growth in per capita GDP (%)	—	–1.17	2.79
Cumulative growth in per capita GDP (%)	—	–5.70	8.20
HDI	2.20[b]	2.60[c]	2.80
Nation-Building Input			
Peak military presence per capita, number of troops per 1,000 inhabitants	0.30		
Peak international civilian police presence per capita, number of police per 1,000 inhabitants	0.02		
Average annual per capita assistance in the first five years (constant 2010 US$)	36.46		

SOURCES: World Bank, undated (d); Freedom House, various years; World Bank, undated (a); IMF, undated; UNDP, undated; Dobbins, Jones, Crane, Chivvis, et al., 2008, Figures 9.2, 9.4, 9.9; UN Peace Operations, various years; World Bank, undated (c).

[a] Civil war in the eastern DRC resumed in 2012, with Rwanda apparently once again backing a rebel force.

[b] Data are for 2000.

[c] Data are for 2005.

NOTE: NA = not available.

Table A.8
Performance Indicators and Nation-Building Inputs for Somalia

Performance Indicator	Year of Intervention (1992)	5 Years Later	10 Years Later
At peace?	—	No	No
Government effectiveness	1.73	1.61	2.62
Freedom Index	1.00	1.00	1.75
PPP per capita income ($)	NA	NA	NA
Average annual rate of growth in per capita GDP (%)	—	NA	NA
Cumulative growth in per capita GDP (%)	—	NA	NA
HDI	NA	NA	NA
Nation-Building Input			
Peak military presence per capita, number of troops per 1,000 inhabitants	5.70		
Peak international civilian police presence per capita, number of police per 1,000 inhabitants	0.01		
Average annual per capita assistance in the first five years (constant 2010 US$)	89.85		

SOURCES: World Bank, undated (d); Freedom House, various years; World Bank, undated (a); IMF, undated; UNDP, undated; Dobbins, Jones, Crane, Chivvis, et al., 2008, Figures 9.2, 9.4, 9.9; UN Peace Operations, various years; World Bank, undated (c).

NOTE: NA = not available.

Table A.9
Performance Indicators and Nation-Building Inputs for Iraq

Performance Indicator	Year of Intervention (2003)	5 Years Later	10 Years Later
At peace?	—	No	No (2012)
Government effectiveness	2.44	3.25	3.29
Freedom Index	1.00	2.50	3.25
PPP per capita income ($)	2,330	3,370	3,770
Average annual rate of growth in per capita GDP (%)	—	12.29	NA
Cumulative growth in per capita GDP (%)	—	78.50	84.40[a]
HDI	5.50[b]	5.60	5.70
Nation-Building Input			
Peak military presence per capita, number of troops per 1,000 inhabitants	6.50		
Peak international civilian police presence per capita, number of police per 1,000 inhabitants	0.00		
Average annual per capita assistance in the first five years (constant 2010 US$)	369.32		

SOURCES: World Bank, undated (d); Freedom House, various years; World Bank, undated (a); IMF, undated; UNDP, undated; Dobbins, Jones, Crane, Chivvis, et al., 2008, Figures 9.2, 9.4, 9.9; UN Peace Operations, various years; World Bank, undated (c).

[a] Based on 2009 data.

[b] Data are for 2005.

NOTE: NA = not available.

Table A.10
Performance Indicators and Nation-Building Inputs for Mozambique

Performance Indicator	Year of Intervention (1992)	5 Years Later	10 Years Later
At peace?	—	Yes	Yes
Government effectiveness	5.24	4.80	4.71
Freedom Index	4.00	6.25	6.25
PPP per capita income ($)	260	360	510
Average annual rate of growth in per capita GDP (%)	—	3.32	3.28
Cumulative growth in per capita GDP (%)	—	27.6	68.8
HDI	2.10[a]	2.50[b]	2.60[c]

Nation-Building Input			
Peak military presence per capita, number of troops per 1,000 inhabitants	0.40		
Peak international civilian police presence per capita, number of police per 1,000 inhabitants	0.07		
Average annual per capita assistance in the first five years (constant 2010 US$)	104.98		

SOURCES: World Bank, undated (d); Freedom House, various years; World Bank, undated (a); IMF, undated; UNDP, undated; Dobbins, Jones, Crane, Chivvis, et al., 2008, Figures 9.2, 9.4, 9.9; UN Peace Operations, various years; World Bank, undated (c).

[a] Data are for 1995.

[b] Data are for 2000.

[c] Data are for 2005.

NOTE: NA = not available.

Table A.11
Performance Indicators and Nation-Building Inputs for Haiti

Performance Indicator	Year of Intervention (2004)	5 Years Later	10 Years Later
At peace?	—	Yes	Yes (2012)
Government effectiveness	2.54	2.81	2.60
Freedom Index	2.50	4.75	4.75
PPP per capita income ($)	1,010	1,170	1,190
Average annual rate of growth in per capita GDP (%)	—	0.41	NA
Cumulative growth in per capita GDP (%)	—	−5.30	−5.30[a]
HDI	4.30[b]	4.50	4.50
Nation-Building Input			
Peak military presence per capita, number of troops per 1,000 inhabitants	0.78		
Peak international civilian police presence per capita, number of police per 1,000 inhabitants	0.19		
Average annual per capita assistance in the first five years (constant 2010 US$)	74.15		

SOURCES: World Bank, undated (d); Freedom House, various years; World Bank, undated (a); IMF, undated; UNDP, undated; Dobbins, Jones, Crane, Chivvis, et al., 2008, Figures 9.2, 9.4, 9.9; UN Peace Operations, various years; World Bank, undated (c).

[a] Based on 2009 data.

[b] Data are for 2005.

NOTE: NA = not available.

Table A.12
Performance Indicators and Nation-Building Inputs for Liberia

Performance Indicator	Year of Intervention (2003)	5 Years Later	10 Years Later
At peace?	—	Yes	Yes (2012)
Government effectiveness	2.81	3.07	3.36
Freedom Index	2.50	6.25	6.25
PPP per capita income ($)	210	370	520
Average annual rate of growth in per capita GDP (%)	—	2.46	NA
Cumulative growth in per capita GDP (%)	—	12.9	16.4[a]
HDI	3.00[b]	3.30	3.30
Nation-Building Input			
Peak military presence per capita, number of troops per 1,000 inhabitants	4.72		
Peak international civilian police presence per capita, number of police per 1,000 inhabitants	0.36		
Average annual per capita assistance in the first five years (constant 2010 US$)	138.59		

SOURCES: World Bank, undated (d); Freedom House, various years; World Bank, undated (a); IMF, undated; UNDP, undated; Dobbins, Jones, Crane, Chivvis, et al., 2008, Figures 9.2, 9.4, 9.9; UN Peace Operations, various years; World Bank, undated (c).

[a] Based on 2010 data.

[b] Data are for 2005.

NOTE: NA = not available.

Table A.13
Performance Indicators and Nation-Building Inputs for El Salvador

Performance Indicator	Year of Intervention (1992)	5 Years Later	10 Years Later
At peace?	—	Yes	Yes
Government effectiveness	4.28	4.58	4.64
Freedom Index	7.00	7.75	7.75
PPP per capita income ($)	2,980	3,990	4,810
Average annual rate of growth in per capita GDP (%)	—	1.66	2.13
Cumulative growth in per capita GDP (%)	—	8.6	20.6
HDI	5.80[a]	6.20[b]	6.50[c]
Nation-Building Input			
Peak military presence per capita, number of troops per 1,000 inhabitants	0.10		
Peak international civilian police presence per capita, number of police per 1,000 inhabitants	0.06		
Average annual per capita assistance in the first five years (constant 2010 US$)	79.57		

SOURCES: World Bank, undated (d); Freedom House, various years; World Bank, undated (a); IMF, undated; UNDP, undated; Dobbins, Jones, Crane, Chivvis, et al., 2008, Figures 9.2, 9.4, 9.9; UN Peace Operations, various years; World Bank, undated (c).

[a] Data are for 1995.

[b] Data are for 2000.

[c] Data are for 2005.

NOTE: NA = not available.

Table A.14
Performance Indicators and Nation-Building Inputs for Namibia

Performance Indicator	Year of Intervention (1988)	5 Years Later	10 Years Later
At peace?	—	Yes	Yes
Government effectiveness	NA	6.42	5.88
Freedom Index	6.25	7.75	7.75
PPP per capita income ($)	2,440	3,270	3,870
Average annual rate of growth in per capita GDP (%)	—	0.79	1.89
Cumulative growth in per capita GDP (%)	—	4.0	14.2
HDI	5.60[a]	5.90[b]	6.10

Nation-Building Input			
Peak military presence per capita, number of troops per 1,000 inhabitants	3.40		
Peak international civilian police presence per capita, number of police per 1,000 inhabitants	1.07		
Average annual per capita assistance in the first five years (constant 2010 US$)	118.10		

SOURCES: World Bank, undated (d); Freedom House, various years; World Bank, undated (a); IMF, undated; UNDP, undated; Dobbins, Jones, Crane, Chivvis, et al., 2008, Figures 9.2, 9.4, 9.9; UN Peace Operations, various years; World Bank, undated (c).

[a] Data are for 1990.

[b] Data are for 1995.

NOTE: NA = not available.

Table A.15
Performance Indicators and Nation-Building Inputs for Cambodia

Performance Indicator	Year of Intervention (1991)	5 Years Later	10 Years Later
At peace?	—	Yes	Yes
Government effectiveness	3.92	3.92	3.99
Freedom Index	2.50	2.50	3.25
PPP per capita income ($)	650	670	960
Average annual rate of growth in per capita GDP (%)	—	3.22	5.55
Cumulative growth in per capita GDP (%)	—	17.20	53.60
HDI	NA	4.20[a]	4.40[b]
Nation-Building Input			
Peak military presence per capita, number of troops per 1,000 inhabitants	1.50		
Peak international civilian police presence per capita, number of police per 1,000 inhabitants	0.50		
Average annual per capita assistance in the first five years (constant 2010 US$)	38.36		

SOURCES: World Bank, undated (d); Freedom House, various years; World Bank, undated (a); IMF, undated; UNDP, undated; Dobbins, Jones, Crane, Chivvis, et al., 2008, Figures 9.2, 9.4, 9.9; UN Peace Operations, various years; World Bank, undated (c).

[a] Data are for 1995.

[b] Data are for 2000.

NOTE: NA = not available.

Table A.16
Performance Indicators and Nation-Building Inputs for Eastern Slavonia

Performance Indicator	Year of Intervention (1995)	5 Years Later	10 Years Later
At peace?	—	Yes	Yes
Government effectiveness	5.62	6.06	6.45
Freedom Index	5.50	7.75	8.50
PPP per capita income ($)	7,990	10,720	14,930
Average annual rate of growth in per capita GDP (%)	—	3.80	5.10
Cumulative growth in per capita GDP (%)	—	20.60	54.50
HDI	7.10	7.80	7.90
Nation-Building Input			
Peak military presence per capita, number of troops per 1,000 inhabitants	35.30		
Peak international civilian police presence per capita, number of police per 1,000 inhabitants	4.35		
Average annual per capita assistance in the first five years (constant 2010 US$)	19.77		

SOURCES: World Bank, undated (d); Freedom House, various years; World Bank, undated (a); IMF, undated; UNDP, undated; Dobbins, Jones, Crane, Chivvis, et al., 2008, Figures 9.2, 9.4, 9.9; UN Peace Operations, various years; World Bank, undated (c).

NOTE: For this region of Croatia, we use data for Croatia. NA = not available.

Table A.17
Performance Indicators and Nation-Building Inputs for Albania

Performance Indicator	Year of Intervention (1997)	5 Years Later	10 Years Later
At peace?	—	Yes	Yes
Government effectiveness	4.06	4.47	4.83
Freedom Index	5.50	7.00	7.00
PPP per capita income ($)	3,090	4,980	7,390
Average annual rate of growth in per capita GDP (%)	—	6.3	5.2
Cumulative growth in per capita GDP (%)	—	35.8	75.3
HDI	6.90[a]	7.20[b]	7.30
Nation-Building Input			
Peak military presence per capita, number of troops per 1,000 inhabitants	2.30		
Peak international civilian police presence per capita, number of police per 1,000 inhabitants	0.08		
Average annual per capita assistance in the first five years (constant 2010 US$)	148.84		

SOURCES: World Bank, undated (d); Freedom House, various years; World Bank, undated (a); IMF, undated; UNDP, undated; Dobbins, Jones, Crane, Chivvis, et al., 2008, Figures 9.2, 9.4, 9.9; UN Peace Operations, various years; World Bank, undated (c).

[a] Data are for 2000.

[b] Data are for 2005.

NOTE: NA = not available.

Table A.18
Performance Indicators and Nation-Building Inputs for Macedonia

Performance Indicator	Year of Intervention (2001)	5 Years Later	10 Years Later
At peace?	—	Yes	Yes
Government effectiveness	4.09	5.37	5.18
Freedom Index	5.50	7.00	7.00
PPP per capita income ($)	5,790	8,730	11,490
Average annual rate of growth in per capita GDP (%)	—	3.30	3.30
Cumulative growth in per capita GDP (%)	—	17.70	35.90
HDI	NA	7.00[a]	7.30
Nation-Building Input			
Peak military presence per capita, number of troops per 1,000 inhabitants	2.40		
Peak international civilian police presence per capita, number of police per 1,000 inhabitants	0.20		
Average annual per capita assistance in the first five years (constant 2010 US$)	161.66		

SOURCES: World Bank, undated (d); Freedom House, various years; World Bank, undated (a); IMF, undated; UNDP, undated; Dobbins, Jones, Crane, Chivvis, et al., 2008, Figures 9.2, 9.4, 9.9; UN Peace Operations, various years; World Bank, undated (c).

[a] Data are for 2005.

NOTE: NA = not available.

Table A.19
Performance Indicators and Nation-Building Inputs for Côte d'Ivoire

Performance Indicator	Year of Intervention (2002)	5 Years Later	10 Years Later
At peace?	—	Yes	Yes
Government effectiveness	3.81	3.25	3.11
Freedom Index	2.50	1.75	2.50
PPP per capita income ($)	1,490	1,670	1,730
Average annual rate of growth in per capita GDP (%)	NA	−1.50	NA
Cumulative growth in per capita GDP (%)	—	−7.40	−7.40[a]
HDI	3.80[b]	3.80	4.00
Nation-Building Input			
Peak military presence per capita, number of troops per 1,000 inhabitants	0.45		
Peak international civilian police presence per capita, number of police per 1,000 inhabitants	0.07		
Average annual per capita assistance in the first five years (constant 2010 US$)	26.40		

SOURCES: World Bank, undated (d); Freedom House, various years; World Bank, undated (a); IMF, undated; UNDP, undated; Dobbins, Jones, Crane, Chivvis, et al., 2008, Figures 9.2, 9.4, 9.9; UN Peace Operations, various years; World Bank, undated (c).

[a] Based on 2008 data.

[b] Data are for 2005.

NOTE: NA = not available.

Table A.20
Performance Indicators and Nation-Building Inputs for Solomon Islands

Performance Indicator	Year of Intervention (2003)	5 Years Later	10 Years Later
At peace?	—	Yes	Yes (2012)
Government effectiveness	1.41	3.72	3.79
Freedom Index	1.75	6.25	6.25
PPP per capita income ($)	1,860	2,250	2,360
Average annual rate of growth in per capita GDP (%)	NA	4.30	NA
Cumulative growth in per capita GDP (%)	—	23.20	20.80[a]
HDI	5.00[b]	5.10	5.10

Nation-Building Input			
Peak military presence per capita, number of troops per 1,000 inhabitants	3.96		
Peak international civilian police presence per capita, number of police per 1,000 inhabitants	0.66		
Average annual per capita assistance in the first five years (constant 2010 US$)	488.58		

SOURCES: World Bank, undated (d); Freedom House, various years; World Bank, undated (a); IMF, undated; UNDP, undated; Dobbins, Jones, Crane, Chivvis, et al., 2008, Figures 9.2, 9.4, 9.9; UN Peace Operations, various years; World Bank, undated (c).

[a] Based on 2009 data.

[b] Data are for 2005.

NOTE: NA = not available.

Economic Growth Statistics for Nation-Building Interventions in Comparative Perspective

Table B.1 shows, for each of the 20 countries discussed in Chapter Nine, cumulative growth in per capita GDP in the first ten years following the start of the nation-building intervention compared with (1) cumulative growth in the same ten-year period for the country's income group among all countries in the world, (2) cumulative growth in the same ten-year period for the geographical region to which the country belongs, and (3) cumulative growth in the whole world in that same time period. The world economic growth data are provided to put into perspective how well or how poorly the income groups and regions performed relative to all countries in the relevant time frames.

The table categorizes the eight countries whose economic growth exceeded that of both their income groups and their regions; the seven countries whose economic growth fell below that of both their income groups and regions; the three that had mixed performance (growth exceeded either income group or region but not both); and the two for which there are insufficient data. Average annual per capita foreign assistance to each of the countries (in the first five years following the date of intervention) is shown to provide a basis for gauging whether there is a relationship between volume of assistance and economic growth performance; as discussed in Chapter Nine, these data do not indicate that aid necessarily propelled growth in these countries.

Table B.1
Comparative Economic Growth Statistics for 20 Major Post–Cold War Nation-Building Interventions

Country	Region and Income Group	Year of Intervention	Growth in per Capita GDP in 1st 10 Years After Intervention (%)	Growth in per Capita GDP for Same Period (%)			Average Annual per Capita Assistance in First 5 Years (constant 2010 US$)
				Income Group	Region	World	
Performed better than peers							
Afghanistan	SA/low income	2001	130.9	38.37	71.06	14.96	62.72
Albania	ECA/lower middle income	1997	75.3	42.02	65.33	20.46	148.84
Bosnia	ECA/upper middle income	1995	213.7	47.16	26	19.02	384.00
Eastern Slavonia	ECA/high income	1995	54.5	27.87	26	19.02	19.77
Iraq	MENA/lower middle income	2003	84.4[a]	45.43	24.29[b]	12.43[c]	369.32
Kosovo	ECA/lower middle income	1999	83.2	46.28	59.40	13.32	273.93
Mozambique	SSA/low income	1992	68.8	13.13	3.82	15.46	104.98
Sierra Leone	SSA/low income	2000	72.7	37.17	24.44	13.66	93.10

Table B.1—Continued

Country	Region and Income Group	Year of Intervention	Growth in per Capita GDP in 1st 10 Years After Intervention (%)	Growth in per Capita GDP for Same Period (%)			Average Annual per Capita Assistance in First 5 Years (constant 2010 US$)
				Income Group	Region	World	
Mixed performance compared with peers							
Cambodia	EAP/low income	1991	53.6	7.97	95.44	15.25	38.36
El Salvador	LAC/lower middle income	1992	20.6	23.74	8.59	15.46	79.57
Namibia	SSA/upper middle income	1988	14.2	22.36	-5.57	13.05	118.10
Performed worse than peers							
East Timor	EAP/lower middle income	1999	42.7	46.28	115.66	13.32	361.00
Côte d'Ivoire	SSA/lower middle income	2002	-7.4[d]	50.82	24.16	14.11	26.40
DRC	SSA/low income	1999	8.2	33.61	22.63	13.32	36.46
Haiti	LAC/low income	2004	-5.3[a]	29.93[c]	23.63[c]	9.42[c]	74.15

Table B.1—Continued

Country	Region and Income Group	Year of Intervention	Growth in per Capita GDP in 1st 10 Years After Intervention (%)	Growth in per Capita GDP for Same Period (%)			Average Annual per Capita Assistance in First 5 Years (constant 2010 US$)
				Income Group	Region	World	
Liberia	SSA/low income	2003	16.4[b]	34.92[c]	22.27[c]	12.43[c]	138.59
Macedonia	ECA/upper middle income	2001	35.9	72.98	62.02	14.96	161.66
Solomon Islands	EAP/lower middle income	2003	20.8[a]	45.43[c]	94.71[c]	12.43[c]	488.58
Insufficient data							
Somalia	SSA/low income	1992	NA	13.13	3.82	15.46	89.85
Sudan	SSA/lower middle income	2005	NA	31.29[c]	14.47[c]	7.03[c]	69.69

SOURCES: IMF, undated; Dobbins, Jones, Crane, Chivvis, et al., 2008, Figure 9.9; World Bank, undated (c).

[a] Based on the most-recent data available (2009).

[b] Based on the most-recent data available (2010).

[c] Based on the most-recent data available (2011).

[d] Based on the most-recent data available (2008).

NOTE: SA = South Asia. ECA = Eastern Europe and Central Asia. MENA = Middle East and North Africa. SSA = sub-Saharan Africa. EAP = East Asia and Pacific. LAC: Latin America and the Caribbean. We use World Bank region and income-group classifications.

References

Abdullah, Ibrahim, "Bush Path to Destruction: The Origin and Character of the Revolutionary United Front/Sierra Leone," *Journal of Modern African Studies*, Vol. 36, No. 2, June 1998, pp. 203–235.

"Achievements and Chronology," *Stability Pact for South Eastern Europe*, undated, referenced August 2012. As of December 3, 2012:
http://www.stabilitypact.org/about/achievements.asp

Albrecht, Peter, *Betwixt and Between: Chiefs and Reform of Sierra Leone's Justice Sector*, Copenhagen: Danish Institute for International Studies, Working Paper 2010:33, 2010. As of December 5, 2012:
http://diis.dk/graphics/Publications/WP2010/
WP2010-33-Albrecht-Betwixt-and-between_web.pdf

Albrecht, Peter, and Paul Jackson, *Security System Transformation in Sierra Leone, 1997–2007*, Birmingham, UK: Global Facilitation Network for Security Sector Reform, University of Birmingham, 2009. As of December 13, 2012:
http://www.ssrnetwork.net/document_library/detail/4680/
security-system-transformation-in-sierra-leone-1997-2007

Anderson, James H., and Cheryl Williamson Gray, *Anticorruption in Transition 3: Who Is Succeeding and Why?* Washington, D.C.: World Bank, 2006.

Andjelic, Neven, *Bosnia-Herzegovina: The End of a Legacy*, London: Frank Cass, 2003.

Andreas, Peter, "The Clandestine Political Economy of War and Peace in Bosnia," *International Studies Quarterly*, Vol. 48, No. 1, March 2004, pp. 29–52.

Arana, Ana, "How the Street Gangs Took Central America," *Foreign Affairs*, Vol. 83, No. 3, May–June 2005.

Asian Legal Resource Centre, "Civil and Political Rights, Including the Question of: Independence of the Judiciary, Administration of Justice, Impunity," written statement submitted to the UN Secretary-General, February 8, 2000.

Aucoin, Louis, and Michele Brandt, "East Timor's Constitutional Passage to Independence," in Laurel Miller and Louis Aucoin, eds., *Framing the State in Times of Transition: Case Studies in Constitution Making*, Washington, D.C.: U.S. Institute of Peace Press, 2010, pp. 245–274.

Australia and the Democratic Republic of Timor-Leste, "Treaty Between Australia and the Democratic Republic of Timor-Leste on Certain Maritime Arrangements in the Timor Sea," *Australian Treaty Series*, Sydney, January 12, 2006. As of December 4, 2012:
http://www.austlii.edu.au/au/other/dfat/treaties/2007/12.html

Autesserre, Séverine, "The Trouble with Congo: How Local Disputes Fuel Regional Conflict," *Foreign Affairs*, Vol. 87, No. 3, May–June 2008, pp. 94–110.

———, "Hobbes and the Congo: Frames, Local Violence, and International Intervention," *International Organization*, Vol. 63, Spring 2009, pp. 249–280.

———, *The Trouble with the Congo: Local Violence and the Failure of International Peacebuilding*, Cambridge, UK: Cambridge University Press, 2010.

Bates, Robert H., *When Things Fell Apart: State Failure in Late-Century Africa*, New York: Cambridge University Press, 2008.

Beaugrand, Philippe, *Zaïre's Hyperinflation, 1990–96*, Washington, D.C.: International Monetary Fund, Working Paper WP/97/50, April 1997. As of December 5, 2012:
http://bibpurl.oclc.org/web/24285/wp9750.pdf

Beauvais, Joel C., "Benevolent Despotism: A Critique of U.N. State-Building in East Timor," *New York University Journal of International Law and Politics*, Vol. 33, Summer 2001, pp. 1101–1178.

Becker, Elizabeth, *When the War Was Over: Cambodia and the Khmer Rouge Revolution*, New York: PublicAffairs, 1998.

Belloni, Roberto, *State Building and International Intervention in Bosnia*, London: Routledge, 2007.

Bellows, John, and Edward Miguel, "War and Institutions: New Evidence from Sierra Leone," *American Economic Review*, Vol. 96, No. 2, 2006, pp. 394–399.

BERCI International, *Peacekeeping Operations in the Democratic Republic of the Congo: The Perception of the Population*, Peacekeeping Best Practices Section, United Nations Department of Peacekeeping Operations, November 2005. As of December 5, 2012:
http://www.peacekeepingbestpractices.unlb.org/PBPS/Library/
MONUC%20perception%20of%20population.pdf

Berdal, Mats R., *Building Peace After War*, Abingdon, UK: Routledge, 2009.

Beyrer, Chris, "Burma and Cambodia: Human Rights, Social Disruption, and the Spread of HIV/AIDS," *Health and Human Rights*, Vol. 2, No. 4, 1998, pp. 84–97.

Blandford, Kristen, "Profile 2011: Timor-Leste," Washington, D.C.: Fund for Peace, Country Profile CCPPR11TL, December 15, 2011. As of December 4, 2012:
http://www.fundforpeace.org/global/?q=states-timorleste2011

Blattman, Christopher, and Edward Miguel, *Civil War: A Review of Fifty Years of Research*, Washington, D.C.: Center for Global Development, Working Paper 166, March 21, 2009. As of December 13, 2012:
http://www.cgdev.org/content/publications/detail/1421335

Blunt, Peter, "The Political Economy of Accountability in Timor-Leste: Implications for Public Policy," *Public Administration and Development*, Vol. 29, 2009, pp. 89–100.

Bockers, Estelle, Nadine Stammel, and Christine Knaevelsrud, "Reconciliation in Cambodia: Thirty Years After the Terror of the Khmer Rouge Regime," *Torture*, Vol. 21, No. 2, 2011, pp. 71–83.

Bolten, Catherine, "The Agricultural Impasse: Creating 'Normal' Post-War Development in Northern Sierra Leone," *Journal of Political Ecology*, Vol. 16, 2009, pp. 70–86.

"Border Dynamics: Mutineers Threaten Security in Eastern DRC," *Jane's Intelligence Review*, July 19, 2012.

Bose, Sumantra, "The Bosnian State a Decade After Dayton," *International Peacekeeping*, Vol. 12, No. 3, Autumn 2005, pp. 322–335.

Boyce, James K., "External Assistance and the Peace Process in El Salvador," *World Development*, Vol. 23, No. 12, December 1995, pp. 2101–2116.

Brinkley, Joel, "Cambodia's Curse: Struggling to Shed the Khmer Rouge's Legacy," *Foreign Affairs*, March–April 2009.

———, *Cambodia's Curse: The Modern History of a Troubled Land*, New York: PublicAffairs, 2011.

Brown, Frederick Z., and David G. Timberman, eds., *Cambodia and the International Community: The Quest for Peace, Development, and Democracy*, Singapore: Institute of Southeast Asian Studies, 1998.

Brown, Taylor, Richard Fanthorpe, Janet Gardener, Lansana Gberie, and M. Gibril Sesay, *Sierra Leone: Drivers of Change*, Bristol, UK: IDL Group, March 2005. As of December 4, 2012:
http://www.theidlgroup.com/documents/
SierraLeoneDriversofChange_june06_.pdf

Buhaug, Halvard, Scott Gates, and Päivi Lujala, "Geography, Rebel Capability, and the Duration of Civil Conflict," *Journal of Conflict Resolution*, Vol. 53, No. 4, August 2009, pp. 544–569.

Byman, Daniel, *Keeping the Peace: Lasting Solutions to Ethnic Conflicts*, Baltimore, Md.: Johns Hopkins University Press, 2002.

Byman, Daniel, and Taylor Seybolt, "Humanitarian Intervention and Communal Civil Wars," *Security Studies*, Vol. 13, No. 1, 2003, pp. 33–78.

Cain, Andrew, "Rebuilt Sarajevo Hosts Balkans Summit: U.S. at Odds with Allies over Kosovo Aid," *Washington Times*, July 30, 1999.

Call, Charles T., "Assessing El Salvador's Transition from Civil War to Peace," in Stephen John Stedman, Donald S. Rothchild, and Elizabeth M. Cousens, eds., *Ending Civil Wars: The Implementation of Peace Agreements*, Boulder, Colo.: Lynn Rienner, 2002, pp. 383–420.

———, "Democratisation, War and State-Building: Constructing the Rule of Law in El Salvador," *Journal of Latin American Studies*, Vol. 35, No. 4, November 2003, pp. 827–862.

Caplan, Richard, *International Governance of War-Torn Territories: Rule and Reconstruction*, New York: Oxford University Press, 2005.

Carney, Timothy, "The Organization of Power," in Karl D. Jackson, ed., *Cambodia, 1975–1978: Rendezvous with Death*, Princeton, N.J.: Princeton University Press, 1989, pp. 13–35.

Cederman, Lars-Erik, and Luc Girardin, "Beyond Fractionalization: Mapping Ethnicity onto Nationalist Insurgencies," *American Political Science Review*, Vol. 101, No. 1, February 2007, pp. 173–185.

Central Intelligence Agency, "Bosnia and Herzegovina," *The World Factbook*, 2012a. As of December 3, 2012:
https://www.cia.gov/library/publications/the-world-factbook/geos/bk.html

———, "Cambodia," *The World Factbook*, 2012b. As of November 30, 2012:
https://www.cia.gov/library/publications/the-world-factbook/geos/cb.html

———, "Congo, Democratic Republic of the," *The World Factbook*, 2012c. As of December 5, 2012:
https://www.cia.gov/library/publications/the-world-factbook/geos/cg.html

———, "El Salvador," *The World Factbook*, 2012d. As of December 3, 2012:
https://www.cia.gov/library/publications/the-world-factbook/geos/es.html

———, "Macedonia," *The World Factbook*, 2012e. As of December 3, 2012:
https://www.cia.gov/library/publications/the-world-factbook/geos/mk.html

———, "Sierra Leone," *The World Factbook*, 2012f. As of December 12, 2012:
https://www.cia.gov/library/publications/the-world-factbook/geos/sl.html

———, "Timor-Leste," *The World Factbook*, 2012g. As of December 4, 2012:
https://www.cia.gov/library/publications/the-world-factbook/geos/tt.html

Cerkez-Robinson, Aida, "Bosnia's Ethnic Divisions Are Evident in Schools," Associated Press, August 23, 2009.

Chandler, David P., "Seeing Red," in David P. Chandler and Ben Kiernan, eds., *Revolution and Its Aftermath in Kampuchea: Eight Essays*, New Haven, Conn.: Yale University Southeast Asia Studies, 1983, pp. 34–56.

Chapman, Nick, and Charlotte Vaillant, *Synthesis of Country Programme Evaluations Conducted in Fragile States*, London: UK Department for International Development, 2010.

Chappell, Derek, "NATO and the Defence Reform Commission: Partners for Progress," *SETimes*, June 2, 2006. As of December 3, 2012: http://www.setimes.com/cocoon/setimes/xhtml/en_GB/features/setimes/special/dayton/peacekeeping/feature-11

Charbonneau, Louis, "Death Toll in Ivory Coast's Abidjan to Rise Sharply: U.N.," Reuters, April 11, 2011. As of December 5, 2012: http://uk.reuters.com/article/2011/04/11/uk-ivorycoast-un-abidjan-security-idUKTRE73A6B020110411

Chávez, Joaquín M., "Perspectives on Demobilisation, Reintegration and Weapons Control in the El Salvador Peace Process," in Cate Buchanan, ed., *Reflections on Guns, Fighters and Armed Violence in Peace Processes*, Geneva: HD Centre for Humanitarian Dialogue, 2008, pp. 13–18.

Cheema, Shabbir, Bertrand de Speville, Terhi Nieminen-Mäkynen, David Mattiske, and Peter Blunt, *Strengthening Accountability and Transparency in Timor-Leste*, Dili: United Nations Office in Timor-Leste, January 27, 2006. As of December 4, 2012: http://siteresources.worldbank.org/INTTIMORLESTE/Resources/Report_of_the_Alkatiri_Initiative_Review_Mission.pdf

Chesterman, Simon, *Justice Under International Administration: Kosovo, East Timor and Afghanistan*, Vienna: International Peace Institute, September 14, 2002. As of December 4, 2012: http://www.ipacademy.org/publication/policy-papers/detail/149-justice-under-international-administration-kosovo-east-timor-and-afghanistan.html

———, "East Timor," in Mats R. Berdal and Spyros Economides, eds., *United Nations Interventionism, 1991–2004*, Cambridge, UK: Cambridge University Press, 2007, pp. 192–216.

Chhun, Chhim, Chhoun Nareth, Em Sorany, Hing Vutha, Huon Chantrea, Joakim Ojendal, Keo Socheat, Khieng Sothy, Kim Sedara, Kim Sour, Koy Ra, Larry Strange, Lun Pide, Nang Phirun, Net Neath, Ros Bansok, Roth Vathana, Saing Chan Hang, Sok Sethea, and Sum Sreymom, *Annual Development Review 2011–12*, Phnom Penh: CDRI, February 2012. As of December 2, 2012: http://www.cdri.org.kh/index.php/home/242-annual-development-review-2011-12

Childress, Michael, *The Effectiveness of U.S. Training Efforts in Internal Defense and Development: The Cases of El Salvador and Honduras*, Santa Monica, Calif.: RAND Corporation, MR-250-USDP, 1995. As of December 3, 2012:
http://www.rand.org/pubs/monograph_reports/MR250.html

Chollet, Derek H., *The Road to the Dayton Accords: A Study of American Statecraft*, New York: Palgrave Macmillan, 2005.

Chong, Daniel P. L., "UNTAC in Cambodia: A New Model for Humanitarian Aid in Failed States?" *Development and Change*, Vol. 33, No. 5, November 2002, pp. 957–978.

Christensen, Maya M., and Mats Utas, "Mercenaries of Democracy: The 'Politricks' of Remobilized Combatants in the 2007 General Elections, Sierra Leone," *African Affairs*, Vol. 107, No. 429, 2008, pp. 515–539.

CIA—*See* Central Intelligence Agency.

Cigar, Norman, *Genocide in Bosnia: The Politics of "Ethnic Cleansing,"* College Station, Texas: Texas A&M University Press, 2000.

Coalition to Stop the Use of Child Soldiers, *Child Soldiers: Global Report 2008*, London, 2008. As of December 4, 2012:
http://www.childsoldiersglobalreport.org/content/sierra-leone

Cohen, David, "Seeking Justice on the Cheap: Is the East Timor Tribunal Really a Model for the Future?" *Asia Pacific Issues*, Vol. 61, August 2002. As of December 4, 2012:
http://www.eastwestcenter.org/fileadmin/stored/pdfs/api061.pdf

Coleman, Peter T., "Characteristics of Protracted, Intractable Conflict: Toward the Development of a Metaframework—I," *Peace and Conflict: Journal of Peace Psychology*, Vol. 9, No. 1, 2003, pp. 1–37.

Collier, Paul, *The Bottom Billion: Why the Poorest Countries Are Failing and What Can Be Done About It*, Oxford, UK: Oxford University Press, 2007.

Collier, Paul, V. L. Elliott, Håvard Hegre, Anke Hoeffler, Marta Reynal-Querol, and Nicholas Sambanis, *Breaking the Conflict Trap: Civil War and Development Policy*, Washington, D.C.: World Bank, 2003.

Collier, Paul, and Anke Hoeffler, "On the Incidence of Civil War in Africa," *Journal of Conflict Resolution*, Vol. 46, No. 1, February 2002, pp. 13–28.

———, *The Challenge of Reducing the Global Incidence of Civil War*, Oxford, UK: Centre for the Study of African Economies, Department of Economics, Oxford University, March 26, 2004a. As of December 6, 2012:
http://www.copenhagenconsensus.com/Files/Filer/CC/Papers/
Conflicts_230404.pdf

———, "Greed and Grievance in Civil War," *Oxford Economic Papers*, Vol. 56, No. 4, October 2004b, pp. 563–595.

Collier, Paul, Anke Hoeffler, and Dominic Rohner, "Beyond Greed and Grievance: Feasibility and Civil War," *Oxford Economic Papers*, Vol. 61, No. 1, 2009, pp. 1–27.

Collier, Paul, Anke Hoeffler, and Måns Söderbom, "Post-Conflict Risks," *Journal of Peace Research*, Vol. 45, No. 4, July 2008, pp. 461–478.

Collier, Paul, and Dominic Rohner, "Democracy, Development, and Conflict," *Journal of the European Economic Association*, Vol. 6, No. 2–3, April–May 2008, pp. 531–540.

Córdova Macías, Ricardo, "Demilitarizing and Democratizing Salvadoran Politics," in Margarita S. Studemeister, ed., *El Salvador: Implementation of the Peace Accords*, Washington, D.C.: U.S. Institute of Peace, Peaceworks 38, January 2001, pp. 27–32. As of December 3, 2012:
http://purl.access.gpo.gov/GPO/LPS11631

Cornwell, Richard, "The Democratic Republic of the Congo: From Fiction to Fact?" *African Security Review*, Vol. 14, No. 4, 2005, pp. 41–42.

CountryWatch, *East Timor: 2012 Country Review*, Houston, Texas, 2012. As of December 4, 2012:
http://www.countrywatch.com/pdfs/reviews/B384564Y.02b.pdf

Cox, Marcus, *State Building and Post-Conflict Reconstruction: Lessons from Bosnia*, Geneva: Centre for Applied Studies in International Negotiations, January 2001.

Crocker, Chester A., Fen Osler Hampson, and Pamela R. Aall, *Grasping the Nettle: Analyzing Cases of Intractable Conflict*, Washington, D.C.: U.S. Institute of Peace Press, 2005.

Cuc, Milan, "Bosnia and Herzegovina: On the Road to EU Accession," *IMF Survey Magazine: Countries and Regions*, November 12, 2008. As of December 3, 2012:
http://www.imf.org/external/pubs/ft/survey/so/2008/CAR111208A.htm

Curtis, Grant, *Cambodia Reborn? The Transition to Democracy and Development*, Washington, D.C.: Brookings Institution, 1998.

Curtis, Mark, *Sierra Leone at the Crossroads: Seizing the Chance to Benefit from Mining*, Freetown: National Advocacy Coalition on Extractives, March 2009.

Cutting, Joel, and Gladwell Otieno, *Annual Review of DFID Support to the Anti-Corruption Commission Phase 2 in Sierra Leone*, London: UK Department for International Development, January 25, 2007.

Dann, Philipp, and Zaid Al-Ali, "The International *Pouvoir Constituant*: Constitution-Making Under External Influence in Iraq, Sudan and East Timor," *Max Planck Yearbook of United Nations Law*, Vol. 10, 2006, pp. 423–463.

Davies, V. A. B., "Sierra Leone: Ironic Tragedy," *Journal of African Economies*, Vol. 9, No. 3, 2000, pp. 349–369.

De Bertodano, Sylvia, "East Timor: Trials and Tribulations," in Cesare Romano, André Nollkaemper, and Jann K. Kleffner, eds., *Internationalized Criminal Courts and Tribunals: Sierra Leone, East Timor, Kosovo, and Cambodia*, Oxford, UK: Oxford University Press, 2004, pp. 79–98.

De Soto, Alvaro, and Graciana del Castillo, "Obstacles to Peacebuilding," *Foreign Policy*, No. 94, Spring 1994, pp. 69–83.

Del Castillo, Graciana, "The Arms-for-Land Deal in El Salvador," in Michael W. Doyle, Ian Johnstone, and Robert C. Orr, eds., *Keeping the Peace: Multidimensional UN Operations in Cambodia and El Salvador*, New York: Cambridge University Press, 1997, pp. 342–366.

———, "Post-Conflict Reconstruction and the Challenge to International Organizations: The Case of El Salvador," *World Development*, Vol. 29, No. 12, December 2001, pp. 1967–1985.

———, "The Political Economy of Peace," *Project Syndicate*, January 12, 2012. As of December 3, 2012:
http://www.project-syndicate.org/commentary/the-political-economy-of-peace

DFID—*See* UK Department for International Development.

Dobbins, James, Seth G. Jones, Keith Crane, Christopher S. Chivvis, Andrew Radin, F. Stephen Larrabee, Nora Bensahel, Brooke Stearns Lawson, and Benjamin W. Goldsmith, *Europe's Role in Nation-Building: From the Balkans to the Congo*, Santa Monica, Calif.: RAND Corporation, MG-722-RC, 2008. As of November 29, 2012:
http://www.rand.org/pubs/monographs/MG722.html

Dobbins, James, Seth G. Jones, Keith Crane, and Beth Cole DeGrasse, *The Beginner's Guide to Nation-Building*, Santa Monica, Calif.: RAND Corporation, MG-557-SRF, 2007. As of November 29, 2012:
http://www.rand.org/pubs/monographs/MG557.html

Dobbins, James, Seth G. Jones, Keith Crane, Andrew Rathmell, Brett Steele, Richard Teltschik, and Anga R. Timilsina, *The UN's Role in Nation-Building: From the Congo to Iraq*, Santa Monica, Calif.: RAND Corporation, MG-304-RC, 2005. As of November 29, 2012:
http://www.rand.org/pubs/monographs/MG304.html

Dobbins, James, John G. McGinn, Keith Crane, Seth G. Jones, Rollie Lal, Andrew Rathmell, Rachel M. Swanger, and Anga R. Timilsina, *America's Role in Nation-Building: From Germany to Iraq*, Santa Monica, Calif.: RAND Corporation, MR-1753-RC, 2003. As of November 29, 2012:
http://www.rand.org/pubs/monograph_reports/MR1753.html

Dodd, Mark, "Give Us a Free Hand or We Quit, E. Timor Leaders Say," *Sydney Morning Herald*, December 5, 2000.

Donais, Timothy, *The Political Economy of Peacebuilding in Post-Dayton Bosnia*, London: Routledge, 2005.

Doyle, Michael W., *UN Peacekeeping in Cambodia: UNTAC's Civil Mandate*, Boulder, Colo.: Lynne Reinner Publishers, 1995.

Doyle, Michael W., and Nicholas Sambanis, *Making War and Building Peace: United Nations Peace Operations*, Princeton, N.J.: Princeton University Press, 2006.

"'Dozens Killed' as Sudan's Army and Rebels Clash," BBC News, September 7, 2012. As of December 6, 2012:
http://www.bbc.co.uk/news/world-africa-19527693

Dube, Oeindrila, and Juan Vargas, *Commodity Price Shocks and Civil Conflict: Evidence from Colombia*, Cambridge, Mass.: Harvard University Press, 2008.

Duggan, Stephen J., "Education, Teacher Training and Prospects for Economic Recovery in Cambodia," *Comparative Education*, Vol. 32, No. 3, November 1996, pp. 361–375.

East Timor Ministry of Finance, *External Trade Statistics: Annual Report 2009*, Dili, 2009.

EBRD—*See* European Bank for Reconstruction and Development.

Economist Intelligence Unit, "Country Report: Sierra Leone," December 2009.

———, "Country Report: Sierra Leone," September 2011.

"Economy: El Salvador," *Jane's Sentinel Security Assessment*, April 11, 2011.

Edelstein, David M., "Occupational Hazards: Why Military Occupations Succeed or Fail," *International Security*, Vol. 29, No. 1, Summer 2004, pp. 49–91.

Effron, Laurie, and F. Stephen O'Brien, *Bosnia and Herzegovina: Post Conflict Reconstruction and the Transition to a Market Economy*, Washington, D.C.: World Bank, 2004.

"El Salvador (El Salvador), World Armies," *Jane's World Armies*, May 16, 2011.

European Bank for Reconstruction and Development, "Bosnia and Herzegovina Economic Overview," web page, date unknown. No longer available online.

———, "Bosnia and Herzegovina Country Assessment," undated, accessed August 2012. As of December 3, 2012:
http://www.ebrd.com/pages/research/publications/flagships/transition/bosniaandherzegovina.shtml

European Stability Initiative, *A Bosnian Fortress: Return, Energy and the Future of Bosnia*, Berlin, December 19, 2007.

"External Affairs (Democratic Republic of Congo)," *Jane's Sentinel Security Assessment: Central Africa*, December 16, 2011.

"External Affairs (East Timor): External Affairs," *Jane's Sentinel Security Assessment: Southeast Asia*, September 5, 2001.

"External Affairs (Indonesia): External Affairs," *Jane's Sentinel Security Assessment: Southeast Asia*, November 28, 2011.

Fagan, Adam, "Civil Society in Bosnia Ten Years After Dayton," *International Peacekeeping*, Vol. 12, No. 3, 2005, pp. 406–419.

Fanthorpe, Richard, *Post-War Reconstruction in Rural Sierra Leone: What Political Structures May Prove Viable? Final Report*, London: UK Department for International Development, 2004. As of December 5, 2012:
http://www.dfid.gov.uk/r4d/Output/175631/Default.aspx

———, "On the Limits of Liberal Peace: Chiefs and Democratic Decentralization in Post-War Sierra Leone," *African Affairs*, Vol. 105, No. 418, January 2006, pp. 27–49.

Fawthrop, Tom, and Helen Jarvis, *Getting Away with Genocide? Elusive Justice and the Khmer Rouge Tribunal*, Sydney, New South Wales: University of New South Wales Press, 2005.

Fearon, James D., "Economic Development, Insurgency, and Civil War," in Elhanan Helpman, ed., *Institutions and Economic Performance*, Cambridge, Mass.: Harvard University Press, 2008, pp. 292–328.

Fearon, James D., and David D. Laitin, "Ethnicity, Insurgency, and Civil War," *American Political Science Review*, Vol. 97, No. 1, February 2003, pp. 75–90.

Fernandes, Clinton, *Reluctant Saviour: Australia, Indonesia, and the Independence of East Timor*, Carlton North, Vic.: Scribe Publications, 2004.

Fortna, Virginia Page, *Does Peacekeeping Work? Shaping Belligerents' Choices After Civil War*, Princeton, N.J.: Princeton University Press, 2008.

Freedom House, *Freedom in the World* reports, various years.

———, "Sierra Leone: Freedom in the World 2008," c. 2008. As of December 4, 2012:
http://www.freedomhouse.org/report/freedom-world/2008/sierra-leone

———, "Sierra Leone: Freedom in the World 2011," c. 2011. As of December 5, 2012:
http://www.freedomhouse.org/report/freedom-world/2011/sierra-leone

———, *Freedom in the World 2012: The Arab Uprisings and Their Global Repercussions*, c. 2012a. As of December 5, 2012:
http://www.freedomhouse.org/report/freedom-world/freedom-world-2012

———, "Sierra Leone: Freedom in the World 2012," c. 2012b. As of December 5, 2012:
http://www.freedomhouse.org/report/freedom-world/2012/sierra-leone

Friedman, Francine, *Bosnia and Herzegovina: A Polity on the Brink*, London: Routledge, 2004.

Frieson, Kate, "Revolution and Rural Response in Cambodia, 1970–1975," in Ben Kiernan, ed., *Genocide and Democracy in Cambodia: The Khmer Rouge, the United Nations, and the International Community*, New Haven, Conn.: Yale University Southeast Asia Studies, 1993, pp. 33–50.

Gallup, Jeffrey, "Cambodia's Electoral System: A Window of Opportunity for Reform," in Aurel Croissant, Gabriele Bruns, and Marei John, eds., *Electoral Politics in Southeast and East Asia*, Singapore: Friedrich Ebert Stiftung, 2002, pp. 25–73.

Gambino, Anthony W., *Congo: Securing Peace, Sustaining Progress*, New York: Council on Foreign Relations, 2008.

"Genocide and Mass Atrocity Warning: Democratic Republic of the Congo—The Kivus," Genocide Watch, October 3, 2012. As of December 6, 2012: http://www.genocidewatch.org/drofcongo.html

Gettleman, Jeffrey, "Congo Slips into Chaos Again as Rebels Gain," *New York Times*, November 25, 2012. As of December 5, 2012: http://www.nytimes.com/2012/11/26/world/africa/ as-rebels-gain-congo-again-slips-into-chaos.html

Ginifer, Jeremy, "The Challenge of the Security Sector and Security Reform Processes in Democratic Transitions: The Case of Sierra Leone," *Democratization*, Vol. 13, No. 5, 2006, pp. 791–810.

Gleditsch, Kristian Skrede, *All International Politics Is Local: The Diffusion of Conflict, Integration, and Democratization*, Ann Arbor, Mich.: University of Michigan Press, 2002.

———, "Transnational Dimensions of Civil War," *Journal of Peace Research*, Vol. 44, No. 3, May 2007, pp. 293–309.

Gligorov, K., "The Economic System of Yugoslavia," in George Macesich, ed., *Essays on the Yugoslav Economic Model*, New York: Praeger, 1989, pp. 1–11.

Global Witness, *Cambodia's Family Trees: Illegal Logging and the Stripping of Public Assets*, Washington, D.C., June 2007. As of December 2, 2012: http://www.globalwitness.org/library/cambodias-family-trees

Goldsmith, Andrew, and Sinclair Dinnen, "Transnational Police Building: Critical Lessons from Timor-Leste and Solomon Islands," *Third World Quarterly*, Vol. 28, No. 6, 2007, pp. 1091–1109.

Gottesman, Evan, *Cambodia After the Khmer Rouge: Inside the Politics of Nation Building*, New Haven, Conn.: Yale University Press, 2003.

Haas, Michael, *Genocide by Proxy: Cambodian Pawn on a Superpower Chessboard*, New York: Praeger, 1991.

Hampson, Fen Osler, "The Pursuit of Human Rights: The United Nations in El Salvador," in William J. Durch, ed., *UN Peacekeeping, American Politics, and the Uncivil Wars of the 1990s*, New York: St. Martin's Press, 1996, pp. 69–102.

Hanlon, Joseph, "Is the International Community Helping to Recreate the Preconditions for War in Sierra Leone?" *Round Table*, Vol. 94, No. 381, September 2005, pp. 459–472.

Harding, Andrew, "Ivory Coast: More Than 100 Bodies Found, Says UN," BBC News, April 8, 2011. As of December 5, 2012: http://www.bbc.co.uk/news/world-africa-13013082

Hegre, Håvard, Tanja Ellingsen, Scott Gates, and Nils Petter Gleditsch, "Toward a Democratic Civil Peace? Democracy, Political Change, and Civil War, 1816–1992," *American Political Science Review*, Vol. 95, No. 1, March 2001, pp. 33–48.

Hegre, Håvard, and Nicholas Sambanis, "Sensitivity Analysis of Empirical Results on Civil War Onset," *Journal of Conflict Resolution*, Vol. 50, No. 4, August 2006, pp. 508–535.

Hendrickson, Dylan, *Safeguarding Peace: Cambodia's Constitutional Challenge*, London, UK: Conciliation Resources, 1998.

Herbst, Jeffrey Ira, *States and Power in Africa: Comparative Lessons in Authority and Control*, Princeton, N.J.: Princeton University Press, 2000.

Hirsch, John L., *Sierra Leone: Diamonds and the Struggle for Democracy*, Boulder, Colo.: Lynne Rienner, 2001.

Holbrooke, Richard C., *To End a War*, New York: Modern Library, 1999.

Hood, Ludovic, "Security Sector Reform in East Timor, 1999–2004," *International Peacekeeping*, Vol. 13, No. 1, 2006, pp. 60–77.

Horn, Adrian, and Funmi Olonisakin, "United Kingdom–Led Security Sector Reform in Sierra Leone," *Civil Wars*, Vol. 8, No. 2, 2006, pp. 109–123.

Howard, Lise Morjé, *UN Peacekeeping in Civil Wars*, Cambridge, UK: Cambridge University Press, 2008.

Hughes, Caroline, *UNTAC in Cambodia: The Impact on Human Rights*, Singapore: Indochina Programme, Institute of Southeast Asian Studies, 1996.

———, *Dependent Communities: Aid and Politics in Cambodia and East Timor*, Ithaca, N.Y.: Southeast Asia Program, Cornell University, 2009a.

———, "Reconstructing Legitimate Political Authority Through Elections?" in Joakim Öjendal and Mona Lilja, eds., *Beyond Democracy in Cambodia: Political Reconstruction in a Post-Conflict Society*, Copenhagen: NIAS Press, 2009b, pp. 31–69.

Human Rights Watch, *Human Rights Watch World Report 2011: Events of 2010*, New York: Seven Stories, 2011.

Hume, Mo, "El Salvador: The Limits of a Violent Peace," in Michael C. Pugh, Neil Cooper, and Mandy Turner, eds., *Whose Peace? Critical Perspectives on the Political Economy of Peacebuilding*, Basingstoke, UK: Palgrave Macmillan, 2008, pp. 318–336.

Humphreys, Macartan, "Natural Resources, Conflict, and Conflict Resolution: Uncovering the Mechanisms," *Journal of Conflict Resolution*, Vol. 49, No. 4, August 2005, pp. 508–537.

Humphreys, Macartan, and Jeremy Weinstein, *What the Fighters Say: A Survey of Ex-Combatants in Sierra Leone, June–August 2003*, New York: Columbia University, Stanford University, and Post-Conflict Reintegration Initiative for Development and Empowerment, July 2004.

Huntington, Samuel P., *The Third Wave: Democratization in the Late Twentieth Century*, Norman, Okla.: University of Oklahoma Press, 1991.

Huxley, Tim, *Disintegrating Indonesia? Implications for Regional Security*, Oxford, UK: Oxford University Press, 2002.

ICTY—*See* International Criminal Tribunal for the Former Yugoslavia.

IMF—*See* International Monetary Fund.

"Internal Affairs (East Timor): Internal Affairs," *Jane's Sentinel Security Assessment: Southeast Asia*, July 11, 2012.

"Internal Affairs (Sierra Leone): Internal Affairs," *Jane's Sentinel Security Assessment: West Africa*, July 28, 2010.

International Criminal Tribunal for the Former Yugoslavia, "The Cost of Justice," undated, accessed November 2012.

International Crisis Group, *Is Dayton Failing? Bosnia Four Years After the Peace Agreement*, Europe Report 80, October 28, 1999. As of December 5, 2012: http://www.crisisgroup.org/en/regions/europe/balkans/bosnia-herzegovina/080-is-dayton-failing-bosnia-four-years-after-the-peace-agreement.aspx

———, *Sierra Leone: Time for a New Military and Political Strategy*, Africa Report 28, April 11, 2001. As of December 5, 2012: http://www.crisisgroup.org/en/regions/africa/west-africa/sierra-leone/028-sierra-leone-time-for-a-new-military-and-political-strategy.aspx

———, *Sierra Leone's Truth and Reconciliation Commission: A Fresh Start?* Africa Briefing 12, December 20, 2002. As of December 5, 2012: http://www.crisisgroup.org/en/regions/africa/west-africa/sierra-leone/B012-sierra-leones-truth-and-reconciliation-commission-a-fresh-start.aspx

————, *The Kivus: The Forgotten Crucible of the Congo Conflict*, Africa Report 56, January 24, 2003a. As of December 5, 2012:
http://www.crisisgroup.org/~/media/Files/africa/central-africa/dr-congo/
The%20Kivus%20The%20Forgotten%20Crucible%20of%20the%20Congo%20
Conflict.pdf

————, *Tackling Liberia: The Eye of the Regional Storm*, Africa Report 662, April 30, 2003b. As of December 5, 2012:
http://www.crisisgroup.org/en/regions/africa/west-africa/liberia/
062-tackling-liberia-the-eye-of-the-regional-storm.aspx

————, *Sierra Leone: The State of Security and Governance*, Africa Report 67, September 2, 2003c. As of December 5, 2012:
http://www.crisisgroup.org/en/regions/africa/west-africa/sierra-leone/
067-sierra-leone-the-state-of-security-and-governance.aspx

————, *Liberia and Sierra Leone: Rebuilding Failed States*, Africa Report 87, December 8, 2004. As of December 5, 2012:
http://www.crisisgroup.org/en/regions/africa/west-africa/sierra-leone/
087-liberia-and-sierra-leone-rebuilding-failed-states.aspx

————, *The Congo's Transition Is Failing: Crisis in the Kivus*, Africa Report 91, March 30, 2005a. As of December 5, 2012:
http://www.crisisgroup.org/en/regions/africa/central-africa/dr-congo/
091-the-congos-transition-is-failing-crisis-in-the-kivus.aspx

————, *Bosnia's Stalled Police Reform: No Progress, No EU*, Europe Report 164, September 6, 2005b. As of December 5, 2012:
http://www.crisisgroup.org/en/regions/europe/balkans/bosnia-herzegovina/
164-bosnias-stalled-police-reform-no-progress-no-eu.aspx

————, *Escaping the Conflict Trap: Promoting Good Governance in the Congo*, Africa Report 114, July 20, 2006. As of December 5, 2012:
http://www.crisisgroup.org/en/regions/africa/central-africa/dr-congo/
114-escaping-the-conflict-trap-promoting-good-governance-in-the-congo.aspx

————, *Congo: Staying Engaged After the Elections*, Africa Briefing 44, January 9, 2007a. As of December 5, 2012:
http://www.crisisgroup.org/en/regions/africa/central-africa/dr-congo/
B044-congo-staying-engaged-after-the-elections.aspx

————, *Ensuring Bosnia's Future: A New International Engagement Strategy*, Europe Report 180, February 15, 2007b. As of December 5, 2012:
http://www.crisisgroup.org/en/regions/europe/balkans/bosnia-herzegovina/
180-ensuring-bosnias-future-a-new-international-engagement-strategy.aspx

————, *Sierra Leone: The Election Opportunity*, Africa Report 129, July 12, 2007c. As of December 5, 2012:
http://www.crisisgroup.org/en/regions/africa/west-africa/sierra-leone/
129-sierra-leone-the-election-opportunity.aspx

———, *Sierra Leone: A New Era of Reform?* Africa Report 143, July 31, 2008. As of December 4, 2012:
http://www.crisisgroup.org/en/regions/africa/west-africa/sierra-leone/143-sierra-leone-a-new-era-of-reform.aspx

———, *Congo: Five Priorities for a Peacebuilding Strategy*, Africa Report 150, May 11, 2009a. As of December 5, 2012:
http://www.crisisgroup.org/en/regions/africa/central-africa/dr-congo/150-congo-five-priorities-for-a-peacebuilding-strategy.aspx

———, *Handing Back Responsibility to Timor-Leste's Police*, December 3, 2009b. As of December 4, 2012:
http://www.crisisgroup.org/~/media/Files/asia/south-east-asia/timor-leste/180_handing_back_responsibility_to_timor_lestes_police.ashx

———, *Eastern Congo: Why Stabilisation Failed*, Africa Briefing 91, October 4, 2012. As of December 5, 2012:
http://www.crisisgroup.org/en/regions/africa/central-africa/dr-congo/b091-eastern-congo-why-stabilisation-failed.aspx

International Monetary Fund, "International Financial Statistics (IFS) Query Builder," undated, referenced 2012. As of November 29, 2012:
http://elibrary-data.imf.org/QueryBuilder.aspx

———, *Bosnia and Herzegovina: Selected Issues*, Washington, D.C., Staff Country Report 98/69, August 1998. As of December 3, 2012:
http://www.imf.org/external/pubs/cat/longres.aspx?sk=2704.0

———, *Bosnia and Herzegovina: 2005 Article IV Consultation—Staff Report, Staff Supplement, Public Information Notice on the Executive Board Discussion, and Statement by the Executive Director for Bosnia and Herzegovina*, Washington, D.C., Country Report 05/199, June 2005. As of December 3, 2012:
http://www.imf.org/external/pubs/ft/scr/2005/cr05199.pdf

———, *Democratic Republic of the Congo: 2007 Article IV Consultation— Staff Report; Staff Supplement; Staff Statement; Public Information Notice on the Executive Board Discussion; and Statement by the Executive Director for the Democratic Republic of the Congo*, Country Report 07/327, September 2007a. As of December 5, 2012:
http://www.imf.org/external/pubs/ft/scr/2007/cr07327.pdf

———, *Democratic Republic of the Congo: Poverty Reduction Strategy Paper*, Country Report 07/330, September 2007b. As of December 13, 2012:
http://www.imf.org/external/pubs/ft/scr/2007/cr07330.pdf

———, *Bosnia and Herzegovina: 2008 Article IV Consultation—Staff Report; Public Information Notice on the Executive Board Discussion; and Statement by the Executive Director for Bosnia and Herzegovina*, Washington, D.C., Country Report 08/327, October 2008. As of December 3, 2012:
http://www.imf.org/external/pubs/ft/scr/2008/cr08327.pdf

International Republican Institute, *Survey of Cambodian Public Opinion, July 31–August 26, 2009*, c. 2009. As of December 2, 2012:
http://www.iri.org/sites/default/files/2010%20February%202%20Survey%20of%20Cambodian%20Public%20Opinion,%20July%2031-August%2026,%20 2009%20--%20Khmer%20and%20English%20version.pdf

"In the Dock, but for What? Enthusiasm Is Flagging for Spectacular Trials to Punish War Crimes and Human-Rights Abuses," *Economist*, November 25, 2010. As of December 3, 2012:
http://www.economist.com/node/17572645?story_id=17572645

"Intrigue in Ruling CPP Detailed," *Phnom Penh Post*, July 13, 2011. As of December 2, 2012:
http://www.phnompenhpost.com/index.php/component/option,com_myblog/Itemid,/show,intrigue-in-ruling-cpp-detailed.html/

Jackson, Karl D., "The Ideology of Total Revolution," in Karl D. Jackson, ed., *Cambodia 1975–1978: Rendezvous with Death*, Princeton, N.J.: Princeton University Press, 1989, pp. 37–78.

Jackson, Paul, "Chiefs, Money and Politicians: Rebuilding Local Government in Post-War Sierra Leone," *Public Administration and Development*, Vol. 25, 2005, pp. 49–58.

———, "Reshuffling an Old Deck of Cards? The Politics of Local Government in Sierra Leone," *Journal of African Economies*, Vol. 106, No. 422, January 2007, pp. 95–111.

Jackson, Stephen, "Making a Killing: Criminality and Coping in the Kivu War Economy," *Review of African Political Economy*, Vol. 29, No. 93–94, September–December 2002, pp. 516–536.

Johnstone, Ian, "Rights and Reconciliation in El Salvador," in Michael W. Doyle, Ian Johnstone, and Robert C. Orr, eds., *Keeping the Peace: Multidimensional UN Operations in Cambodia and El Salvador*, New York: Cambridge University Press, 1997, pp. 312–341.

Jolliffe, Jill, "Jail Breakout over Delays," *Age*, August 17, 2002. As of December 4, 2012:
http://www.theage.com.au/articles/2002/08/16/1029114013075.html

Kalyvas, Stathis N., *The Logic of Violence in Civil War*, Cambridge, UK: Cambridge University Press, 2006.

———, "Civil Wars," in Carles Boix and Susan Carol Stokes, eds., *The Oxford Handbook of Comparative Politics*, Oxford, UK: Oxford University Press, 2007, pp. 416–434.

Kamputsea-tutkimuskomission, *Kampuchea in the Seventies: Report of a Finnish Inquiry Commission*, Helsinki: Kampuchean Inquiry Commission, 1982.

Kaplan, Seth, "The Wrong Prescription for the Congo," *Orbis*, Vol. 51, No. 2, 2007, pp. 299–311.

Karatnycky, Adrian, *Freedom in the World: The Annual Survey of Political Rights and Civil Liberties, 1999–2000*, New York: Freedom House, 2000.

Katzenstein, Suzanne, "Hybrid Tribunals: Searching for Justice in East Timor," *Harvard Human Rights Journal*, Vol. 16, 2003, pp. 245–278.

Kaufman, Stuart J., *Modern Hatreds: The Symbolic Politics of Ethnic War*, New York: Cornell University Press, 2001.

Kaufmann, Chaim, "Rational Choice and Progress in the Study of Ethnic Conflict: A Review Essay," *Security Studies*, Vol. 14, No. 1, January–March 2005, pp. 178–207.

Kaufmann, Daniel, Aart Kraay, and Massimo Mastruzzi, *Governance Matters VII: Aggregate and Individual Governance Indicators, 1996–2007*, Washington, D.C.: World Bank, World Bank Institute, Global Programs Division, and Development Research Group, Macroeconomics and Growth Team, 2008.

Keen, David, "Greed and Grievance in Civil War," *International Affairs*, Vol. 88, No. 4, July 2012, pp. 757–777.

Kennelly, Kevin G., *The Role of NATO and the EU in Resolving Frozen Conflicts*, Monterey, Calif.: Naval Postgraduate School, 2006. As of November 30, 2012: http://edocs.nps.edu/npspubs/scholarly/theses/2006/Dec/06Dec_Kennelly.pdf

Kerr, Rachel, and Jessica Lincoln, *The Special Court for Sierra Leone: Outreach, Legacy and Impact—Final Report*, London: King's College London, War Crimes Research Group, Department of War Studies, February 2008. As of December 5, 2012: http://www.kcl.ac.uk/sspp/departments/warstudies/research/groups/wc/slfinalreport.pdf

Kilcullen, David, *The Accidental Guerrilla: Fighting Small Wars in the Midst of a Big One*, Oxford, UK: Oxford University Press, 2009.

Kingsbury, Damien, *East Timor: The Price of Liberty*, Houndmills, UK: Palgrave Macmillan, 2009.

Kraay, Aart, Daniel Kaufmann, and Massimo Mastruzzi, *The Worldwide Governance Indicators: Methodology and Analytical Issues*, Washington, D.C.: World Bank, 2010.

Krasno, Jean, *Public Opinion Survey of UNAMSIL's Work in Sierra Leone*, United Nations Peacekeeping Best Practices Unit, July 2005. As of December 5, 2012: http://pbpu.unlb.org/PBPS/Pages/PUBLIC/ViewDocument.aspx?docid=655&cat=1&scat=111&menukey=_6_2_17

Krause, Keith, Robert Muggah, and Elisabeth Gilgen, eds., *Global Burden of Armed Violence 2011: Lethal Encounters*, Cambridge, UK: Cambridge University Press, 2011.

Kriesberg, Louis, Terrell A. Northrup, and Stuart J. Thorson, *Intractable Conflicts and Their Transformation*, Syracuse, N.Y.: Syracuse University Press, 1989.

Lacina, Bethany, and Nils Gleditsch, "Monitoring Trends in Global Combat: A New Dataset of Battle Deaths," *European Journal of Population*, Vol. 21, No. 2–3, June 2005, pp. 145–166.

Lampe, John R., *Yugoslavia as History: Twice There Was a Country*, Cambridge, UK: Cambridge University Press, 1996.

Landler, Mark, "Newcomer Charges Bosnia Business Barricades," *New York Times*, June 25, 2003. As of December 3, 2012:
http://www.nytimes.com/2003/06/25/business/
newcomer-charges-bosnia-business-barricades.html

Latinobarómetro, "Análisis de resultados en línea," data set from various years, accessed February 2012. As of December 3, 2012:
http://www.latinobarometro.org/latino/LATAnalize.jsp

Leitenberg, Milton, *Death in Wars and Conflicts in the 20th Century*, Ithaca, N.Y.: Cornell University, Peace Studies Program, 2006.

Lemarchand, René, *The Dynamics of Violence in Central Africa*, Philadelphia, Pa.: University of Pennsylvania Press, 2009.

Lemay-Hébert, Nicolas, "UNPOL and Police Reform in Timor-Leste: Accomplishments and Setbacks," *International Peacekeeping*, Vol. 16, No. 3, 2009, pp. 393–406.

Levine, Mark, "Peacemaking in El Salvador," in Michael W. Doyle, Ian Johnstone, and Robert C. Orr, *Keeping the Peace: Multidimensional UN Operations in Cambodia and El Salvador*, New York: Cambridge University Press, 1997, pp. 227–254.

Londoño de la Cuesta, Juan Luis, and Rodrigo Guerrero, *Violencia en América Latina: Epidemiología y costos*, Washington, D.C.: Banco Interamericano de Desarrollo, Oficina del Economista Jefe, August 1999.

Luke, David Fashole, and Stephen P. Riley, "The Politics of Economic Decline in Sierra Leone," *Journal of Modern African Studies*, Vol. 27, No. 1, March 1989, pp. 133–141.

Lukic, Renéo, and Allen Lynch, *Europe from the Balkans to the Urals: The Disintegration of Yugoslavia and the Soviet Union*, Oxford, UK: Oxford University Press, 1996.

MacKenzie, Megan, "Securitization and Desecuritization: Female Soldiers and the Reconstruction of Women in Post-Conflict Sierra Leone," *Security Studies*, Vol. 18, No. 2, 2009, pp. 241–261.

Malcolm, Noel, *Bosnia: A Short History*, New York: New York University Press, 1994.

Mansfield, Edward D., and Jack Snyder, "Democratization and the Danger of War," *International Security*, Vol. 20, No. 1, Summer 1995, pp. 5–38.

Marshall, Monty, and Benjamin R. Cole, *Global Report 2011: Conflict, Governance, and State Fragility*, Vienna, Va.: Center for Systemic Peace, December 1, 2011. As of December 5, 2012:
http://www.systemicpeace.org/GlobalReport2011.pdf

McCartan, Brian, "Cambodia Shrugs Off Aid Curb," *Asia Times*, August 23, 2011. As of December 2, 2012:
http://www.atimes.com/atimes/Southeast_Asia/MH23Ae02.html

McCormick, David H., "From Peacekeeping to Peacebuilding: Restructuring Military and Police Institutions in El Salvador," in Michael W. Doyle, Ian Johnstone, and Robert C. Orr, eds., *Keeping the Peace: Multidimensional UN Operations in Cambodia and El Salvador*, New York: Cambridge University Press, 1997, pp. 282–311.

McDonald, Hamish, D. Ball, G. van Klinken, D. Bouurshier, D. Kammen, and R. Tanter, *Masters of Terror: Indonesia's Military and Violence in East Timor in 1999*, Canberra: Strategic and Defence Studies Centre, Australian National University, 2002.

McGrew, Laura, "Re-Establishing Legitimacy Through the Extraordinary Chambers in the Courts of Cambodia," in Joakim Öjendal and Mona Lilja, eds., *Beyond Democracy in Cambodia: Political Reconstruction in a Post-Conflict Society*, Copenhagen: NIAS Press, 2009, pp. 250–296.

Meek, Sarah, "Policing Sierra Leone," in Mark Malan, Sarah Meek, Thokozani Thusi, Jeremy Ginifer, and Patrick Coker, eds., *Sierra Leone: Building the Road to Recovery*, Pretoria: Institute for Security Studies, Monograph 80, March 1, 2003, pp. 105–116.

Memisevic, Tija, "EU Conditionality in Bosnia and Herzegovina: Police Reform and the Legacy of War Crimes," in Judy Batt and Jelena Obradovic-Wochnik, eds., *War Crimes, Conditionality and EU Integration in the Western Balkans*, Paris: Institute for Security Studies, European Union, Chaillot Paper 116, June 2009, pp. 49–66. As of December 3, 2012:
http://www.iss.europa.eu/uploads/media/cp116.pdf

Messner, J. J., Nate Haken, Joelle Burbank, Kristen Blandford, Annie Janus, Melody Knight, and Kendall Lawrence, *The Failed States Index 2011*, Washington, D.C.: Fund for Peace, CR-11-14-FS, June 20, 2011. As of December 4, 2012:
http://www.fundforpeace.org/global/?q=cr-11-14-fs

Miguel, Edward, Shanker Satyanath, and Ernest Sergenti, "Economic Shocks and Civil Conflict: An Instrumental Variables Approach," *Journal of Political Economy*, Vol. 122, No. 4, August 2004, pp. 725–753.

Montalvo, José G., and Marta Reynal-Querol, "Ethnic Polarization, Potential Conflict, and Civil Wars," *American Economic Review*, Vol. 95, No. 3, June 2005, pp. 797–816.

Montgomery, Tommie Sue, *Revolution in El Salvador: From Civil Strife to Civil Peace*, Boulder, Colo.: Westview Press, 1995.

MONUSCO—*See* United Nations Organization Stabilization Mission in the Democratic Republic of the Congo.

Moore, Karen, Chris Squire, and Foday MacBailey, *Sierra Leone National Recovery Strategy Assessment*, Freetown: Government of Sierra Leone, December 24, 2003.

Murray, Kevin, *El Salvador: Peace on Trial*, Oxford, UK: Oxfam UK and Ireland, 1997.

Narayan, Deepa, and Patti Petesch, eds., *Moving Out of Poverty*, Vol. 4: *Rising from the Ashes of Conflict*, Washington, D.C.: World Bank, 2009.

NationMaster, undated home page. As of November 30, 2012:
http://www.nationmaster.com/

Nossiter, Adam, "Hundreds Killed in Ivory Coast Town as Conflict Intensifies," *New York Times*, April 2, 2011. As of December 5, 2012:
http://www.nytimes.com/2011/04/03/world/africa/03ivory.html

Nuamah, Kwaku, and I. William Zartman, *Case Study: Intervention in Sierra Leone*, case study prepared for the conference on Intervention in Internal Conflict, Center for International and Security Studies at Maryland, University of Maryland, December 7, 2001.

Obradovic, Josip, and William N. Dunn, eds., *Worker's Self-Management and Organizational Power in Yugoslavia*, Pittsburgh, Pa.: University Center for International Studies, University of Pittsburgh, 1978.

Office of the High Representative, "The General Framework Agreement: Annex 7," December 14, 1995. As of December 3, 2012:
http://www.ohr.int/dpa/default.asp?content_id=375

———, *34th Report of the High Representative for Implementation of the Peace Agreement on Bosnia and Herzegovina to the Secretary-General of the United Nations*, November 21, 2008. As of December 3, 2012:
http://www.ohr.int/other-doc/hr-reports/default.asp?content_id=42739

OHR—*See* Office of the High Representative.

Olsson, Ola, "Conflict Diamonds," *Journal of Development Economics*, Vol. 82, No. 2, March 2007, pp. 267–286.

"Opposition Highs and Lows," *Phnom Penh Post*, July 14, 2011. As of December 2, 2012:
http://www.phnompenhpost.com/index.php/component/option,com_myblog/Itemid,/show,opposition-highs-and-lows.html/

Organisation for Economic Co-operation and Development, *Concepts and Dilemmas of State Building in Fragile Situations: From Fragility to Resilience*, Paris, 2009. As of November 30, 2012:
http://www.oecd.org/development/conflictandfragility/41100930.pdf

―――, *Do No Harm: International Support for Statebuilding*, Paris, November 1, 2010. As of November 30, 2012:
http://www.oecd.org/dac/conflictandfragility/donoharminternationalsupportforstatebuilding.htm

Owen, Taylor, and Ben Kiernan, "Bombs over Cambodia," *Walrus*, October 2006, pp. 62–69.

Paris, Roland, *At War's End: Building Peace After Civil Conflict*, Cambridge, UK: Cambridge University Press, 2004.

Partnership Africa Canada, *Diamonds and Human Security: Annual Review 2009*, 2009. As of December 4, 2012:
http://www.pacweb.org/Documents/annual-reviews-diamonds/AR_diamonds_2009_eng.pdf

Pearce, Jenny, "Peace-Building in the Periphery: Lessons from Central America," *Third World Quarterly*, Vol. 20, No. 1, February 1999, pp. 51–68.

Peeters, Pia, Wendy Cunningham, Gayatri Acharya, and Arvil Van Adams, *Youth Employment in Sierra Leone: Sustainable Livelihood Opportunities in a Post-Conflict Setting*, Washington, D.C.: World Bank, 2009.

Peou, Sorpong, "Hun Sen's Pre-Emptive Coup 1997: Causes and Consequences," in Derek da Cunha and John Funston, eds., *Southeast Asian Affairs: 1998*, Singapore: ISEAS, 1998, pp. 86–102.

Perlez, Jane, "In East Timor, Refugees Born of Chaos, Carnage and Fear," *New York Times*, May 29, 2006. As of December 4, 2012:
http://www.nytimes.com/2006/05/29/world/asia/29timor.html

Perry, Valery, "Democratization in Brcko and Bosnia," in Michael A. Innes, ed., *Bosnian Security After Dayton: New Perspectives*, London: Routledge, 2006, pp. 51–70.

Peters, Krijn, and Paul Richards, "'Why We Fight': Voices of Youth Combatants in Sierra Leone," *Africa: Journal of the International African Institute*, Vol. 68, No. 2, 1998, pp. 183–210.

Posen, Barry R., "The Security Dilemma and Ethnic Conflict," *Survival*, Vol. 35, No. 1, Spring 1993, pp. 27–47.

Power, Samantha, *Chasing the Flame: One Man's Fight to Save the World*, New York: Penguin Books, 2008.

Prunier, Gérard, *Africa's World War: Congo, the Rwandan Genocide, and the Making of a Continental Catastrophe*, Oxford, UK: Oxford University Press, 2009.

Pugh, Michael, "Rubbing Salt into War Wounds: Shadow Economies and Peacebuilding in Bosnia and Kosovo," *Problems of Post-Communism*, Vol. 51, No. 3, May–June 2004, pp. 53–60.

Ramet, Sabrina P., *Thinking About Yugoslavia: Scholarly Debates About the Yugoslav Breakup and the Wars in Bosnia and Kosovo*, Cambridge, UK: Cambridge University Press, 2005.

Ratner, Steven R., *The New UN Peacekeeping: Building Peace in Lands of Conflict After the Cold War*, New York: St. Martin's Press, 1995.

Reno, William, *Corruption and State Politics in Sierra Leone*, Cambridge, UK: Cambridge University Press, 1995.

———, *Warlord Politics and African States*, Boulder, Colo.: Lynne Rienner Publishers, 1998.

———, *Warlord Politics and African States*, Boulder, Colo.: Lynne Rienner Publishers, 1999.

Richards, Paul, *Fighting for the Rain Forest: War, Youth and Resources in Sierra Leone*, Oxford, UK: International African Institute in association with James Currey, 1996.

Robinson, Courtland, "Refugee Warriors at the Thai-Cambodian Border," *Refugee Survey Quarterly*, Vol. 19, No. 1, 2000, pp. 23–37.

Robson, Peter, "The Mano River Union," *Journal of Modern African Studies*, Vol. 20, No. 4, December 1982, pp. 613–628.

Rodgers, Dennis, Robert Muggah, and Chris Stevenson, *Gangs of Central America: Causes, Costs, and Interventions*, Geneva: Small Arms Survey, Graduate Institute of International and Development Studies, Occasional Paper 23, May 2009. As of December 13, 2012:
http://www.smallarmssurvey.org/fileadmin/docs/B-Occasional-papers/SAS-OP23-Gangs-Central-America.pdf

Rohland, Klaus, and Sarah Cliffe, *The East Timor Reconstruction Program: Successes, Problems and Tradeoffs*, Washington, D.C.: IBRD, 2002.

Ron, James, "Paradigm in Distress? Primary Commodities and Civil War," *Journal of Conflict Resolution*, Vol. 49, No. 4, August 2005, pp. 443–450.

Rose, William, "The Security Dilemma and Ethnic Conflict: Some New Hypotheses," *Security Studies*, Vol. 9, No. 4, Summer 2000, pp. 1–51.

Ross, Michael L., "What Do We Know About Natural Resources and Civil War?" *Journal of Peace Research*, Vol. 41, No. 3, May 2004, pp. 337–356.

Ross, Russell R., *Cambodia: A Country Study*, Washington, D.C.: Federal Research Division, 1990. As of November 30, 2012: http://purl.access.gpo.gov/GPO/LPS76121

Sambanis, Nicholas, "Partition as a Solution to Ethnic War: An Empirical Critique of the Theoretical Literature," *World Politics*, Vol. 52, No. 4, 2000, pp. 437–483.

———, "Do Ethnic and Nonethnic Civil Wars Have the Same Causes? A Theoretical and Empirical Inquiry (Part 1)," *Journal of Conflict Resolution*, Vol. 45, No. 3, June 2001, pp. 259–282.

Sarkees, Meredith Reid, *The COW Typology of War: Defining and Categorizing Wars (version 4 of the data)*, undated. As of December 5, 2012: http://www.correlatesofwar.org/COW2%20Data/WarData_NEW/COW%20Website%20-%20Typology%20of%20war.pdf

Sawyer, Edward, "Remove or Reform? A Case for (Restructuring) Chiefdom Governance in Post-Conflict Sierra Leone," *African Affairs*, Vol. 107, No. 428, 2008, pp. 387–403.

Schroeder, Ursula C., and Cornelius Friesendorf, "State-Building and Organized Crime: Implementing the International Law Enforcement Agenda in Bosnia," *Journal of International Relations and Development*, Vol. 12, 2009, pp. 137–167.

Schwarz, Benjamin, *American Counterinsurgency Doctrine and El Salvador: The Frustrations of Reform and the Illusions of Nation Building*, Santa Monica, Calif.: RAND Corporation, R-4042-USDP, 1991. As of December 3, 2012: http://www.rand.org/pubs/reports/R4042.html

Seligson, Mitchell A., "Thirty Years of Transformation in the Agrarian Sector of El Salvador, 1961–1991," *Latin American Research Review*, Vol. 30, No. 3, 1995, pp. 43–74.

Sharp, Bruce, "Counting Hell," *Mekong.net*, last updated June 9, 2008. As of November 30, 2012: http://www.mekong.net/cambodia/deaths.htm

Shawcross, William, *Sideshow: Kissinger, Nixon and the Destruction of Cambodia*, New York: Simon and Schuster, 1979.

"Sierra Leone: Disarmament and Rehabilation [sic] Completed After Five Years," Integrated Regional Information Networks, February 4, 2004. As of December 4, 2012: http://www.irinnews.org/Report/48444/SIERRA-LEONE-Disarmament-and-rehabilation-completed-after-five-years

"Sierra Leone: Fighting for Women's Right to Land," Integrated Regional Information Networks, June 22, 2012.

Silber, Laura, and Allan Little, *Yugoslavia: Death of a Nation*, New York: TV Books, 1996.

Silove, Derrick, "Conflict in East Timor: Genocide or Expansionist Occupation?" *Human Rights Review*, Vol. 1, No. 3, April–June 2000, pp. 62–79.

Simons, Marlise, and J. David Goodman, "Ex–Liberian Leader Gets 50 Years for War Crimes," *New York Times*, May 30, 2012. As of December 5, 2012: http://www.nytimes.com/2012/05/31/world/africa/ charles-taylor-sentenced-to-50-years-for-war-crimes.html

Simonsen, Sven Gunnar, "The Authoritarian Temptation in East Timor: Nationbuilding and the Need for Inclusive Governance," *Asian Survey*, Vol. 46, No. 4, July–August 2006, pp. 575–596.

Smillie, Ian, Lansana Gberie, and Ralph Hazleton, *The Heart of the Matter: Sierra Leone, Diamonds and Human Security—Completed Report*, Ottawa: Partnership Africa Canada, 2000.

Smith, Michael G., and Moreen Dee, "East Timor," in William J. Durch, ed., *Twenty-First-Century Peace Operations*, Washington, D.C.: U.S. Institute of Peace and Henry L. Stimson Center, 2006, pp. 389–466.

Solà-Martín, Andreu, "Is Peacebuilding Sustainable in Sierra Leone?" *Global Change, Peace and Security*, Vol. 21, No. 3, October 2009, pp. 291–307.

"South Sudan Horror at Deadly Cattle Vendetta," BBC News, January 16, 2012. As of December 6, 2012: http://www.bbc.co.uk/news/world-africa-16575153

Stanley, William Deane, "Building New Police Forces in El Salvador and Guatemala: Learning and Counter-Learning," *International Peacekeeping*, Vol. 6, No. 4, 1999, pp. 113–134.

———, "El Salvador: State-Building Before and After Democratisation, 1980– 95," *Third World Quarterly*, Vol. 27, No. 1, 2006, pp. 101–114.

Stewart, Rory, and Gerald Knaus, *Can Intervention Work?* New York: W. W. Norton and Company, 2011.

"Sudan and South Sudan in Fierce Oil Border Clashes," BBC News, March 27, 2012. As of December 6, 2012: http://www.bbc.co.uk/news/world-africa-17515209

Suhrke, Astri, and Ingrid Samset, "What's in a Figure? Estimating Recurrence of Civil War," *International Peacekeeping*, Vol. 14, No. 2, April 2007, pp. 195–203.

Swarns, Rachel L., "Congo and Its Rebels Sign Accord to End War," *New York Times*, December 18, 2002. As of December 5, 2012: http://www.nytimes.com/2002/12/18/world/ congo-and-its-rebels-sign-accord-to-end-war.html

Thayer, Nate, "U.N., Government Reports Cite Killings by Cambodian Military Officials," *Washington Post*, August 13, 1994.

———, "Pol Pot, I Presume," *Wall Street Journal*, August 1, 1997.

———, "'I'm Tired of Talking About It': Excerpts from Interview with Pol Pot October 16, 1997," *Nate Thayer*, November 9, 2011. As of November 30, 2012: http://natethayer.typepad.com/blog/2011/11/ im-tired-of-talking-about-itexcerpts-from-interview-with-pol-pot-by-nate-thayer. html

Themnér, Lotta, and Peter Wallensteen, "Armed Conflict, 1946–2010," *Journal of Peace Research*, Vol. 48, No. 4, July 2011, pp. 525–536.

Thion, Serge, *Watching Cambodia: Ten Paths to Enter the Cambodian Tangle*, Bangkok, Thailand: Cheney, 1993.

Thomson, Brian, *Sierra Leone: Reform or Relapse? Conflict and Governance Reform*, London: Chatham House, June 2007. As of December 4, 2012: http://www.chathamhouse.org/publications/papers/view/108540

Timilsina, Anga R., *Getting the Policies Right: The Prioritization and Sequencing of Policies in Post-Conflict Countries*, Santa Monica, Calif.: RAND Corporation, RGSD-222, 2007. As of December 2, 2012: http://www.rand.org/pubs/rgs_dissertations/RGSD222.html

Torres-Rivas, Edelberto, "Insurrection and Civil War in El Salvador," in Michael W. Doyle, Ian Johnstone, and Robert C. Orr, eds., *Keeping the Peace: Multidimensional UN Operations in Cambodia and El Salvador*, New York: Cambridge University Press, 1997, pp. 209–226.

Transparency International, *Corruption Perceptions Index 2003*, 2003. As of December 5, 2012: http://archive.transparency.org/policy_research/surveys_indices/cpi/2003

———, *Corruption Perceptions Index 2009*, 2009. As of December 5, 2012: http://archive.transparency.org/policy_research/surveys_indices/cpi/2009

———, *Corruption Perceptions Index 2011*, 2011. As of December 2, 2012: http://cpi.transparency.org/cpi2011/results/

———, *Corruption Perceptions Index 2012*, 2012. As of December 12, 2012: http://cpi.transparency.org/cpi2012/

Trefon, Theodore, Van Hoyweghen Saskia, and Stefaan Smis, "Editorial: State Failure in the Congo—Perceptions and Realities," *Review of African Political Economy*, Vol. 29, No. 93–94, September–December 2002, pp. 379–388.

Trenkov-Wermuth, Calin, *United Nations Justice: Legal and Judicial Reform in Governance Operations*, Shibuya-ku, Japan: UN University Press, 2010.

Tutusaus, Jean Pierre, Sue Nelson, and Arthur Abadje, *USAID/Sierra Leone Diamond Sector Program Evaluation*, Washington, D.C.: U.S. Agency for International Development, July 20, 2007. As of December 4, 2012: http://transition.usaid.gov/sl/contracting/mission/refmaterials/USAIDSierraLeoneDiamondProgramEvaluationreport_final.pdf

UK Department for International Development, *Bosnia and Herzegovina*, London, Country Strategy Paper, 2000.

Un, Kheang, "The Judicial System and Democratization in Post-Conflict Cambodia," in Joakim Öjendal and Mona Lilja, eds., *Beyond Democracy in Cambodia: Political Reconstruction in a Post-Conflict Society*, Copenhagen: NIAS Press, 2009, pp. 70–100.

UNDP—*See* United Nations Development Programme.

UNHCR—*See* United Nations High Commissioner for Refugees.

United Nations, "Cambodia–UNTAC: Background," undated. As of November 30, 2012: http://www.un.org/en/peacekeeping/missions/past/untacbackgr2.html

United Nations Department of Economic and Social Affairs, *World Population Prospects, the 2010 Revision*, updated October 20, 2011. As of December 5, 2012: http://esa.un.org/unpd/wpp/index.htm

United Nations Department of Economic and Social Affairs and United Nations Development Programme, *The Challenges of Restoring Governance in Crisis and Post-Conflict Countries*, Seventh Global Forum on Reinventing Government: Building Trust in Government, Vienna, ST/ESA/PAD/SER.E/101, June 26–29, 2007. As of December 3, 2012: http://bibpurl.oclc.org/web/20692

United Nations Department of Public Information, *United Nations Transitional Authority in Cambodia*, New York, 1992.

United Nations Development Programme, "International Human Development Indicators: Do-It-Yourself Data Tables," undated. As of December 6, 2012: http://hdrstats.undp.org/en/tables/

———, *Human Development Report 1991: Financing Human Development*, New York: Oxford University Press, 1991. As of December 4, 2012: http://hdr.undp.org/en/reports/global/hdr1991/

———, *Early Warning System: Annual Report 2002*, May 20, 2003. As of December 3, 2012: http://www.undp.ba/index.aspx?PID=36&RID=8

———, *Early Warning System: Annual Report 2003*, 2004.

————, *Early Warning System: Annual Report 2004*, June 24, 2005. As of December 3, 2012:
http://www.undp.ba/index.aspx?PID=36&RID=47

————, *Early Warning System: Annual Report 2005*, May 17, 2006. As of December 3, 2012:
http://www.undp.ba/index.aspx?PID=36&RID=54

————, *Early Warning System: Annual Report 2006*, May 17, 2007. As of December 3, 2012:
http://www.undp.ba/index.aspx?PID=36&RID=64

————, *Early Warning System: Annual Report 2007*, May 6, 2008. As of December 3, 2012:
http://www.undp.ba/index.aspx?PID=36&RID=74

————, *Early Warning System: Annual Report 2008*, April 22, 2009. As of December 3, 2012:
http://www.undp.ba/index.aspx?PID=36&RID=87

————, *Human Development Report 2011: Sustainability and Equity—A Better Future for All*, New York, 2011. As of December 2, 2012:
http://hdr.undp.org/en/reports/global/hdr2011/

United Nations Educational, Scientific and Cultural Organization Institute for Statistics, "Education (all levels) Profile: Sierra Leone," *UIS Statistics in Brief*, undated, referenced November 16, 2011. As of December 4, 2012:
http://stats.uis.unesco.org/unesco/TableViewer/document.
aspx?ReportId=121&IF_Language=eng&BR_Country=6940&BR_Region=40540

United Nations General Assembly, "Financing of the Support Account for Peacekeeping Operations and the United Nations Logistics Base at Brindisi, Italy: Note by the Secretary-General," A/C.5/66/17, June 12, 2012. As of December 5, 2012:
http://www.un.org/ga/search/view_doc.asp?symbol=A/C.5/66/17

United Nations General Assembly Security Council, *Question of East Timor: Report of the Secretary-General*, S/1999/513, May 5, 1999.

United Nations High Commissioner for Refugees, *The State of the World's Refugees 2000: Fifty Years of Humanitarian Action*, Geneva, January 1, 2000. As of December 13, 2012:
http://www.unhcr.org/4a4c754a9.html

————, "East Timorese Refugee Saga Comes to an End," Geneva, December 30, 2002. As of December 4, 2012:
http://www.unhcr.org/3e1060c84.html

United Nations Integrated Mission in Timor-Leste, "Closure of UNMIT," c. 2012. As of January 11, 2013:
http://www.un.org/en/peacekeeping/missions/past/unmit/

United Nations Joint Human Rights Office, *Report of the United Nations Joint Human Rights Office on Human Rights Violations Perpetrated by Armed Groups During Attacks on Villages in Ufamandu I and II, Nyamaboko I and II and Kibabi Groupements, Masisi Territory, North Kivu Province, Between April and September 2012*, November 2012. As of December 6, 2012:
http://www.ohchr.org/Documents/Countries/ZR/UNJHRO_HRVMasisi_en.pdf

United Nations Mission in Liberia, "UNMIL Background," undated. As of December 4, 2012:
http://www.un.org/en/peacekeeping/missions/unmil/background.shtml

United Nations Office on Drugs and Crime, *Drug Trafficking as a Security Threat in West Africa*, October 28, 2008. As of December 5, 2012:
http://www.unodc.org/unodc/en/frontpage/
drug-trafficking-as-a-security-threat-in-west-africa.html

———, *Transnational Organized Crime in Central America and the Caribbean: A Threat Assessment*, Vienna, 2012.

United Nations Organization Stabilization Mission in the Democratic Republic of the Congo, "MONUSCO Facts and Figures," undated, referenced July 4, 2012. As of December 5, 2012:
http://www.un.org/en/peacekeeping/missions/monusco/facts.shtml

United Nations Peace Operations, *Year in Review 2003*, c. 2004.

———, *Year in Review 2004*, January 2005. As of November 29, 2012:
http://www.un.org/en/peacekeeping/publications/yir/2004/

———, *Year in Review 2005*, c. 2006. As of November 29, 2012:
http://www.un.org/en/peacekeeping/publications/yir/2005/

———, *Year in Review 2007*, March 2008. As of November 29, 2012:
http://www.un.org/en/peacekeeping/publications/yir/yir2007.pdf

United Nations Secretary-General, *United Nations Integrated Mission in Timor-Leste (for the period from 20 September 2011 to 6 January 2012)*, S/2012/43, January 18, 2012.

———, *United Nations Integrated Office in Sierra Leone (third report)*, S/2006/922, November 18, 2006.

United Nations Security Council, Resolution 1272 (1999), October 25, 1999. As of December 3, 2012:
http://www.un.org/docs/scres/1999/sc99.htm

———, *Twenty-Seventh Report of the Secretary-General on the United Nations Mission in Sierra Leone*, S/2005/777, December 12, 2005. As of December 4, 2012:
http://unipsil.unmissions.org/portals/unipsil/media/documents/scrpt/sgrsl12.pdf

————, *First Report of the Secretary-General on the United Nations Integrated Office in Sierra Leone*, S/2006/269, April 28, 2006. As of December 4, 2012:
http://www.unhcr.org/refworld/publisher,UNSC,,SLE,453785572,0.html

————, *Report of the Secretary-General Pursuant to Paragraph 8 of Resolution 1698 (2006) Concerning the Democratic Republic of the Congo*, S/2007/68, February 8, 2007. As of December 5, 2012:
http://www.un.org/Docs/journal/asp/ws.asp?m=S/2007/68

————, *Sixth Report of the Secretary-General on the United Nations Integrated Office in Sierra Leone*, S/2008/281, April 29, 2008a. As of December 5, 2012:
http://www.un.org/Docs/journal/asp/ws.asp?m=S/2008/281

————, *Report of the Secretary-General on the Deployment of the African Union–United Nations Hybrid Operation in Darfur*, S/2008/443, July 7, 2008b.

————, *Fourth Special Report of the Secretary-General on the United Nations Organization Mission in the Democratic Republic of the Congo*, S/2008/728, November 21, 2008c.

————, *First Report of the Secretary-General on the United Nations Integrated Peacebuilding Office in Sierra Leone*, S/2009/59, January 30, 2009a. As of December 5, 2012:
http://www.un.org/Docs/journal/asp/ws.asp?m=S/2009/59

————, *Twenty-Eighth Report of the Secretary-General on the United Nations Organization Mission in the Democratic Republic of the Congo*, S/2009/335, June 30, 2009b. As of December 5, 2012:
http://www.un.org/Docs/journal/asp/ws.asp?m=S/2009/335

————, *Third Report of the Secretary-General on the United Nations Integrated Peacebuilding Office in Sierra Leone*, S/2009/438, September 1, 2009c. As of December 5, 2012:
http://www.un.org/Docs/journal/asp/ws.asp?m=S/2009/438

————, *Thirtieth Report of the Secretary-General on the United Nations Organization Mission in the Democratic Republic of the Congo*, S/2009/623, December 4, 2009d. As of December 5, 2012:
http://www.un.org/Docs/journal/asp/ws.asp?m=S/2009/623

————, *Sixth Report of the Secretary-General on the United Nations Integrated Peacebuilding Office in Sierra Leone*, S/2011/119, March 9, 2011. As of December 13, 2012:
http://unipsil.unmissions.org/portals/unipsil/media/documents/scrpt/SL_2011_119.pdf

United Nations Transitional Administration in East Timor, *On the Establishment of the National Consultative Council*, UNTAET/REG/1999/2, December 2, 1999.

———, *On the Establishment of a Central Payments Office of East Timor*, UNTAET/REG/2000/6, January 22, 2000a. As of December 4, 2012: http://www.un.org/en/peacekeeping/missions/past/etimor/untaetR/Reg006E.pdf

———, *On the Establishment of the Cabinet of the Transitional Government in East Timor*, UNTAET/REG/2000/23, July 14, 2000b.

———, *On the Establishment of a National Council*, UNTAET/REG/2000/24, July 14, 2000c. As of December 4, 2012: http://www.un.org/en/peacekeeping/missions/past/etimor/untaetR/Reg2400E.pdf

———, *On the Establishment of a Defence Force for East Timor*, UNTAET/REG/2001/1, January 31, 2001a. As of December 4, 2012: http://www.un.org/en/peacekeeping/missions/past/etimor/untaetR/reg20011.htm

———, *On the Establishment of a Commission for Reception, Truth and Reconciliation in East Timor*, UNTAET/REG/2001/10, July 13, 2001b. As of December 4, 2012: http://www.un.org/en/peacekeeping/missions/past/etimor/untaetR/Reg10e.pdf

———, *On the Establishment of the Council of Ministers*, UNTAET/REG/2001/28, September 19, 2001c. As of December 4, 2012: http://www.unmit.org/legal/UNTAET-Law/Regulations%20English/Reg2001-28.pdf

UNMIL—*See* United Nations Mission in Liberia.

UNODC—*See* United Nations Office on Drugs and Crime.

UNTAET—*See* United Nations Transitional Administration in East Timor.

U.S. Department of State, *2010 Human Rights Report: Sierra Leone*, Washington, D.C., April 8, 2011a. As of December 5, 2012: http://www.state.gov/j/drl/rls/hrrpt/2010/af/154368.htm

———, "Timor-Leste (10/11/11)," Background Note, October 11, 2011b. As of December 4, 2012: http://www.state.gov/outofdate/bgn/timorleste/191073.htm

———, "Congo, Democratic Republic of the (04/30/12)," April 30, 2012. As of December 5, 2012: http://www.state.gov/outofdate/bgn/congokinshasa/200313.htm

U.S. Institute of Peace, "Peace Agreements: Cambodia," undated. As of November 30, 2012: http://www.usip.org/publications/peace-agreements-cambodia

Van de Walle, Nicolas, *Overcoming Stagnation in Aid-Dependent Countries*, Washington, D.C.: Center for Global Development, 2005.

Vieira de Mello, Sérgio, press briefing, Dili, April 5, 2000. As of December 4, 2012: http://www.un.org/en/peacekeeping/missions/past/etimor/DB/PC050400.HTM

Vinck, Patrick, Phuong N. Pham, Mychelle Balthazard, and Sokhom Hean, *After the First Trial: A Population-Based Survey on Knowledge and Perception of Justice and the Extraordinary Chambers in the Courts of Cambodia*, Berkeley, Calif.: Human Rights Center, University of California Berkeley, June 2011. As of December 2, 2012:
http://www.escholarship.org/uc/item/2f42q5vx

Vlassenroot, Koen, and Timothy Raeymaekers, eds., *Conflict and Social Transformation in Eastern DR Congo*, Gent: Academia Press Scientific Publishers, 2004.

Walter, Barbara F., "Does Conflict Beget Conflict? Explaining Recurring Civil War," *Journal of Peace Research*, Vol. 41, No. 3, May 2004, pp. 371–388.

———, *Conflict Relapse and the Sustainability of Post-Conflict Peace*, World Bank, World Development Report 2011, background paper, September 13, 2010. As of November 30, 2012:
https://openknowledge.worldbank.org/bitstream/handle/10986/9069/WDR2011_0008.pdf?sequence=1

Waltz, Kenneth Neal, *Theory of International Politics*, New York: McGraw-Hill, 1979.

Ward, Michael D., Brian D. Greenhill, and Kristin M. Bakke, "The Perils of Policy by P-Value: Predicting Civil Conflicts," *Journal of Peace Research*, Vol. 47, No. 4, July 2010, pp. 363–375.

"West Africa: Cote d'Ivore [sic] Joins MRU Today," *News* (Monrovia), May 15, 2008.

Whaites, Alan, *States in Development: Understanding State-Building*, UK Department for International Development, working paper, 2008.

Widyono, Benny, *Dancing in Shadows: Sihanouk, the Khmer Rouge, and the United Nations in Cambodia*, Lanham, Md.: Rowman and Littlefield Publishers, 2008.

Wilkins, Timothy A., "The El Salvador Peace Accords: Using International and Domestic Law Norms to Build Peace," in Michael W. Doyle, Ian Johnstone, and Robert C. Orr, eds., *Keeping the Peace: Multidimensional UN Operations in Cambodia and El Salvador*, New York: Cambridge University Press, 1997, pp. 255–281.

Williams, Paul, "Fighting for Freetown: British Military Intervention in Sierra Leone," *Contemporary Security Policy*, Vol. 22, No. 3, 2001, pp. 140–168.

Wood, Elisabeth Jean, *Forging Democracy from Below: Insurgent Transitions in South Africa and El Salvador*, Cambridge, UK: Cambridge University Press, 2000.

Woodward, Susan, *Balkan Tragedy: Chaos and Dissolution After the Cold War*, Washington, D.C.: Brookings Institution, 1995.

————, "Bosnia and Herzegovina: How Not to End Civil War," in Barbara F. Walter and Jack Snyder, eds., *Civil Wars, Insecurity, and Intervention*, New York: Columbia University Press, 1999, pp. 73–115.

World Bank, "GNI per Capita, PPP (current international $)," undated (a). As of November 29, 2012:
http://data.worldbank.org/indicator/NY.GNP.PCAP.PP.CD

————, "World DataBank," undated (b), referenced August 2012. As of December 5, 2012:
http://databank.worldbank.org/data/home.aspx

————, "World Development Indicators," undated (c). As of November 29, 2012:
http://data.worldbank.org/data-catalog/world-development-indicators

————, "Worldwide Governance Indicators," undated (d), referenced August 2012. As of November 29, 2012:
http://info.worldbank.org/governance/wgi/index.asp

————, *East Timor: Building a Nation—A Framework for Reconstruction and Development*, Governance Background Paper, November 1999. As of December 3, 2012:
http://siteresources.worldbank.org/INTTIMORLESTE/Resources/Governance.pdf

————, *Transitional Support Strategy for the Democratic Republic of the Congo*, Report 27751, January 26, 2004. As of December 5, 2012:
http://www-wds.worldbank.org/external/default/WDSContentServer/WDSP/IB/2005/03/09/000012009_20050309120753/Rendered/PDF/27751.pdf

————, *International Development Association Country Assistance Strategy for the Democratic Republic of the Congo for the Period FY08–FY11*, Vol. I, Report 41474-ZR, November 16, 2007. As of December 5, 2012:
http://www-wds.worldbank.org/external/default/WDSContentServer/WDSP/IB/2007/11/30/000020439_20071130135944/Rendered/PDF/414740ZR.pdf

World Bank, European Commission, and European Bank for Reconstruction and Development, *Bosnia and Herzegovina: Toward Economic Recovery*, Washington, D.C.: World Bank, 1996.

Young, Eoin, "Launch of Overall Strategy in the Fight Against Sexual Violence in the DRC," United Nations Organization Mission in the Democratic Republic of the Congo, April 2, 2009.

Zack-Williams, Alfred B., "Sierra Leone: The Political Economy of Civil War, 1991–98," *Third World Quarterly*, Vol. 20, No. 1, February 1999, pp. 143–162.

Zhou, Yongmei, ed., *Decentralization, Democracy, and Development: Recent Experience from Sierra Leone*, Washington, D.C.: World Bank, 2009.